50% OFF Online CLT Prep Course!

Dear Customer,

We consider it an honor and a privilege that you chose our CLT Study Guide. As a way of showing our appreciation and to help us better serve you, we have partnered with Mometrix Test Preparation to offer you **50% off their online CLT Prep Course**. Many CLT courses are needlessly expensive and don't deliver enough value. With their course, you get access to the best CLT prep material, and **you only pay half price**.

Mometrix has structured their online course to perfectly complement your printed study guide. The CLT Prep Course contains **in-depth lessons** that cover all the most important topics, 220+ **video reviews** that explain difficult concepts, **over 250 practice questions** to ensure you feel prepared, and more than **430 digital flashcards**, so you can study while you're on the go.

Online NCE Prep Course

Topics Covered:
- Verbal Reasoning
  - Word Roots and Prefixes and Suffixes
  - Nuance and Word Meanings
- Grammar and Writing
  - Parts of Speech
  - Subject, Predicates, & Subject-Verb Agreement
- Essay
  - The Writing Process
  - Writing Style and Form
- Quantitive Reasoning
  - Math Reasoning
  - Algebra

Course Features:
- CLT Study Guide
  - Get content that complements our best-selling study guide.
- 2 Full-Length Practice Tests
  - With over 250 practice questions, you can test yourself again and again.
- Mobile Friendly
  - If you need to study on the go, the course is easily accessible from your mobile device.
- CLT Flashcards
  - Their course includes a flashcard mode with over 430 content cards to help you study.

To receive this discount, visit http://www.mometrix.com/university/clt or scan the QR code with your phone. At the checkout page, enter the discount code: **CLT50TPB**

If you have any questions or concerns, please contact Mometrix at support@mometrix.com.

Sincerely,

 in partnership with

FREE Test Taking Tips Video/DVD Offer

To better serve you, we created videos covering test taking tips that we want to give you for FREE. **These videos cover world-class tips that will help you succeed on your test.**

We just ask that you send us feedback about this product. Please let us know what you thought about it—whether good, bad, or indifferent.

To get your **FREE videos**, you can use the QR code below or email freevideos@studyguideteam.com with "Free Videos" in the subject line and the following information in the body of the email:

   a. The title of your product

   b. Your product rating on a scale of 1-5, with 5 being the highest

   c. Your feedback about the product

If you have any questions or concerns, please don't hesitate to contact us at info@studyguideteam.com.

Thank you!

CLT Study Guide

2 Practice Exams and Prep Book
for the Classical Learning Test
[Includes Detailed Answer Explanations]

Lydia Morrison

Copyright © 2024 by TPB Publishing

All rights reserved. No part of this publication may be reproduced, distributed, or transmitted in any form or by any means, including photocopying, recording, or other electronic or mechanical methods, without the prior written permission of the publisher, except in the case of brief quotations embodied in critical reviews and certain other noncommercial uses permitted by copyright law.

Written and edited by TPB Publishing.

TPB Publishing is not associated with or endorsed by any official testing organization. TPB Publishing is a publisher of unofficial educational products. All test and organization names are trademarks of their respective owners. Content in this book is included for utilitarian purposes only and does not constitute an endorsement by TPB Publishing of any particular point of view.

Interested in buying more than 10 copies of our product? Contact us about bulk discounts:
bulkorders@studyguideteam.com

ISBN 13: 9781637759417

Table of Contents

Welcome --- 1
   FREE Videos/DVD OFFER --- 1

Quick Overview --- 2

Test-Taking Strategies --- 3

Bonus Content --- 7

Introduction to the CLT --- 8

Study Prep Plan for the CLT Test --- 10

Verbal Reasoning Section --- 15
   Comprehension --- 15
   Analysis --- 25
   Analogies --- 35
   Practice Quiz --- 38
   Answer Explanations --- 41

Grammar and Writing Section --- 42
   Practice Quiz --- 68
   Answer Explanations --- 71

Quantitative Reasoning Section --- 72
   General Mathematics --- 72
   Arithmetic and Operations --- 80
   Algebraic Expressions and Equations --- 86
   Algebra and Functions: Linear and Quadratic Equations and Inequalities 99
   Geometry --- 112
   Functions --- 138

Practice Quiz	154
Answer Explanations	155

Practice Test #1 — 156

Verbal Reasoning	156
Grammar and Writing	167
Quantitative Reasoning	179

Answer Explanations #1 — 187

Verbal Reasoning	187
Grammar and Writing	192
Quantitative Reasoning	198

Practice Test #2 — 204

Verbal Reasoning	204
Grammar and Writing	215
Quantitative Reasoning	227

Answer Explanations #2 — 235

Verbal Reasoning	235
Grammar and Writing	240
Quantitative Reasoning	246

Welcome

Dear Reader,

Welcome to your new Test Prep Books study guide! We are pleased that you chose us to help you prepare for your exam. There are many study options to choose from, and we appreciate you choosing us. Studying can be a daunting task, but we have designed a smart, effective study guide to help prepare you for what lies ahead.

Whether you're a parent helping your child learn and grow, a high school student working hard to get into your dream college, or a nursing student studying for a complex exam, we want to help give you the tools you need to succeed. We hope this study guide gives you the skills and the confidence to thrive, and we can't thank you enough for allowing us to be part of your journey.

In an effort to continue to improve our products, we welcome feedback from our customers. We look forward to hearing from you. Suggestions, success stories, and criticisms can all be communicated by emailing us at info@studyguideteam.com.

Sincerely,
Test Prep Books Team

FREE Videos/DVD OFFER

Doing well on your exam requires both knowing the test content and understanding how to use that knowledge to do well on the test. We offer completely FREE test taking tip videos. **These videos cover world-class tips that you can use to succeed on your test.**

To get your **FREE videos**, you can use the QR code below or email freevideos@studyguideteam.com with "Free Videos" in the subject line and the following information in the body of the email:

    a. The title of your product
    b. Your product rating on a scale of 1-5, with 5 being the highest
    c. Your feedback about the product

If you have any questions or concerns, please don't hesitate to contact us at info@studyguideteam.com.

Quick Overview

As you draw closer to taking your exam, effective preparation becomes more and more important. Thankfully, you have this study guide to help you get ready. Use this guide to help keep your studying on track and refer to it often.

This study guide contains several key sections that will help you be successful on your exam. The guide contains tips for what you should do the night before and the day of the test. Also included are test-taking tips. Knowing the right information is not always enough. Many well-prepared test takers struggle with exams. These tips will help equip you to accurately read, assess, and answer test questions.

A large part of the guide is devoted to showing you what content to expect on the exam and to helping you better understand that content. In this guide are practice test questions so that you can see how well you have grasped the content. Then, answer explanations are provided so that you can understand why you missed certain questions.

Don't try to cram the night before you take your exam. This is not a wise strategy for a few reasons. First, your retention of the information will be low. Your time would be better used by reviewing information you already know rather than trying to learn a lot of new information. Second, you will likely become stressed as you try to gain a large amount of knowledge in a short amount of time. Third, you will be depriving yourself of sleep. So be sure to go to bed at a reasonable time the night before. Being well-rested helps you focus and remain calm.

Be sure to eat a substantial breakfast the morning of the exam. If you are taking the exam in the afternoon, be sure to have a good lunch as well. Being hungry is distracting and can make it difficult to focus. You have hopefully spent lots of time preparing for the exam. Don't let an empty stomach get in the way of success!

When travelling to the testing center, leave earlier than needed. That way, you have a buffer in case you experience any delays. This will help you remain calm and will keep you from missing your appointment time at the testing center.

Be sure to pace yourself during the exam. Don't try to rush through the exam. There is no need to risk performing poorly on the exam just so you can leave the testing center early. Allow yourself to use all of the allotted time if needed.

Remain positive while taking the exam even if you feel like you are performing poorly. Thinking about the content you should have mastered will not help you perform better on the exam.

Once the exam is complete, take some time to relax. Even if you feel that you need to take the exam again, you will be well served by some down time before you begin studying again. It's often easier to convince yourself to study if you know that it will come with a reward!

Test-Taking Strategies

1. Predicting the Answer

When you feel confident in your preparation for a multiple-choice test, try predicting the answer before reading the answer choices. This is especially useful on questions that test objective factual knowledge. By predicting the answer before reading the available choices, you eliminate the possibility that you will be distracted or led astray by an incorrect answer choice. You will feel more confident in your selection if you read the question, predict the answer, and then find your prediction among the answer choices. After using this strategy, be sure to still read all of the answer choices carefully and completely. If you feel unprepared, you should not attempt to predict the answers. This would be a waste of time and an opportunity for your mind to wander in the wrong direction.

2. Reading the Whole Question

Too often, test takers scan a multiple-choice question, recognize a few familiar words, and immediately jump to the answer choices. Test authors are aware of this common impatience, and they will sometimes prey upon it. For instance, a test author might subtly turn the question into a negative, or he or she might redirect the focus of the question right at the end. The only way to avoid falling into these traps is to read the entirety of the question carefully before reading the answer choices.

3. Looking for Wrong Answers

Long and complicated multiple-choice questions can be intimidating. One way to simplify a difficult multiple-choice question is to eliminate all of the answer choices that are clearly wrong. In most sets of answers, there will be at least one selection that can be dismissed right away. If the test is administered on paper, the test taker could draw a line through it to indicate that it may be ignored; otherwise, the test taker will have to perform this operation mentally or on scratch paper. In either case, once the obviously incorrect answers have been eliminated, the remaining choices may be considered. Sometimes identifying the clearly wrong answers will give the test taker some information about the correct answer. For instance, if one of the remaining answer choices is a direct opposite of one of the eliminated answer choices, it may well be the correct answer. The opposite of obviously wrong is obviously right! Of course, this is not always the case. Some answers are obviously incorrect simply because they are irrelevant to the question being asked. Still, identifying and eliminating some incorrect answer choices is a good way to simplify a multiple-choice question.

4. Don't Overanalyze

Anxious test takers often overanalyze questions. When you are nervous, your brain will often run wild, causing you to make associations and discover clues that don't actually exist. If you feel that this may be a problem for you, do whatever you can to slow down during the test. Try taking a deep breath or counting to ten. As you read and consider the question, restrict yourself to the particular words used by the author. Avoid thought tangents about what the author *really* meant, or what he or she was *trying* to say. The only things that matter on a multiple-choice test are the words that are actually in the question. You must avoid reading too much into a multiple-choice question, or supposing that the writer meant something other than what he or she wrote.

5. No Need for Panic

It is wise to learn as many strategies as possible before taking a multiple-choice test, but it is likely that you will come across a few questions for which you simply don't know the answer. In this situation, avoid panicking. Because most multiple-choice tests include dozens of questions, the relative value of a single wrong answer is small. As much as possible, you should compartmentalize each question on a multiple-choice test. In other words, you should not allow your feelings about one question to affect your success on the others. When you find a question that you either don't understand or don't know how to answer, just take a deep breath and do your best. Read the entire question slowly and carefully. Try rephrasing the question a couple of different ways. Then, read all of the answer choices carefully. After eliminating obviously wrong answers, make a selection and move on to the next question.

6. Confusing Answer Choices

When working on a difficult multiple-choice question, there may be a tendency to focus on the answer choices that are the easiest to understand. Many people, whether consciously or not, gravitate to the answer choices that require the least concentration, knowledge, and memory. This is a mistake. When you come across an answer choice that is confusing, you should give it extra attention. A question might be confusing because you do not know the subject matter to which it refers. If this is the case, don't

eliminate the answer before you have affirmatively settled on another. When you come across an answer choice of this type, set it aside as you look at the remaining choices. If you can confidently assert that one of the other choices is correct, you can leave the confusing answer aside. Otherwise, you will need to take a moment to try to better understand the confusing answer choice. Rephrasing is one way to tease out the sense of a confusing answer choice.

7. Your First Instinct

Many people struggle with multiple-choice tests because they overthink the questions. If you have studied sufficiently for the test, you should be prepared to trust your first instinct once you have carefully and completely read the question and all of the answer choices. There is a great deal of research suggesting that the mind can come to the correct conclusion very quickly once it has obtained all of the relevant information. At times, it may seem to you as if your intuition is working faster even than your reasoning mind. This may in fact be true. The knowledge you obtain while studying may be retrieved from your subconscious before you have a chance to work out the associations that support it. Verify your instinct by working out the reasons that it should be trusted.

8. Key Words

Many test takers struggle with multiple-choice questions because they have poor reading comprehension skills. Quickly reading and understanding a multiple-choice question requires a mixture of skill and experience. To help with this, try jotting down a few key words and phrases on a piece of scrap paper. Doing this concentrates the process of reading and forces the mind to weigh the relative importance of the question's parts. In selecting words and phrases to write down, the test taker thinks about the question more deeply and carefully. This is especially true for multiple-choice questions that are preceded by a long prompt.

9. Subtle Negatives

One of the oldest tricks in the multiple-choice test writer's book is to subtly reverse the meaning of a question with a word like *not* or *except*. If you are not paying attention to each word in the question, you can easily be led astray by this trick. For instance, a common question format is, "Which of the following is…?" Obviously, if the question instead is, "Which of the following is not…?," then the answer will be quite different. Even worse, the test makers are aware of the potential for this mistake and will include one answer choice that would be correct if the question were not negated or reversed. A test taker who misses the reversal will find what he or she believes to be a correct answer and will be so confident that he or she will fail to reread the question and discover the original error. The only way to avoid this is to practice a wide variety of multiple-choice questions and to pay close attention to each and every word.

10. Reading Every Answer Choice

It may seem obvious, but you should always read every one of the answer choices! Too many test takers fall into the habit of scanning the question and assuming that they understand the question because they recognize a few key words. From there, they pick the first answer choice that answers the question they believe they have read. Test takers who read all of the answer choices might discover that one of the latter answer choices is actually *more* correct. Moreover, reading all of the answer choices can remind you of facts related to the question that can help you arrive at the correct answer. Sometimes, a misstatement or incorrect detail in one of the latter answer choices will trigger your memory of the subject and will enable you to find the right answer. Failing to read all of the answer choices is like not reading all of the items on a restaurant menu: you might miss out on the perfect choice.

11. Spot the Hedges

One of the keys to success on multiple-choice tests is paying close attention to every word. This is never truer than with words like *almost*, *most*, *some*, and *sometimes*. These words are called "hedges" because they indicate that a statement is not totally true or not true in every place and time. An absolute statement will contain no hedges, but in many subjects, the answers are not always straightforward or absolute. There are always exceptions to the rules in these subjects. For this reason,

you should favor those multiple-choice questions that contain hedging language. The presence of qualifying words indicates that the author is taking special care with his or her words, which is certainly important when composing the right answer. After all, there are many ways to be wrong, but there is only one way to be right! For this reason, it is wise to avoid answers that are absolute when taking a multiple-choice test. An absolute answer is one that says things are either all one way or all another. They often include words like *every*, *always*, *best*, and *never*. If you are taking a multiple-choice test in a subject that doesn't lend itself to absolute answers, be on your guard if you see any of these words.

12. Long Answers

In many subject areas, the answers are not simple. As already mentioned, the right answer often requires hedges. Another common feature of the answers to a complex or subjective question are qualifying clauses, which are groups of words that subtly modify the meaning of the sentence. If the question or answer choice describes a rule to which there are exceptions or the subject matter is complicated, ambiguous, or confusing, the correct answer will require many words in order to be expressed clearly and accurately. In essence, you should not be deterred by answer choices that seem excessively long. Oftentimes, the author of the text will not be able to write the correct answer without offering some qualifications and modifications. Your job is to read the answer choices thoroughly and completely and to select the one that most accurately and precisely answers the question.

13. Restating to Understand

Sometimes, a question on a multiple-choice test is difficult not because of what it asks but because of how it is written. If this is the case, restate the question or answer choice in different words. This process serves a couple of important purposes. First, it forces you to concentrate on the core of the question. In order to rephrase the question accurately, you have to understand it well. Rephrasing the question will concentrate your mind on the key words and ideas. Second, it will present the information to your mind in a fresh way. This process may trigger your memory and render some useful scrap of information picked up while studying.

14. True Statements

Sometimes an answer choice will be true in itself, but it does not answer the question. This is one of the main reasons why it is essential to read the question carefully and completely before proceeding to the answer choices. Too often, test takers skip ahead to the answer choices and look for true statements. Having found one of these, they are content to select it without reference to the question above. The savvy test taker will always read the entire question before turning to the answer choices. Then, having settled on a correct answer choice, he or she will refer to the original question and ensure that the selected answer is relevant. The mistake of choosing a correct-but-irrelevant answer choice is especially common on questions related to specific pieces of objective knowledge.

15. No Patterns

One of the more dangerous ideas that circulates about multiple-choice tests is that the correct answers tend to fall into patterns. These erroneous ideas range from a belief that B and C are the most common right answers, to the idea that an unprepared test-taker should answer "A-B-A-C-A-D-A-B-A." It cannot be emphasized enough that pattern-seeking of this type is exactly the WRONG way to approach a multiple-choice test. To begin with, it is highly unlikely that the test maker will plot the correct answers according to some predetermined pattern. The questions are scrambled and delivered in a random order. Furthermore, even if the test maker was following a pattern in the assignation of correct answers, there is no reason why the test taker would know which pattern he or she was using. Any attempt to discern a pattern in the answer choices is a waste of time and a distraction from the real work of taking the test. A test taker would be much better served by extra preparation before the test than by reliance on a pattern in the answers.

Bonus Content

In addition to being in the book, both practice tests can be found online in digital format along with other bonus items. Scan the QR code or go to this link to access this content:

testprepbooks.com/bonus/clt

The first time you access the tests, you will need to register as a "new user" and verify your email address.

If you have any issues, please email support@testprepbooks.com.

Introduction to the CLT

Function of the Test

The Classic Learning Test (CLT) is designed to be an objective measure for a student's college readiness. The test is taken by 11th and 12th graders across the United States, and its results are accepted at hundreds of colleges across the country.

Created in 2015, the CLT offers an alternative option for college admissions testing designed to be rigorous and challenging. The CLT uses passages from a variety of history's greatest writers, scientists, and thinkers. The test aims to reward students who can grapple with these primary sources instead of focusing on rote memorization or general test-taking training. Engaging with these historical texts offers a broad and comprehensive assessment, which benefits both students and academic institutions.

Test Administration

The CLT is usually offered online (and is often taken at home), but it is sometimes offered in schools that have partnered with the CLT. Online tests are proctored remotely while tests administered in-school are proctored by school staff. Students with documented disabilities are granted reasonable accommodations either online or in person as needed.

Test Format

The CLT consists of 120 multiple-choice questions in three subject areas: Verbal Reasoning, Grammar & Writing, and Quantitative Reasoning. Two hours are provided for completion of the test, divided among the three sections. These sections must be completed in order.

Included passages are primarily drawn from texts written by figures in the Author Bank, a list of historical writers—both religious and secular—that have shaped the modern world. These passages make up the first two sections: Verbal Reasoning and Grammar & Writing.

The Verbal Reasoning section takes one passage each from Literature, Science, Philosophy or Religion, and Historical or Founding Documents. Each passage (or pair of passages in the case of Historical or Founding Documents) has ten questions that draw from it. These questions are divided between general comprehension of the passage and deeper analysis. Additionally, the final two questions from each passage are analogy-based. 40 minutes are allotted for the 40 questions in the Verbal Reasoning section.

Similarly, the Grammar and Writing Section also has four passage, with one each from Philosophy or Religion, Science, and a Modern or Influential Thinker, as well as a Historical Profile written about a prominent figure in history. Each of these passages serves as the basis for ten questions relating to grammar or writing. 35 minutes are allotted for the 40 questions in the Grammar and Writing section.

The Quantitative Reasoning portion of the exam tests a number of related mathematical disciplines. While a series of basic formulas are provided for reference, calculators are not permitted. Some questions are related to general algebra, some feature geometry (including trigonometry), and some questions examine general mathematical reasoning through logic and word problems. 45 minutes are allotted for the 40 questions in the Quantitative Reasoning section.

Introduction to the CLT

There is an optional essay section available in some formats, but this essay has no bearing on the student's overall score.

Section	Length	Questions
Verbal Reasoning	40 minutes	40
Grammar and Writing	35 minutes	40
Quantitative Reasoning	45 minutes	40
Essay (optional)	30 minutes	1 essay

Scoring

Test scores for the CLT range from 0-120. This is not directly divisible to achieve a percentage score, as some sections are scaled and your score in each section is adjusted appropriately. Along with your scores is an indication of your national percentile. This percentile shows your projected score as it compares to a national sample of scores for the same test. Scores are also shown as a projected score compared to the score you would likely receive on the SAT or ACT test, based on your CLT results.

Tests scores are generally released within three weeks of completion. Online test results are released more quickly than paper tests. Once released, test scores can be submitted online to CLT Partner Colleges.

Study Prep Plan for the CLT Test

1 **Schedule** - Use one of our study schedules below or come up with one of your own.

2 **Relax** - Test anxiety can hurt even the best students. There are many ways to reduce stress. Find the one that works best for you.

3 **Execute** - Once you have a good plan in place, be sure to stick to it.

One Week Study Schedule		
	Day 1	Verbal Reasoning Section
	Day 2	Grammar and Writing Section
	Day 3	Quantitative Reasoning Section
	Day 4	Algebra and Functions: Linear and Quadratic...
	Day 5	Practice Test 1
	Day 6	Practice Test 2
	Day 7	Take Your Exam!

Two Week Study Schedule				
	Day 1	Verbal Reasoning Section	Day 8	Functions
	Day 2	Analysis	Day 9	Trigonometric Functions
	Day 3	Grammar and Writing Section	Day 10	Practice Test 1
	Day 4	Direct Objects	Day 11	Answer Explanations 1
	Day 5	Quantitative Reasoning Section	Day 12	Practice Test 2
	Day 6	Algebra and Functions: Linear and Quadratic...	Day 13	Answer Explanations 2
	Day 7	Geometry	Day 14	Take Your Exam!

Study Prep Plan for the CLT Test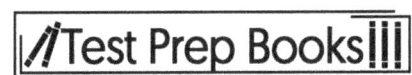

One Month Study Schedule

Day 1	Verbal Reasoning Section	Day 11	Faulty Parallelism	Day 21	Congruence and Similarity in Terms...
Day 2	Meaning of Words and Phrases	Day 12	Quantitative Reasoning Section	Day 22	Perimeter and Area
Day 3	Analysis	Day 13	Properties of Exponents	Day 23	Functions
Day 4	Inferring the Traits, Feelings...	Day 14	Converting Between Fractions, Decimals...	Day 24	Trigonometric Functions
Day 5	Analogies	Day 15	Algebraic Expressions and Equations	Day 25	Solving Trigonometric Functions
Day 6	Grammar and Writing Section	Day 16	Rate of Change	Day 26	Practice Test 1
Day 7	Capitalization Rules	Day 17	Algebra and Functions: Linear and Quadratic...	Day 27	Answer Explanations 1
Day 8	Apostrophes	Day 18	Solving Equations	Day 28	Practice Test 2
Day 9	Direct Objects	Day 19	Geometry	Day 29	Answer Explanations 2
Day 10	Absolute Phrases	Day 20	Polygons and Solids	Day 30	Take Your Exam!

Build your own prep plan by visiting:

testprepbooks.com/prep

As you study for your test, we'd like to take the opportunity to remind you that you are capable of great things! With the right tools and dedication, you truly can do anything you set your mind to. The fact that you are holding this book right now shows how committed you are. In case no one has told you lately, you've got this! Our intention behind including this coloring page is to give you the chance to take some time to engage your creative side when you need a little brain-break from studying. As a company, we want to encourage people like you to achieve their dreams by providing good quality study materials for the tests and certifications that improve careers and change lives. As individuals, many of us have taken such tests in our careers, and we know how challenging this process can be. While we can't come alongside you and cheer you on personally, we can offer you the space to recall your purpose, reconnect with your passion, and refresh your brain through an artistic practice. We wish you every success, and happy studying!

Verbal Reasoning Section

Comprehension

Comprehension is a fundamental skill that leads to academic and professional success. The ability to comprehend the deepest meaning of a passage is crucial. This is true whether the reader is a student learning about a new subject or a professional analyzing studies that affect their work. Reading comprehension involves understanding the passage's structure, making connections between different parts of the passage, and determining the main ideas and concepts. The reader can employ multiple techniques to increase comprehension and navigate content with ease.

Understanding Explicit Details

Readers want to draw a conclusion about what the author has presented. Drawing a conclusion will help the reader to understand what the writer intended as well as whether he or she agrees with what the author has said. There are a few ways to determine the logical conclusion, but careful reading is the most important. The passage may be read several times, and readers should mentally highlight or take notes on the details that they deem important to the meaning of the piece. Readers may draw a conclusion that is different than what the writer intended, or they may draw more than one conclusion. Readers should look carefully at the details to see if their conclusion matches up with what the writer has presented and intended for readers to understand.

Textual evidence can help readers to draw a conclusion about a passage. **Textual evidence** refers to information such as facts and examples that support the main point; it will likely come from outside sources and can be in the form of quoted or paraphrased material. Details should be precise, descriptive, and factual. Readers should look to this evidence and its credibility and validity in relation to the main idea to draw a conclusion about the writing.

The author may state the conclusion directly in the passage. Inferring the author's conclusion is useful, especially when it is not overtly stated, but inferences should not outweigh the information that is directly stated. Alternatively, when readers are trying to draw a conclusion about a text, it may not always be directly stated.

As mentioned before, summary is another effective way to draw a conclusion from a passage. Summary is a shortened version of the original text, written in one's own words. It should focus on the main points of the original text, including only the relevant details. It's important to be brief but thorough in a summary. While the summary should always be shorter than the original passage, it should still retain the meaning of the original source.

Like summary, paraphrasing can also help a reader to fully understand a part of a reading. Paraphrase calls for the reader to take a small part of the passage and to say it in their own words. Paraphrase is more than rewording the original passage, though. It should be written in one's own way, while still retaining the meaning of the original source. When a reader's goal is to write something in their own words, deeper understanding of the original source is required. Again, applying summary and paraphrase to the passages during the test may not be the most efficient use of the test taker's time. However, these tools should be considered when one is practicing comprehending passages. Test takers who are familiar with carefully selecting important aspects of the passage will benefit from this experience on test day.

Topic, Main Idea, and Theme

In order to understand any text, readers first must determine the **topic**, or what the text is about. In non-fiction writing, the topic can generally be expressed in a few words. For example, a passage might be about college education, moving to a new neighborhood, or dog breeds. Slightly more specific information is found in the **main idea**, or what the writer wants readers to know about the topic. An article might be about the history of popular dog breeds; another article might tell how certain dog breeds are unfairly stereotyped. In both cases, the topic is the same—dog breeds—but the main ideas are quite different.

Each writer has a distinct purpose for writing and a different set of details for what they want us to know about dog breeds. When a writer expresses their main idea in one sentence, this is known as a **thesis statement**. If a writer uses a thesis statement, it can generally be found at the beginning of the passage. Finally, the most specific information in a text is in the **supporting details**. An article about dog breed stereotyping might discuss a case study of pit bulls and provide statistics about how many dog attacks are caused by pit bulls versus other breeds.

Below is a diagram showcasing a topic with the main idea and supporting details. The topic is a single word (Cheetahs). The main idea tells us *what about* cheetahs the essay will be discussing. The supporting details offer proof that the main idea is true.

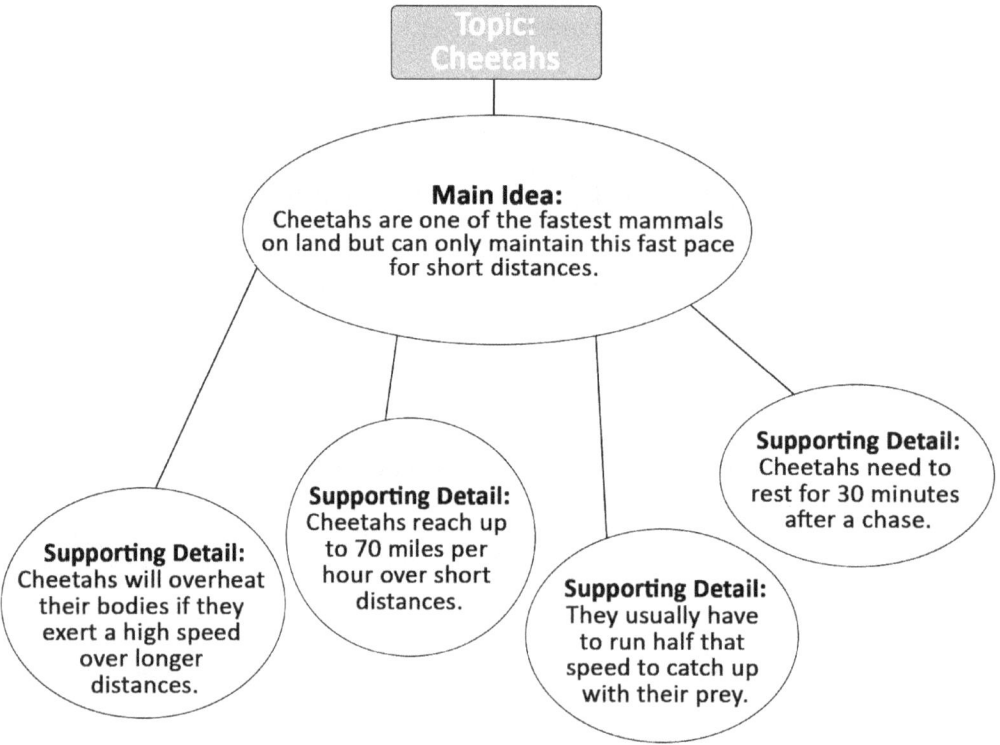

In contrast to informative writing, literary texts contain *themes*. A **theme** is a general way to describe the ideas and questions raised in a piece of literature. Like a topic, a theme can often be expressed in just one word or a few words rather than a full sentence. However, due to the complex nature of literature, most texts contain more than one theme. Some examples of literary themes include isolation, sacrifice, and vengeance. A text's theme might also explore the relationship between two contrasting ideas: ignorance versus knowledge, nature versus technology, science versus religion.

A theme generally expresses a relatively broad and abstract idea about the text—so don't confuse a text's theme with its subject. Both theme and subject can answer the question, "What's the story about?" but the subject answers the question in a concrete way while the theme answers more abstractly. For example, the subject of *Hamlet* is Hamlet's investigation of his father's death (a concrete idea of what happens in the story). However, its themes—that is, the ideas explored through the story—include indecision and revenge, fundamental concepts that unite the events of the story. Because the theme is usually abstract, it might seem difficult to identify. Readers can ask themselves several questions to get a better idea of the theme:

- What observations does the writer make about human behavior?
- How do specific events of this story relate to society in general?
- What forces drive the characters' actions and decisions?
- How did the characters change or what did they learn during the story?

Style, Structure, Mood, and Tone

Readers should be able to identify the components of a writer's **style**. Think about someone's fashion style—a person might dress casually or formally; they might wear trendy clothes or classic clothes; they might prefer simple looks or flashy ones. And the way a person styles their fashion often determines the impression they give to other people. Similarly, writers combine elements of structure, diction, and figurative and connotative language to create their own style.

Structure refers to how a writer organizes ideas. In literature, a text may be either *prose* or *poetry*. Poetry relies on careful word choice (especially in terms of sound and emotional meaning) and rhythm in order to communicate a special feeling or idea. Contrary to the popular assumption, poetry doesn't have to rhyme or follow a strict structure. In fact, there are two types of poetic form: **open form** and **closed form**. In closed form, the poet follows a predictable and repetitive structure, perhaps by using a fixed number of syllables in each line or repeating the same rhyme scheme.

Examples of closed-form structure include sonnets and haiku, both of which require the poet to follow an established pattern of rhythm or rhyme. Open-form poetry doesn't have restrictions on length, the number of syllables or pattern of stress in each line (also known as meter), or the rhyme pattern. Open-form poetry has a structure, but it's more flexible and open to the creative whims of the poet. When a poet uses open form, changes in structure can reflect changes in emotion. For example, if a poem starts out with blunt, brief lines but then develops into long and complex lines, it might represent the speaker becoming more open and expressive of emotions that they had previously been reluctant to share.

Prose is regular written language without any meter or rhythmic form. Literary prose includes novels, short stories, and memoirs. An author may choose prose over poetry when they want to communicate in colloquial language, or when they want to convey information that is more straightforward (but of course, both poetry and prose can be emotional and creative). It's also possible to combine prose and poetry. In Shakespeare's plays, for example, some characters speak in metered lines while other characters speak in prose. This separation may indicate the topic under discussion.

For example, in *Julius Caesar*, Brutus' speech is in prose, while Marc Antony's speech is written in iambic pentameter, a common poetic meter. Antony's speech begins with "Friends, Romans, countrymen, lend me your ears; / I come to bury Caesar, not to praise him." The cadence and stress of the language in Antony's speech makes for a more powerful listening device compared to Brutus' opening, "Romans, countrymen, and friends! Listen to my reasons and be silent so you can hear." In this way, employing prose or poetry can influence the impression that readers get from a text or drama. The crowd, in *Julius Caesar*, is persuaded by Marc Antony's speech in the end, for all its rhetorical glory.

There are also different story structures, or ways for the writer to present their narrative. A story can be either **linear** (told in the same order that events happened) or **non-linear** (the events are presented to the reader out of order). In a non-linear structure, the author may use flashbacks, when the timeline of the story shifts backwards to reveal earlier events. Non-linear storytelling is common in mystery or suspense writing, where the author keeps some information or events hidden from the reader until later in the story.

An author's style can also come from *diction*, or word choice. Just like a person's fashion style can be casual or formal depending on the event, an author's writing style can be anywhere from conversational to academic, elevated to colloquial, reflecting the audience and subject matter. For example, a chemistry textbook is going to contain more academic language and scientific terminology than a newspaper article, which is likely to contain common expressions and easier vocabulary. **Colloquial language** refers to the informal language of normal speech, and may include elements of non-standard pronunciation or grammar (words like "y'all," for example). Colloquialisms can often be found in "local color" pieces where the writer wants the reader to feel directly involved in the everyday lives and conversations of people or characters in the text.

Diction also contributes to the *tone* of the text. Keys to recognizing an author's tone include paying attention to any connotative or emotional language as well as what types of details and information are included (or if any important information seems to be missing). If an article about a proposal to build a new highway only includes information about how the highway will increase traffic congestion and negatively impact the environment, readers can feel the author's critical tone towards the subject. On the other hand, if the article also mentions research about how the highway could direct more customers to local businesses and boost the town's economy, the author's tone will probably seem more balanced.

A text's **mood** is the general feeling or atmosphere created by the author's descriptions and imagery (and, again, it relies on diction and selection of details). **Imagery** refers to all of the details in a text that appeal to any of the five senses; it's how the author helps draw a picture in the reader's mind. Imagine a story that starts with, "It was a dark and stormy night..." and includes descriptions of the howling wind outside, the dim flicker of candlelight, the mysterious creak of unknown footsteps coming upstairs. All of this imagery comes together to create a mood of creepiness and mystery.

Literary Devices

A **rhetorical device** is the phrasing and presentation of an idea that reinforces and emphasizes a point in an argument. A rhetorical device is often quite memorable. One famous use of a rhetorical device is in John F. Kennedy's 1961 inaugural address: "Ask not what your country can do for you, ask what you can do for your country." The contrast of ideas presented in the phrasing is an example of the rhetorical device of antimetabole. Some other common examples are provided below, but test takers should be aware that this is not a complete list.

Verbal Reasoning Section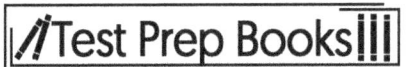

Device	Definition	Example
Alliteration	Repeating the same beginning sound or letter in a phrase for emphasis	The busy baby babbled.
Allusion	A reference to a famous person, event, or significant literary text as a form of significant comparison	"We are apt to shut our eyes against a painful truth, and listen to the song of that siren till she transforms us into beasts." Patrick Henry
Anaphora	The repetition of the same words at the beginning of successive words, phrases, or clauses, designed to emphasize an idea	"We shall not flag or fail. We shall go on to the end. We shall fight in France, we shall fight on the seas and oceans, we shall fight with growing confidence … we shall fight in the fields and in the streets, we shall fight in the hills. We shall never surrender." Winston Churchill
Antithesis	A part of speech where a contrast of ideas is expressed by a pair of words that are opposite of each other.	"That's one small step for man, one giant leap for mankind." Neil Armstrong
Foreshadowing	Giving an indication that something is going to happen later in the story	I wasn't aware at the time, but I would come to regret those words.
Hyperbole	Using exaggeration not meant to be taken literally	The girl weighed less than a feather.
Idiom	Using words with predictable meanings to create a phrase with a different meaning	The world is your oyster.
Imagery	Appealing to the senses by using descriptive language	The sky was painted with red and pink and streaked with orange.
Metaphor	Compares two things as if they are the same	He was a giant teddy bear.
Onomatopoeia	Using words that imitate sound	The tire went off with a bang and a crunch.
Parallelism	A syntactical similarity in a structure or series of structures used for impact of an idea, making it memorable	"A penny saved is a penny earned." Ben Franklin
Personification	Attributing human characteristics to an object or an animal	The house glowered menacingly with a dark smile.

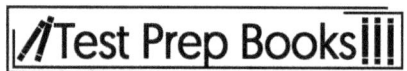

Device	Definition	Example
Rhetorical question	A question posed that is not answered by the writer though there is a desired response, most often designed to emphasize a point	"Can anyone look at our reduced standing in the world today and say, 'Let's have four more years of this?'" Ronald Reagan
Simile	Compares two things using "like" or "as"	Her hair was like gold.
Symbolism	Using symbols to represent ideas and provide a different meaning	The ring represented the bond between us.
Understatement	A statement meant to portray a situation as less important than it actually is to create an ironic effect	"The war in the Pacific has not necessarily developed in Japan's favor." Emperor Hirohito, surrendering Japan in World War II

Sarcasm

Depending on the tone of voice or the words used, sarcasm can be expressed in many different ways. **Sarcasm** is defined as a bitter or ambiguous declaration that intends to cut or taunt. Most of the ways we use sarcasm is saying something and not really meaning it. In a way, sarcasm is a contradiction that is understood by both the speaker and the listener to convey the opposite meaning. For example, let's say Bobby is struggling to learn how to play the trumpet. His sister, Gloria, walks in and tells him: "What a great trumpet player you've become!" This is a sort of verbal irony known as sarcasm. Gloria is speaking a contradiction, but Bobby and Gloria both know the truth behind what she's saying: that Bobby is not a good trumpet player. Sarcasm can also be accompanied by nonverbal language, such as a smirk or a head tilt. Remember that sarcasm is not always clear to the listener; sometimes sarcasm can be expressed by the speaker but lost on the listener.

Irony

Irony is a device that authors use when pitting two contrasting items or ideas against each other in order to create an effect. It's frequently used when an author wants to employ humor or convey a sarcastic tone. Additionally, it's often used in fictional works to build tension between characters, or between a particular character and the reader. An author may use **verbal irony** (sarcasm), **situational irony** (where actions or events have the opposite effect than what's expected), and **dramatic irony** (where the reader knows something a character does not). Examples of irony include:

- Dramatic Irony: An author describing the presence of a hidden killer in a murder mystery, unbeknownst to the characters but known to the reader.

- Situational Irony: An author relating the tale of a fire captain who loses her home in a five-alarm conflagration.

- Verbal Irony: This is where an author or character says one thing but means another. For example, telling a police officer "Thanks a lot" after receiving a ticket.

Verbal Reasoning Section

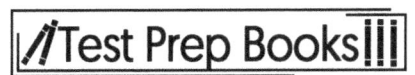

Understatement

Making an **understatement** means making a statement that gives the illusion of something being smaller than it actually is. Understatement is used, in some instances, as a humorous rhetorical device. Let's say that there are two friends. One of the friends, Kate, meets the other friend's, Jasmine's, boyfriend. Jasmine's boyfriend, in Kate's opinion, is attractive, funny, and intelligent. After Kate meets her friend's boyfriend, Kate says to Jasmine, "You could do worse." Kate and Jasmine both know from Kate's tone that this means Kate is being ironic—Jasmine could do much, much worse, because her boyfriend is considered a "good catch." The understatement was a rhetorical device used by Kate to let Jasmine know she approves.

Meaning of Words and Phrases

A useful vocabulary skill is being able to understand meaning in context. A word's **context** refers to other words and information surrounding it, which can have a big impact on how readers interpret that word's meaning. Of course, many words have more than one definition. For example, consider the meaning of the word *engaged*. The first definition that comes to mind might be "promised to be married," but consider the following sentences:

a. The two armies engaged in a conflict that lasted all night.

b. The three-hour lecture flew by because students were so engaged in the material.

c. The busy executive engaged a new assistant to help with his workload.

Were any of those sentences related to marriage? In fact, *engaged* has a variety of other meanings. In these sentences, respectively, it can mean: "battled," "interested or involved," and "appointed or employed." Readers may wonder how to decide which definition to apply. The appropriate meaning is prioritized based on context. For example, sentence C mentions *executive*, *assistant*, and *workload*, so readers can assume that *engaged* has something to do with work—in which case, "appointed or employed" is the best definition for this context. Context clues can also be found in sentence A. Words like *armies* and *conflicts* show that this sentence is about a military situation, so in this context, *engaged* is closest in meaning to "battled." By using context clues—the surrounding words in the sentence—readers can easily select the most appropriate definition.

Context clues can also help readers when they don't know *any* meanings for a certain word. Test writers will deliberately ask about unfamiliar vocabulary to measure your ability to use context to make an educated guess about a word's meaning. Look at the following sentence:

The *loquacious* professor was notorious for always taking too long to finish his lectures.

Even if the word *loquacious* seems completely new, it's possible to utilize context to make a good guess about the word's meaning. Grammatically, it's apparent that *loquacious* is an adjective that modifies the noun *professor*—so *loquacious* must be some kind of quality or characteristic. A clue in this sentence is "taking too long to finish his lectures." Readers should then consider qualities that might cause a professor's lectures to run long. Perhaps he's disorganized, slow, or talkative—all words that might still make sense in this sentence. Choice *D*, therefore, is a logical choice for this sentence—the professor talks too much, so his lectures run late. In fact, *loquacious* means "talkative or wordy."

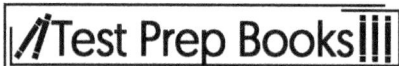

One way to use context clues is to think of potential replacement words before considering the answer choices. You can also turn to the answer choices first and try to replace each of them in the sentence to see if the sentence is logical and retains the same meaning.

Another way to use context clues is to consider clues in the word itself. Most students are familiar with prefixes, suffixes, and root words—the building blocks of many English words. A little knowledge goes a long way when it comes to these components of English vocabulary, and these words can point readers in the right direction when they need help finding an appropriate definition.

Word Choices

Just as one word may have different meanings, the same meaning can be conveyed by different words or synonyms. However, there are very few synonyms that have *exactly* the same definition. Rather, there are slight nuances in usage and meaning. In this case, a writer's **diction**, or word choice, is important to the meaning meant to be conveyed.

Many words have a surface *denotation* and a deeper *connotation*. A word's **denotation** is the literal definition of a word that can be found in any dictionary (an easy way to remember this is that "denotation" and "dictionary definition" all begin with the letter "D"). For example, if someone looked up the word "snake" in the dictionary, they'd learn that a snake is a common reptile with scales, a long body, and no limbs.

A word's **connotation** refers to its emotional and cultural associations, beyond its literal definition. Some connotations are universal, some are common within a particular cultural group, and some are more personal. Let's go back to the word "snake." A reader probably already knows its denotation—a slithering animal—but readers should also take a moment to consider its possible connotations. For readers from a Judeo-Christian culture, they might associate a snake with the serpent from the Garden of Eden who tempts Adam and Eve into eating the forbidden fruit. In this case, a snake's connotations might include deceit, danger, and sneakiness.

Consider the following character description:

> He slithered into the room like a snake.

Does this sound like a character who can be trusted? It's the connotation of the word "snake" that implies untrustworthiness. Connotative language, then, helps writers to communicate a deeper, more emotional meaning.

Read the following excerpt from "The Lamb," a poem by William Blake.

> Little lamb, who made thee?
> Dost thou know who made thee,
> Gave thee life, and bid thee feed
> By the stream and o'er the mead;
> Gave thee clothing of delight,
> Softest clothing, woolly, bright;
> Gave thee such a tender voice,
> Making all the vales rejoice?
> Little lamb, who made thee?
> Dost thou know who made thee?

Think about the connotations of a *lamb*. Whereas a snake might make readers think of something dangerous and dishonest, a lamb tends to carry a different connotation: innocence and purity. Blake's poem contains other emotional language—*delight, softest, tender, rejoice*—to support this impression.

Some words have similar denotations but very different connotations. *Weird* and *unique* can both describe something distinctive and unlike the norm. But they convey different emotions:

> You have such a weird fashion sense!

> You have such a unique fashion sense!

Which sentence is a compliment? Which sentence is an insult? *Weird* generally has more negative connotations, whereas *unique* is more positive. In this way, connotative language is a powerful way for writers to evoke emotion.

A writer's diction also informs their tone. **Tone** refers to the author's attitude toward their subject. A writer's tone might be critical, curious, respectful, dismissive, or any other possible attitude. The key to understanding tone is focusing not just on <u>what</u> is said, but on <u>how</u> it's said.

> a. Although the latest drug trial did not produce a successful vaccine, medical researchers are one step further on the path to eradicating this deadly virus.

> b. Doctors faced yet another disappointing setback in their losing battle against the killer virus; their most recent drug trial has proved as unsuccessful as the last.

Both sentences report the same information: the latest drug trial was a failure. However, each sentence presents this information in a different way, revealing the writer's tone. The first sentence has a more hopeful and confident tone, downplaying the doctors' failure ("although" it failed) and emphasizing their progress ("one step further"). The second sentence has a decidedly more pessimistic and defeatist tone, using phrases like "disappointing setback" and "losing battle." The details a writer chooses to include can also help readers to identify their attitude towards their subject matter.

Identifying emotional or connotative language can be useful in determining the tone of a text. Readers can also consider questions such as, "Who is the speaker?" or "Who is their audience?" (Remember, particularly in fiction, that the speaker or narrator may not be the same person as the author.) For example, in an article about military conflict written by a notable anti-war activist, readers might expect their tone to be critical, harsh, or cynical. If they are presented with a poem written between newlyweds, readers might expect the tone to be loving, sensitive, or infatuated. If the tone seems wildly different from what's expected, consider if the writer is using **irony**. When a writer uses irony, they say one thing but imply the opposite meaning.

Matching the Tone of a Passage

Understanding the tone of a passage is crucial for complete reading comprehension. The tone of a text refers to the attitude that the words in the text convey. This attitude comes from the author's emotions and perspective about the subject matter. The tone determines the mood and atmosphere of the work. This affects how the reader engages with the text as well.

Authors craft the tone of their text through careful word choice. Word choice is a pivotal tool in identifying the tone of the work. Connotations associated with certain words contribute to the overall

tone. Positive word choice can indicate a tone that is uplifting and optimistic. A text that leans toward harsh or critical language is likely to have a negative tone. For example, if an environmentalist is writing about a corporation that is causing massive amounts of pollution, they may use words such as *careless* or *immoral* in their text. Such a text's tone could be described as critical or scathing.

Tone is also associated with sentence structure. A text that uses short, choppy sentences may be conveying a point with urgency. The tone of that work may lean toward being assertive or demanding. A text that uses long, complex language is keying the reader into the fact that the writing is addressing a multifaceted topic. The emotions and ideas being conveyed likely require a significant amount of attention.

To match the tone of a text, it is important to identify and analyze the tone using the information described above. Once the tone has been established, one should take note of the vocabulary used and mirror it with similar wording. The rhetorical devices and structure used should be emulated while keeping in mind the audience of the original text.

Compare and Contrast

In order to understand the relationship between ideas, readers should be able to *compare* and *contrast*. Comparing two things means identifying their similarities, while contrasting two things means finding their differences. Recall the excerpt from "The Lamb" by William Blake:

> Little lamb, who made thee?
> Dost thou know who made thee,
> Gave thee life, and bid thee feed
> By the stream and o'er the mead;
> Gave thee clothing of delight,
> Softest clothing, woolly, bright;
> Gave thee such a tender voice,
> Making all the vales rejoice?
> Little lamb, who made thee?
> Dost thou know who made thee?

Consider that poem alongside an excerpt from another work by Blake called "The Tyger."

> Tyger! Tyger! burning bright
> In the forests of the night,
> What immortal hand or eye
> Could frame thy fearful symmetry?
> […]
> What the hammer? what the chain?
> In what furnace was thy brain?
> What the anvil? what dread grasp
> Dare its deadly terrors clasp?
> When the stars threw down their spears,
> And watered heaven with their tears,
> Did he smile his work to see?
> Did he who made the Lamb make thee?

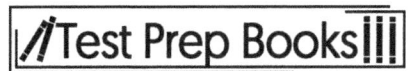

These poems have quite a few things in common. Each poem's subject is an animal—a lamb and a tiger, respectively—and each poem addresses the same question to the animal: "Who created you?" In fact, both poems are formed primarily of questions.

However, the poems also exhibit many differences. For example, it's easy to contrast the tone and word choice in each poem. Whereas "The Lamb" uses words with positive and gentle connotations to create a tone of innocence and serenity, "The Tyger" gives a completely different impression. Some strongly connotative words that stand out include *night*, *fearful*, and *deadly terrors*, all of which contribute to a tone that's tense and full of danger.

When taken together, then, the two poems address the same question—who created the world and all of its creatures?—from two different perspectives. "The Lamb" considers all of the sweet and delightful things that exist, leaving "The Tyger" to ponder the problem of why evil exists. In fact, Blake relies on the contrast between the two poems to fully communicate his dilemma over the paradox of creation—"Did he who make the Lamb make thee?" Although the poems present a strong contrast to one another, it's also possible to find similarities in their subject matter.

Authors often intentionally use contrast in order to ask readers to delve deeper into the qualities of the two things being compared. When an author deliberately places two things (characters, settings, etc.) side-by-side for readers to compare, it's known as **juxtaposition**. An example of juxtaposition can be found in Emily Bronte's *Wuthering Heights*, a novel in which the protagonist Cathy is caught in a love triangle between two romantic interests, Heathcliff and Edgar Linton, who are complete opposites. Cathy compares her feelings for each man in her memorable speech:

> My love for Linton is like the foliage in the woods: time will change it, I'm well aware, as winter changes the trees. My love for Heathcliff resembles the eternal rocks beneath: a source of little visible delight, but necessary. Nelly, I *am* Heathcliff! He's always, always in my mind: not as a pleasure, any more than I am always a pleasure to myself, but as my own being.

When these two characters are placed next to each other, it's easier for readers to grasp their notable characteristics. Edgar is gentle and sophisticated in comparison to Heathcliff, who is rough and wild. Here, Cathy also juxtaposes her feelings about each character. Her love for Edgar is fresh and harmless, like the new spring leaves on trees; but come winter, it will fade away. Her love for Heathcliff might be less conventionally appealing, like the rocks that form the earth; but, just like those rocks, that love forms the foundation of Cathy's being and is essential to her life. By juxtaposing these two men, Cathy is better able to express her thoughts about them.

Analysis

Once basic comprehension has been reached, the reader can dive into making inferences from the text. This is a skill that requires the reader to look beyond the surface of the passage. While basic comprehension helps the reader understand explicit information, passages also include implicit information. This includes the underlying meaning in the text that is not directly stated by the author. To make inferences, readers will draw conclusions based on implicit information. Inferences from the text require a more nuanced understanding of the author's intent and how they are conveying that through language and data.

In order to make inferences in the text, the reader must look at the verbal evidence used. This includes the tone of the text, connotations, and descriptive language. If an author is describing a character's actions with phrases such as *frantic pacing*, *wild hand gestures*, and *heavy breathing*, a reader may infer that the character is feeling anxious. This verbal evidence allows the reader to draw a conclusion that is not explicitly stated.

Readers can also use quantitative data. The way this data is presented will affect the reader's interpretation. Is the data shared as a graph, chart, or table? Different presentations may emphasize the data or minimize the data based on the appearance. For example, showing two opposing data points on a graph may emphasize their difference. However, presenting them in a table would not have the same visual impact. Paying close attention to how data is presented will help with understanding the author's intent, which can contribute to creating inferences of the text.

An example could be a historical text that discusses the possibility of a volcanic eruption near the reader's town. It may not explicitly state that a volcanic eruption is imminent. However, it shows data that the volcano erupts every 1500 years. The reader can then calculate that it has been 1485 years since the last eruption. The author goes into detail about the devastating destruction to local communities that the volcanic eruption would bring. From this, the reader could infer that an eruption will occur soon and that the local communities should prepare for the aftermath of the eruption. In this case, the reader's inference is incredibly important and is required in order for them to take appropriate action in a real-life scenario. This shows that making inferences is a multifaceted skill that can enhance an individual's critical thinking and affect their perspective.

Identifying the Author's Purpose

When it comes to an author's writing, readers should always identify a **position** or **stance**. No matter how objective a text may seem, readers should assume the author has preconceived beliefs. One can reduce the likelihood of accepting an invalid argument by looking for multiple articles on the topic, including those with varying opinions. If several opinions point in the same direction and are backed by reputable peer-reviewed sources, it's more likely that the author has a valid argument. Positions that run contrary to widely held beliefs and existing data should invite scrutiny. There are exceptions to the rule, so readers should be careful consumers of information.

While themes, symbols, and motifs are buried deep within the text and can sometimes be difficult to infer, an author's **purpose** is usually obvious from the beginning. There are four purposes of writing: to inform, to persuade, to describe, and to entertain. **Informative** writing presents facts in an accessible way. **Persuasive** writing appeals to emotions and logic to inspire the reader to adopt a specific stance. Readers should be wary of this type of writing, as it can mask a lack of objectivity with powerful emotion. **Descriptive** writing is designed to paint a picture in the reader's mind, while texts that **entertain** are often narratives designed to engage and delight the reader.

The various writing styles are usually blended, with one purpose dominating the rest. A persuasive text, for example, might begin with a humorous tale to make readers more receptive to the persuasive message, or a recipe in a cookbook designed to inform might be preceded by an entertaining anecdote that makes the recipes more appealing.

Author's Position and Response to Different Viewpoints

If an author presents a differing opinion or a counterargument in order to refute it, the reader should consider how and why the information is being presented. It is meant to strengthen the original argument and shouldn't be confused with the author's intended conclusion, but it should also be considered in the reader's final evaluation.

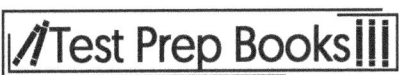

Authors can also use bias if they ignore the opposing viewpoint or present their side in an unbalanced way. A strong argument considers the opposition and finds a way to refute it. Critical readers should look for an unfair or one-sided presentation of the argument and be skeptical, as a bias may be present. Even if this bias is unintentional, if it exists in the writing, the reader should be wary of the validity of the argument. Readers should also look for the use of stereotypes, which refer to specific groups. Stereotypes are often negative connotations about a person or place and should always be avoided. When a critical reader finds stereotypes in a piece of writing, they should be critical of the argument, and consider the validity of anything the author presents. Stereotypes reveal a flaw in the writer's thinking and may suggest a lack of knowledge or understanding about the subject.

Inferring the Author's Purpose in the Passage

In nonfiction writing, authors employ argumentative techniques to present their opinion to readers in the most convincing way. First of all, persuasive writing usually includes at least one type of appeal: an appeal to logic (**logos**), emotion (**pathos**), or credibility and trustworthiness (**ethos**). When a writer appeals to logic, they are asking readers to agree with them based on research, evidence, and an established line of reasoning. An author's argument might also appeal to readers' emotions, perhaps by including personal stories and anecdotes (a short narrative of a specific event). A final type of appeal—appeal to authority—asks the reader to agree with the author's argument on the basis of their expertise or credentials. Consider three different approaches to arguing the same opinion:

Logic (Logos)

Below is an example of an appeal to logic. The author uses evidence to disprove the logic of the school's rule (the rule was supposed to reduce discipline problems; the number of problems has not been reduced; therefore, the rule is not working) and he or she calls for its repeal.

> Our school should abolish its current ban on campus cell phone use. The ban was adopted last year as an attempt to reduce class disruptions and help students focus more on their lessons. However, since the rule was enacted, there has been no change in the number of disciplinary problems in class. Therefore, the rule is ineffective and should be done away with.

Emotion (Pathos)

An author's argument might also appeal to readers' emotions, perhaps by including personal stories and anecdotes. The next example presents an appeal to emotion. By sharing the personal anecdote of one student and speaking about emotional topics like family relationships, the author invokes the reader's empathy in asking them to reconsider the school rule.

> Our school should abolish its current ban on campus cell phone use. If students aren't able to use their phones during the school day, many of them feel isolated from their loved ones. For example, last semester, one student's grandmother had a heart attack in the morning. However, because he couldn't use his cell phone, the student didn't know about his grandmother's condition until the end of the day—when she had already passed away and it was too late to say goodbye. By preventing students from contacting their friends and family, our school is placing undue stress and anxiety on students.

Credibility (Ethos)

Finally, an appeal to authority includes a statement from a relevant expert. In this case, the author uses a doctor in the field of education to support the argument. All three examples begin from the same

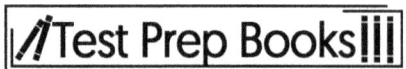

opinion—the school's phone ban needs to change—but rely on different argumentative styles to persuade the reader.

> Our school should abolish its current ban on campus cell phone use. According to Dr. Bartholomew Everett, a leading educational expert, "Research studies show that cell phone usage has no real impact on student attentiveness. Rather, phones provide a valuable technological resource for learning. Schools need to learn how to integrate this new technology into their curriculum." Rather than banning phones altogether, our school should follow the advice of experts and allow students to use phones as part of their learning.

Rhetorical Questions

Another commonly used argumentative technique is asking **rhetorical questions**, questions that do not actually require an answer but that push the reader to consider the topic further.

> I wholly disagree with the proposal to ban restaurants from serving foods with high sugar and sodium contents. Do we really want to live in a world where the government can control what we eat? I prefer to make my own food choices.

Here, the author's rhetorical question prompts readers to put themselves in a hypothetical situation and imagine how they would feel about it.

Inferences from the Text

Readers should be able to make **inferences**. Making an inference requires the reader to read between the lines and look for what's *implied* rather than what's directly stated. Using information that is known from the text, the reader is able to make a logical assumption about information that isn't directly stated but is probably true.

Making inferences is crucial for readers because literary texts often avoid presenting complete and direct information about characters' thoughts or feelings, leaving the reader to interpret clues in the text. In order to make inferences, readers should ask:

- What details are presented in the text?
- Is there any important information that seems to be missing?
- Based on the information that the author does include, what else is probably true?
- Is this inference reasonable based on what is already known?

Drawing Conclusions Not Explicitly Present in the Text

It's also useful to infer meaning from informative texts. Scientists and researchers make inferences every day in order to develop new theories based on facts and observations. Readers of informative texts should also understand how inferences are applied in academic research. Generally speaking, there are two main types of reasoning—*deductive* and *inductive*. An inference based on **deductive reasoning** considers a principle that is generally believed to be true and then applies it to a specific situation ("All English majors love reading. Annabelle is an English major. Therefore, I can infer that Annabelle loves reading."). **Inductive reasoning** makes an inference by using specific evidence to make a general inference ("Trina, Arnold, and Uchenna are all from Florida. Trina, Arnold, and Uchenna all love to swim. Therefore, I can infer that people from Florida usually love swimming."). Both deductive and inductive reasoning use what is *known* to be true to make a logical guess about what is *probably* true.

Verbal Reasoning Section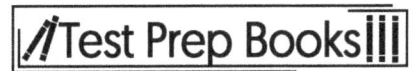

Inferring the Traits, Feelings, and Motives of Characters

Inferences are useful in gaining a deeper understanding of characters in a narrative. Readers can use the same strategies outlined above—paying attention to details and using them to make reasonable guesses about the text—to read between the lines and get a more complete picture of how (and why) characters are thinking, feeling, and acting. Read the following passage from O. Henry's story "The Gift of the Magi":

> One dollar and eighty-seven cents. That was all. And sixty cents of it was in pennies. Pennies saved one and two at a time by bulldozing the grocer and the vegetable man and the butcher until one's cheeks burned with the silent imputation of parsimony that such close dealing implied. Three times Della counted it. One dollar and eighty-seven cents. And the next day would be Christmas.

> There was clearly nothing to do but flop down on the shabby little couch and howl. So Della did it.

These paragraphs introduce the reader to the character Della. Even though the author doesn't include a direct description of Della, the reader can already form a general impression of her personality and emotions. One detail that should stick out to the reader is repetition: "one dollar and eighty-seven cents." This amount is repeated twice in the first paragraph, along with other descriptions of money: "sixty cents of it was in pennies," "pennies saved one and two at a time." The story's preoccupation with money parallels how Della herself is constantly thinking about her finances—"three times Della counted" her meager savings. Already the reader can guess that Della is having money problems. Next, think about her emotions.

The first paragraph describes haggling over groceries "until one's cheeks burned"—another way to describe blushing. People tend to blush when they are embarrassed or ashamed, so readers can infer that Della is ashamed by her financial situation. This inference is also supported by the second paragraph, when she flops down and howls on her "shabby little couch." Clearly, she's in distress. Without saying, "Della has no money and is embarrassed to be poor," O. Henry is able to communicate the same impression to readers through his careful inclusion of details.

A character's **motive** is their reason for acting a certain way. Usually, characters are motivated by something that they want. In the passage above, why is Della upset about not having enough money? There's an important detail at the end of the first paragraph: "the next day would be Christmas." Why is money especially important around Christmas? Christmas is a holiday when people exchange gifts. If Della is struggling with money, she's probably also struggling to buy gifts. So a shrewd reader should be able to guess that Della's motivation is wanting to buy a gift for someone—but she's currently unable to afford it, leading to feelings of shame and frustration.

In order to understand characters in a text, readers should keep the following questions in mind:

- What words does the author use to describe the character? Are these words related to any specific emotions or personality traits (for example, characteristics like rude, friendly, unapproachable, or innocent)?

- What does the character say? Does their dialogue seem to be straightforward, or are they hiding some thoughts or emotions?

- What actions can be observed from this character? How do their actions reflect their feelings?
- What does the character want? What do they do to get it?

Interpreting Nonliteral Language

It's important to be able to recognize and interpret **figurative**, or non-literal, language. Literal statements rely directly on the denotations of words and express exactly what's happening in reality. Figurative language uses non-literal expressions to present information in a creative way. Consider the following sentences:

   a. His pillow was very soft, and he fell asleep quickly.

   b. His pillow was a fluffy cloud, and he floated away on it to the dream world.

Sentence A is literal, employing only the real meanings of each word. Sentence B is figurative. It employs a metaphor by stating that his pillow was a cloud. Of course, he isn't actually sleeping on a cloud, but the reader can draw on images of clouds as light, soft, fluffy, and relaxing to get a sense of how the character felt as he fell asleep. Also, in sentence B, the pillow becomes a vehicle that transports him to a magical dream world. The character isn't literally floating through the air—he's simply falling asleep! But by utilizing figurative language, the author creates a scene of peace, comfort, and relaxation that conveys stronger emotions and more creative imagery than the purely literal sentence. While there are countless types of figurative language, there are a few common ones that any reader should recognize.

Simile and *metaphor* are comparisons between two things, but their formats differ slightly. A **simile** says that two things are *similar* and makes a comparison using "like" or "as"—A is like B, or A is as [some characteristic] as B—whereas a metaphor states that two things are exactly the same—A is B. In both cases, simile and **metaphor** invite the reader to think more deeply about the characteristics of the two subjects and consider where they overlap. An example of metaphor can be found in the above sentence about the sleeper ("His pillow was a fluffy cloud"). For an example of simile, look at the first line of Robert Burns' famous poem:

   My love is like a red, red rose

This is comparison using "like," and the two things being compared are love and a rose. Some characteristics of a rose are that it's fragrant, beautiful, blossoming, colorful, vibrant—by comparing his love to a rose, Burns asks the reader to apply these qualities to his love. In this way, he implies that his love is also fresh, blossoming, and brilliant.

Similes can also compare things that appear dissimilar. Here's a song lyric from Florence and the Machine:

   Happiness hit her like a bullet in the back

"Happiness" has a very positive connotation, but getting "a bullet in the back" seems violent and aggressive, not at all related to happiness. By using an unexpected comparison, the writer forces readers to think more deeply about the comparison and ask themselves how could getting shot be similar to feeling happy. "A bullet in the back" is something that she doesn't see coming; it's sudden and forceful; and presumably, it has a strong impact on her life. So, in this way, the author seems to be saying that unexpected happiness made a sudden and powerful change in her life.

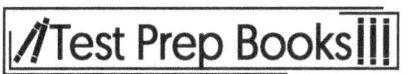

Another common form of figurative language is **personification**, when a non-human object is given human characteristics. William Blake uses personification here:

> ... the stars threw down their spears,
>
> And watered heaven with their tears

He imagines the stars as combatants in a heavenly battle, giving them both action (throwing down their spears) and emotion (the sadness and disappointment of their tears). Personification helps to add emotion or develop relationships between characters and non-human objects. In fact, most people use personification in their everyday lives:

> My alarm clock betrayed me! It didn't go off this morning!
>
> The last piece of chocolate cake was staring at me from the refrigerator.

Next is **hyperbole**, a type of figurative language that uses extreme exaggeration. Sentences like, "I love you to the moon and back," or "I will love you for a million years," are examples of hyperbole. They aren't literally true—unfortunately, people cannot jump to outer space or live for a million years—but they're creative expressions that communicate the depth of feeling of the author.

Another way that writers add deeper meaning to their work is through *allusions*. An **allusion** is a reference to something from history, literature, or another cultural source. When the text is from a different culture or a time period, readers may not be familiar with every allusion. However, allusions tend to be well-known because the author wants the reader to make a connection between what's happening in the text and what's being referenced.

> I can't believe my best friend told our professor that I was skipping class to finish my final project! What a Judas!

This sentence contains a Biblical allusion to Judas, a friend and follower of Jesus who betrayed Jesus to the Romans. In this case, the allusion to Judas is used to give a deeper impression of betrayal and disloyalty from a trusted friend. Commonly used allusions in Western texts may come from the Bible, Greek or Roman mythology, or well-known literature such as Shakespeare. By familiarizing themselves with these touchstones of history and culture, readers can be more prepared to recognize allusions.

Analyzing Individuals, Events, and Ideas Over the Course of a Text

Transitions are the glue that holds the writing together. They function to purposefully incorporate new topics and supporting details in a smooth and coherent way. Transitions and the corresponding structure they create can be used to determine how individuals, events, and ideas change and develop over the course of the text.

Transition words can be categorized based on the relationships they create between ideas:

- **General order**: signaling elaboration of an idea to emphasize a point—e.g., *for example, for instance, to demonstrate, including, such as, in other words, that is, in fact, also, furthermore, likewise, and, truly, so, surely, certainly, obviously, doubtless*

- **Chronological order**: referencing the time frame in which the main event or idea occurs—e.g., *before, after, first, while, soon, shortly thereafter, meanwhile*

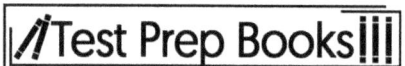

- **Numerical order/order of importance**: indicating that related ideas, supporting details, or events will be described in a sequence, possibly in order of importance—e.g., *first, second, also, finally, another, in addition, equally important, less importantly, most significantly, the main reason, last but not least*

- **Spatial order**: referring to the space and location of something or where things are located in relation to each other—e.g., *inside, outside, above, below, within, close, under, over, far, next to, adjacent to*

- **Cause and effect order**: signaling a causal relationship between events or ideas—e.g., *thus, therefore, since, resulted in, for this reason, as a result, consequently, hence, for, so*

- **Compare and contrast order**: identifying the similarities and differences between two or more objects, ideas, or lines of thought—e.g., *like, as, similarly, equally, just as, unlike, however, but, although, conversely, on the other hand, on the contrary*

- **Summary order**: indicating that a particular idea is coming to a close—e.g., *in conclusion, to sum up, in other words, ultimately, above all*

Evidence

Effective writing relies on its ability to present strong, convincing evidence to the reader. This applies to writing on all subjects and at all academic levels. The strength of evidence directly correlates with the credibility and persuasiveness of the writing. Thus, it is important that writers select relevant, reliable evidence that supports the main purpose of the writing.

Evidence should be thoroughly researched before including it in writing. It should come from reliable sources that are known to be academically sound. This may include academic journals, scientific studies, or other reputable publications. The information provided in the evidence should cross-reference other accurate sources, particularly those that have been peer reviewed. Peer-reviewed sources are checked for biases and incorrect information that need to be eliminated.

Once a writer has a grasp on what strong evidence looks like, the next step is to look for information that is relevant to the writing. Evidence should support the main points and purpose of the writing. Writers should consider what the audience of the writing needs to know. It is helpful to choose evidence that speaks to the audience's needs. For example, if the writing's purpose is to pitch a new technology to corporate businesses, it would be beneficial to include evidence on the costs and revenue of that new technology.

Once effective sources for the writing have been selected, they must be integrated into the writing. This means using the evidence in the portions of the writing that present relevant ideas. For example, if a paragraph is about geothermal energy, it would be appropriate to include statistical information that was found in an article from the Department of Energy. There should be an apparent connection between the writing and the evidence. The reader should not have to guess at the argument or how the evidence relates to it.

To strengthen the writing and the evidence being shared, the writer should analyze the evidence and how it relates to the main purpose of their work. They should explicitly explain the meaning of what they are sharing with the reader. The writer can then further evaluate why the information is significant and why the audience should care about what they are reading. Pointing out the importance of the evidence and the broader purpose of the work helps create a bigger impact on the reader. It is essential to also keep in mind the academic level of the audience, as it may be necessary to simplify or elevate the language for their needs.

Most importantly, the reader should be given evidential context. Information from a source should not be dropped randomly into the writing. Instead, quotes or data from the source should be provided with proper citation. There are numerous citation styles, and they vary depending on the subject of the writing and the requirements of the assignment. However, citations are always necessary, as they provide the original author with proper credit. This ensures that the audience does not believe that the cited information came from the work that they are reading. Plagiarism should be avoided at all costs.

Drawing Conclusions and Making Generalizations

As readers are presented with new information, they should organize it, make sense of it, and reflect on what they learned from the text. Readers draw conclusions at the end of a text by bringing together all of the details, descriptions, facts, and/or opinions presented by the author and asking, "What did I gain from reading this text? How have my ideas or emotions changed? What was the author's overall purpose for writing?" In this case, a **conclusion** is a unifying idea or final thought about the text that the reader can form after they are done reading. As discussed earlier, sometimes writers are very explicit in stating what conclusions should be drawn from a text and what readers are meant to have learned. However, more often than not, writers simply present descriptions or information and then leave it up to readers to draw their own conclusions. As with making inferences, though, readers always need to base their conclusions on textual evidence rather than simply guessing or making random statements.

> When the school district's uniform policy was first introduced fifteen years ago, parents and students alike were incredibly enthusiastic about it. Some of the most appealing arguments in favor of enforcing school uniforms was to create an equal learning environment for all students, to eliminate the focus on fashion and appearance, and to simplify students' morning routine by removing the need to pick a different outfit every day. However, despite this promising beginning, the uniform policy has steadily lost favor over the years. First of all, schools did not notice a significant drop in examples of bullying at school, and students continue to report that they feel judged on their appearance based on things like weight and hairstyle. This seems to indicate that uniforms have not been particularly effective at removing the social pressure that teens feel to appear a certain way in front of their peers. Also, many parents have complained that the school's required uniform pieces like jackets, sweaters, and neckties can only be purchased from one specific clothing shop. Because this retailer has cornered the market on school uniforms, they are operating under a total monopoly, and disgruntled parents feel that they are being grossly overcharged for school clothing for their children. The uniform policy is set to be debated at the upcoming school board meeting, and many expect it to be overturned.

After reading this article, a reader might conclude any of the following: that ideas that start with popular support might become unpopular over time; or that there are several compelling counterarguments to the benefits of school uniforms; or that this school district is open to new ideas but also open to criticism. While each conclusion is slightly different, they are all based on information and evidence from the article, and therefore all are plausible. Each conclusion sums up what the reader learned from the passage and what overall idea the writer seems to be communicating.

Another way for readers to make sense of information in a text is to make **generalizations**. This is somewhat related to the concept of inductive reasoning, by which readers move from specific evidence

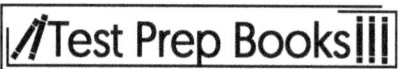

Verbal Reasoning Section

to a more general idea. When readers generalize, they take the specific content of a text and apply it to a larger context or to a different situation. Let's make a generalization from the topic, the bystander effect:

> A bystander is simply a person who watches something happen. Paradoxically, the more people who witness an accident happen, the less likely each individual is to actually intervene and offer assistance. This is known as the bystander effect. Psychologists attribute the bystander effect to something called "diffusion of responsibility." If one individual witnesses an accident, that single person feels the whole burden of responsibility to respond to the accident. However, if there are many witnesses, each person feels that responsibility has been divided amongst many people, so their individual sense of responsibility is much lower and they are less likely to offer help.

This article describes one very specific psychological phenomenon known as the "bystander effect." However, based on this specific information, a reader could form a more general psychological statement such as, "Humans sometimes behave differently when they are alone and when they are in a group."

It's also possible to make generalizations from literary texts. This is a particularly useful reading skill when evaluating the collective works of a particular writer or when forming a general characterization of texts from a particular genre or time period. For example, after reading a handful of novels by Jane Austen, all of which feature clever female protagonists and contain several examples of cynical or unflattering depictions of marriage, a reader can form a general impression of Jane Austen's thoughts on women's social roles. An overarching generalization from these novels might be that, "Education is just as important for women as marriage," or "Marriage isn't a guarantee of happiness or satisfaction." Being able to form generalizations is an important step in drawing connections and establishing relationships between texts.

Making Predictions

When readers make **predictions**, they try to anticipate what will happen next in the text. Think about how weather forecasters make predictions for future weather conditions. It's not purely guesswork. Rather, they gather a wide variety of relevant data, analyze the information they've collected, and also compare it with previous weather patterns. Finally, they're able to make a well-researched prediction with a high rate of probability. Readers must do the same when making predictions in a text—rather than simply guessing, they draw information from earlier in the text and use preexisting knowledge to form a prediction that's reasonably likely to be true.

In literary texts, authors tend to give clues that guide readers through the narrative. One method is *foreshadowing*, where the author hints at what will happen next in the story. Consider these lines from *Romeo and Juliet* in which Juliet desires to learn more about Romeo.

She says to her nurse:

> Go ask his name.—If he be married.
>
> My grave is like to be my wedding bed.

At this point in the play, Juliet's lines simply mean that she would be sorely disappointed to learn that Romeo was already attached to another woman. However, for readers who already know how the play ends, this sentence carries another level of meaning—Juliet's marital choices will go hand in hand with her death. In this way, Shakespeare foreshadows the tragic end of Juliet's love story at the very moment it begins.

Of course, authors sometimes give false hints that lead readers to dead ends. This type of misdirection is especially commonplace in genres like mystery and suspense, where the author wants to keep the reader guessing until the very end. A distracting hint that turns out to be false is known as a **red herring**. However, if readers are aware that certain genres are likely to contain red herrings, then readers can be more cautious in evaluating hints. If a clue seems too obvious, it might be a red herring! In a roundabout way, then, red herrings can actually *help* readers make predictions by forcing them to look beyond the most obvious details.

In addition to clues sprinkled throughout the text, readers can also make predictions by considering the tone and mood of a text. For example, if a story has an overall gloomy mood or its diction creates a tone that is melancholy and foreboding, readers will expect that dark or depressing events will follow. On the other hand, if the tone is playful and lighthearted, readers are less likely to expect tragedy and might instead predict a comic or happy outcome. If the outcome of the story is vastly different from what either readers or the story's characters themselves are expecting, the author is probably using irony.

It's also possible to make predictions in non-literary texts. Consider a persuasive article that opens with the following thesis statement:

> There are countless reasons why closing down the city's only public dog park is a bad idea for local citizens.

Readers can expect that the rest of the essay will contain evidence that supports the author's opinion. The same is also true of informative texts. Imagine a scientific article that contains this sentence:

> Surprising new evidence challenges long-held beliefs about the cognitive capabilities of non-human animals.

In the paragraphs that follow, readers might expect to find any of the following: background on previously accepted theories of animal cognition, description of new scientific research or experimentation, and interpretation and discussion of the experiment's results. By making these predictions whenever they encounter a new text, readers will be more prepared to understand new information and opinions. Also, making predictions about information is especially useful when readers have a limited amount of time to read a text for relevant details. By reading either the thesis statement of the article or the topic sentences of each paragraph, readers can then make logical predictions about what information might be discussed later without having to read the entire text first.

Analogies

Analogies are used to connect various concepts and relationships in a way that deepens our understanding. They are a powerful tool that is used to draw parallels within language. By finding similarities between ideas, it becomes possible to compare their relationship to other concepts that may also be related. Analogies are highly diverse in their possible applications.

The standard structure of an analogy is represented as *A : B :: C : D*, which may look a bit confusing. However, this structure establishes that *A* and *B* have a relationship that is similar to that of *C* and *D*. To

begin, an example of a basic analogy may help clarify their function. For this example, *A* represents *tree*, *B* represents *leaf*, *C* represents *flower*, and *D* represents *petal*. So, the structure would appear as *Tree : Leaf :: Flower : Petal*. The relationship here is that a leaf is something that grows from a tree. This works as an analogy for the flower and petal, as a petal is something that grows from a flower. The relationship between *A* and *B* is parallel to the relationship between *C* and *D*. This is an appropriate use of the analogy.

There are multiple types of analogies. These types are based on the relationship between the terms being used. Firstly, there are synonymous analogies. These are analogies where the relationship between the terms mirrors the relationship of the analogue terms. These analogies highlight similarities. An example of this would be *Good : Wonderful :: Bad : Horrible*, where each pair of words are synonymous. On the other end, there are antonymous analogies. This is where the words in the analogy are antonyms. An example of this would be *Lazy : Hardworking :: Rude : Kind*, in which each pair of words are antonymous with each other.

Other analogies feature a cause-and-effect relationship. These analogies show how one action can lead to another. An example of this would be *Rainstorm : Flood :: Earthquake : Tsunami,* which functions because rainstorms lead to floods and earthquakes lead to tsunamis. Analogies can also display part-to-whole relationships. For example, *Roof : House :: Engine : Car* functions because a roof is a part of a house, and an engine is a part of a car. These terms are all analogous. The earlier example about trees, leaves, flowers, and petals could be considered a part-to-whole analogy.

Additional analogy types include object-to-purpose and tool-to-user. An object-to-purpose analogy shows the relationship between an item and its intended use. For example, *Knife : Cut :: Pencil : Write* shows what each item is designed to do. A tool-to-user analogy is specific to the human-related function of the item. For example, *Paintbrush : Artist :: Gavel : Judge* shows the primary item used in a specific role.

One thing to keep in mind with analogy types is that the order may be reversed. An example of this would be with the tool-to-user analogy. Instead of *Paintbrush : Artist :: Gavel : Judge* it could also read as *Artist: Paintbrush :: Judge : Gavel*, in which the order would then be user to tool. Ultimately these are the same, they are just formatted differently. The meaning and connection between the terms is unchanged despite the difference in order.

As mentioned earlier, analogies break down complex or abstract concepts by linking easier to understand ideas. They create a bridge in the mind that connects the known and unknown. They are an effective way of conquering challenging material. This makes them an invaluable tool in the classroom. This is true for both teachers and students. Teachers can use analogies to keep lessons engaging while promoting creativity. Asking students to come up with analogous terms allows them to tap into numerous subjects that they are familiar with. This in turn helps the student to connect new ideas with prior knowledge.

Analogies can also be useful in everyday life. Concepts and tools used in one area of life can be applied to other similar situations. For example, somebody who played on a sports team growing up may recognize that teamwork in their workplace is extremely similar. Thus, they can make an analogous connection with the type of communication and collaboration efforts they should use. Another example would be an interior designer that is learning how to design a website. They can make analogous connections regarding aesthetic design and functionality, despite the two mediums being completely different. This type of thinking can be applied to life skills, hobbies, and more. Drawing similarities between the known and unknown can speed up progress and efficiency in numerous parts of life.

Analogies also have the ability to improve communication. Complex ideas and feelings can be made more understandable through the use of analogies. This is especially effective when dealing with a diverse audience. This could include aiding in the explanation of cultural gaps or personal experiences. Analogies can create shared perspectives which help forge stronger connections. They can also be persuasive. For example, to persuade their clients to take care of their body by eating good foods and getting exercise, a gym trainer may analogize the human body to that of a car that requires high-quality fuel and maintenance.

As explained in this guide, analogies are useful tools that can be applied to educational, professional, and personal situations. They are especially effective at connecting prior knowledge with new ideas. Analogies of all types are expressed in the format *A : B :: C : D*. These types include synonymous, antonymous, cause-and-effect, part-to-whole, and more. The order of the analogy may switch, but the meaning behind the comparison will remain the same.

Practice Quiz

Passage

This passage is adapted from Frankenstein *by Mary Shelley, originally published in 1818.*

[1] I sat one evening in my laboratory; the sun had set, and the moon was just rising from the sea; I had not sufficient light for my employment, and I remained idle, in a pause of consideration of whether I should leave my labor for the night or hasten its conclusion by an unremitting attention to it. As I sat, a train of reflection occurred to me which led me to consider the effects of what I was now doing. Three years before, I was engaged in the same manner and had created a fiend whose unparalleled barbarity had desolated my heart and filled it forever with the bitterest remorse. I was now about to form another being of whose dispositions I was alike ignorant; she might become ten thousand times more malignant than her mate and delight, for its own sake, in murder and wretchedness. He had sworn to quit the neighborhood of man and hide himself in deserts, but she had not; and she, who in all probability was to become a thinking and reasoning animal, might refuse to comply with a compact made before her creation. They might even hate each other; the creature who already lived loathed his own deformity, and might he not conceive a greater abhorrence for it when it came before his eyes in the female form? She also might turn with disgust from him to the superior beauty of man; she might quit him, and he be again alone, exasperated by the fresh provocation of being deserted by one of his own species.

[2] Even if they were to leave Europe and inhabit the deserts of the new world, yet one of the first results of those sympathies for which the dæmon thirsted would be children, and a race of devils would be propagated upon the earth who might make the very existence of the species of man a condition precarious and full of terror. Had I right, for my own benefit, to inflict this curse upon everlasting generations? I had before been moved by the sophisms of the being I had created; I had been struck senseless by his fiendish threats; but now, for the first time, the wickedness of my promise burst upon me; I shuddered to think that future ages might curse me as their pest, whose selfishness had not hesitated to buy its own peace at the price, perhaps, of the existence of the whole human race.

[3] I trembled and my heart failed within me, when, on looking up, I saw by the light of the moon the dæmon at the casement. A ghastly grin wrinkled his lips as he gazed on me, where I sat fulfilling the task which he had allotted to me. Yes, he had followed me in my travels; he had loitered in forests, hid himself in caves, or taken refuge in wide and desert heaths; and he now came to mark my progress and claim the fulfilment of my promise.

[4] As I looked on him, his countenance expressed the utmost extent of malice and treachery. I thought with a sensation of madness on my promise of creating another like to him, and trembling with passion, tore to pieces the thing on which I was engaged. The wretch saw me destroy the creature on whose future existence he depended for happiness, and with a howl of devilish despair and revenge, withdrew.

[5] I left the room, and locking the door, made a solemn vow in my own heart never to resume my labors; and then, with trembling steps, I sought my own apartment. I was alone; none were near me to dissipate the gloom and relieve me from the sickening oppression of the most terrible reveries.

[6] Several hours passed, and I remained near my window gazing on the sea; it was almost motionless, for the winds were hushed, and all nature reposed under the eye of the quiet moon. A few fishing vessels alone specked the water, and now and then the gentle breeze wafted the sound of voices as the fishermen called to one another. I felt the silence, although I was hardly conscious of its extreme profundity, until my ear was suddenly arrested by the paddling of oars near the shore, and a person landed close to my house.

[7] In a few minutes after, I heard the creaking of my door, as if someone endeavored to open it softly. I trembled from head to foot; I felt a presentiment of who it was and wished to rouse one of the peasants who dwelt in a cottage not far from mine; but I was overcome by the sensation of helplessness, so often felt in frightful dreams, when you in vain endeavor to fly from an impending danger, and was rooted to the spot.

[8] Presently I heard the sound of footsteps along the passage; the door opened, and the wretch whom I dreaded appeared. Shutting the door, he approached me and said in a smothered voice,

[9] "You have destroyed the work which you began; what is it that you intend? Do you dare to break your promise? I have endured toil and misery; I left Switzerland with you; I crept along the shores of the Rhine, among its willow islands and over the summits of its hills. I have dwelt many months in the heaths of England and among the deserts of Scotland. I have endured incalculable fatigue, and cold, and hunger; do you dare destroy my hopes?"

[10] "Begone! I do break my promise; never will I create another like yourself, equal in deformity and wickedness."

1. Which choice best describes the tone of the passage?
    a. Darkly contemplating the predilections of a potential monster
    b. Sensationalizing a known monster's wicked deeds
    c. Tensely describing the events that inspired a conflict between a scientist and his creation
    d. Crafting an intricate portrait of a morally conflicted scientist and his devilish creation

2. Which lines in the passage most clearly provide the reason for the conflict between Dr. Frankenstein and his monster?
    a. Paragraph 2, Sentence 1 ("Even if...terror.")
    b. Paragraph 1, Sentence 3 ("Three years...remorse.")
    c. Paragraph 3, Sentence 3 ("Yes...promise.")
    d. Paragraph 4, Sentence 2 ("I thought...engaged.")

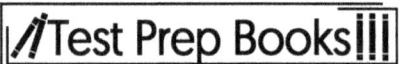

3. The word *failed* in Paragraph 3, Sentence 1 most closely means
    a. broke.
    b. faltered.
    c. thumped.
    d. sped up.

4. virus : plague victims ::
    a. the monsters : humanity
    b. the act of creation : the monsters
    c. evil : the monsters
    d. Dr. Frankenstein : the monsters

5. creator : betrayer ::
    a. Dr. Frankenstein : monster
    b. scientist : laborer
    c. Dr. Frankenstein : himself
    d. monster : laborer

See answers on the next page.

Answer Explanations

1. C: Choice *C* correctly notes the tense tone of the passage as Dr. Frankenstein's narration describes his destruction of the creature on the table and his fearful wait for the monster to confront him afterward. Choices *A* and *B* would require the passage to be composed entirely of reflections on the potential actions of the new monster and the past deeds of the living monster, respectively. Choice *D* would mean that the passage was devoted to descriptions of its characters rather than to the action of the creature's destruction and the start of the confrontation between Frankenstein and his monster.

2. D: Choice *D* narrates the action of the creature's destruction, the reason for the conflict between creator and monster. Choice *A* contemplates the potential future actions of the creature on the table, and Choices *B* and *C* are about things that Frankenstein and his monster have done in the past.

3. B: Choice *B* indicates Dr. Frankenstein's heart weakening at the horror of the sight. Choice *A* would signify sorrow rather than the dread and fear shown in the passage. Choices *C* and *D* pertain to a heart that is strong and active and are not in line with the idea of something failing.

4. A: Choice *A* reflects Dr. Frankenstein's view that the monsters would bring suffering and ruin upon mankind if allowed to reproduce. Choices *B*, *C*, and *D* require viewing the monsters as victims, while Dr. Frankenstein sees them as the potential scourge of humanity. Also, for Choice *D* to be accurate, Dr. Frankenstein would somehow have to proliferate and multiply within the monsters the way he feared the monsters would multiply among the helpless masses of mankind.

5. C: Choice *C* acknowledges that Dr. Frankenstein created his monster and also betrayed him by destroying the creature on the table. Choice *A* would require the monster to have betrayed Frankenstein, and Choices *B* and *D* equate labor with betrayal, while the passage does not.

Grammar and Writing Section

Types of Sentences

There isn't an overabundance of absolutes in grammar, but here is one: every sentence in the English language falls into one of four categories.

- **Declarative:** a simple statement that ends with a period

    The price of milk per gallon is the same as the price of gasoline.

- **Imperative:** a command, instruction, or request that ends with a period

    Buy milk when you stop to fill up your car with gas.

- **Interrogative:** a question that ends with a question mark

    Will you buy the milk?

- **Exclamatory:** a statement or command that expresses emotions like anger, urgency, or surprise and ends with an exclamation mark

    Buy the milk now!

Declarative sentences are the most common type, probably because they are comprised of the most general content, without any of the bells and whistles that the other three types contain. They are, simply, declarations or statements of any degree of seriousness, importance, or information.

Imperative sentences often seem to be missing a subject. The subject is there, though; it is just not visible or audible because it is *implied*. Look at the imperative example sentence.

   Buy the milk when you fill up your car with gas.

You is the implied subject, the one to whom the command is issued. This is sometimes called **the understood you** because it is understood that *you* is the subject of the sentence.

Interrogative sentences—those that ask questions—are defined as such from the idea of the word **interrogation**, the action of questions being asked of suspects by investigators. Although that is serious business, interrogative sentences apply to all kinds of questions.

To exclaim is at the root of **exclamatory** sentences. These are made with strong emotions behind them. The only technical difference between a declarative or imperative sentence and an exclamatory one is the exclamation mark at the end. The example declarative and imperative sentences can both become an exclamatory one simply by putting an exclamation mark at the end of the sentences.

   The price of milk per gallon is the same as the price of gasoline!
   Buy milk when you stop to fill up your car with gas!

After all, someone might be really excited by the price of gas or milk, or they could be mad at the person that will be buying the milk! However, as stated before, exclamation marks in abundance defeat their

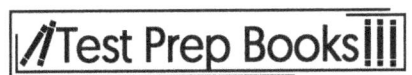

own purpose! After a while, they begin to cause fatigue! When used only for their intended purpose, they can have their expected and desired effect.

Parts of Speech

Nouns

A **noun** is a person, place, thing, or idea. All nouns fit into one of two types, common or proper.

A **common noun** is a word that identifies any of a class of people, places, or things. Examples include numbers, objects, animals, feelings, concepts, qualities, and actions. *A, an,* or *the* usually precedes the common noun. These parts of speech are called *articles*. Here are some examples of sentences using nouns preceded by articles.

A building is under construction.
The girl would like to move to *the* city.

A **proper noun** (also called a **proper name**) is used for the specific name of an individual person, place, or organization. The first letter in a proper noun is capitalized. "My name is *Mary*." "I work for *Walmart*."

Nouns sometimes serve as adjectives (which themselves describe nouns), such as "hockey player" and "state government."

- An **abstract noun** is an idea, state, or quality. It is something that can't be touched, such as happiness, courage, evil, or humor.

A **concrete noun** is something that can be experienced through the senses (touch, taste, hear, smell, see). Examples of concrete nouns are birds, skateboard, pie, and car.

A **collective noun** refers to a collection of people, places, or things that act as one. Examples of collective nouns are as follows: team, class, jury, family, audience, and flock.

Pronouns

A word used in place of a noun is known as a **pronoun**. Pronouns are words like *I, mine, hers,* and *us*.

Pronouns can be split into different classifications (seen below) which make them easier to learn; however, it's not important to memorize the classifications.

- **Personal pronouns:** refer to people, places, things, etc.
  - **First person:** we, I, our, mine
  - **Second person:** you, yours
  - **Third person:** he, them
- **Possessive pronouns:** demonstrate ownership (mine, his, hers, its, ours, theirs, yours)
- **Interrogative pronouns:** ask questions (what, which, who, whom, whose)
- **Relative pronouns:** include the five interrogative pronouns and others that are relative (whoever, whomever, that, when, where)
- **Demonstrative pronouns:** replace something specific (this, that, those, these)
- **Reciprocal pronouns:** indicate something was done or given in return (each other, one another)
- **Indefinite pronouns:** have a nonspecific status (anybody, whoever, someone, everybody, somebody)

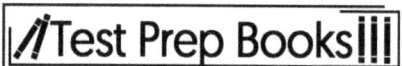

Indefinite pronouns such as *anybody, whoever, someone, everybody,* and *somebody* command a singular verb form, but others such as *all, none,* and *some* could require a singular or plural verb form.

Antecedents

An **antecedent** is the noun to which a pronoun refers; it needs to be written or spoken before the pronoun is used. For many pronouns, antecedents are imperative for clarity. In particular, many of the personal, possessive, and demonstrative pronouns need antecedents. Otherwise, it would be unclear who or what someone is referring to when they use a pronoun like *he* or *this*.

Pronoun reference means that the pronoun should refer clearly to one, clear, unmistakable noun (the antecedent).

Pronoun-antecedent agreement refers to the need for the antecedent and the corresponding pronoun to agree in gender, person, and number. Here are some examples:

> The *kidneys* (plural antecedent) are part of the urinary system. *They* (plural pronoun) serve several roles.

> The kidneys are part of the *urinary system* (singular antecedent). *It* (singular pronoun) is also known as the renal system.

Pronoun Cases

The subjective pronouns —*I, you, he/she/it, we, they,* and *who*—are the subjects of the sentence.

> Example: *They* have a new house.

The objective pronouns—*me, you* (singular)*, him/her, us, them,* and *whom*—are used when something is being done for or given to someone; they are objects of the action.

> Example: The teacher has an apple for *us*.

The possessive pronouns—*mine, my, your, yours, his, hers, its, their, theirs, our,* and *ours*—are used to denote that something (or someone) belongs to someone (or something).

> Example: It's *their* chocolate cake.
> Even Better Example: It's *my* chocolate cake!

One of the greatest challenges and worst abuses of pronouns concerns *who* and *whom*. Just knowing the following rule can eliminate confusion. *Who* is a subjective-case pronoun used only as a subject or subject complement. *Whom* is only objective-case and, therefore, the object of the verb or preposition.

> *Who* is going to the concert?

> You are going to the concert with *whom*?

Hint: When using *who* or *whom*, think of whether someone would say *he* or *him*. If the answer is *he*, use *who*. If the answer is *him*, use *whom*. This trick is easy to remember because *he* and *who* both end in vowels, and *him* and *whom* both end in the letter *M*.

Verbs

A **verb** is the part of speech that describes an action, state of being, or occurrence.

A verb forms the main part of a predicate of a sentence. This means that the verb explains what the noun (which will be discussed shortly) is doing. A simple example is *time flies*. The verb *flies* explains what the action of the noun, *time*, is doing. This example is a *main* verb.

Helping (auxiliary) verbs are words like *have, do, be, can, may, should, must,* and *will*. "I *should* go to the store." Helping verbs assist main verbs in expressing tense, ability, possibility, permission, or obligation.

Particles are minor function words like *not, in, out, up,* or *down* that become part of the verb itself. "I might *not*."

Participles are words formed from verbs that are often used to modify a noun, noun phrase, verb, or verb phrase.

>   The *running* teenager collided with the cyclist.

Participles can also create compound verb forms.

>   He is *speaking*.

Verbs have five basic forms: the **base** form, the **-s** form, the **-ing** form, the **past** form, and the **past participle** form.

The past forms are either **regular** (*love/loved; hate/hated*) or **irregular** because they don't end by adding the common past tense suffix "-ed" (*go/went; fall/fell; set/set*).

Verb Forms

Shifting verb forms entails **conjugation,** which is used to indicate tense, voice, or mood.

Verb tense is used to show when the action in the sentence took place. There are several different verb tenses, and it is important to know how and when to use them. Some verb tenses can be achieved by changing the form of the verb, while others require the use of helping verbs (e.g., *is, was,* or *has*).

Present tense shows the action is happening currently or is ongoing:

>   I walk to work every morning.

>   She is stressed about the deadline.

Past tense shows that the action happened in the past or that the state of being is in the past:

>   I walked to work yesterday morning.

>   She was stressed about the deadline.

Future tense shows that the action will happen in the future or is a future state of being:

>   I will walk to work tomorrow morning.

>   She will be stressed about the deadline.

Present perfect tense shows action that began in the past, but continues into the present:

>   I have walked to work all week.

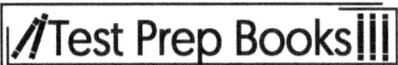

Grammar and Writing Section

She has been stressed about the deadline.

Past perfect tense shows an action was finished before another took place:

I had walked all week until I sprained my ankle.

She had been stressed about the deadline until we talked about it.

Future perfect tense shows an action that will be completed at some point in the future:

By the time the bus arrives, I will have walked to work already.

Voice

Verbs can be in the active or passive voice. When the subject completes the action, the verb is in **active voice**. When the subject receives the action of the sentence, the verb is in **passive voice**.

Active: Jamie ate the ice cream.

Passive: The ice cream was eaten by Jamie.

In active voice, the subject (*Jamie*) is the "do-er" of the action (*ate*). In passive voice, the subject *ice cream* receives the action of being eaten.

While passive voice can add variety to writing, active voice is the generally preferred sentence structure.

Mood

Mood is used to show the speaker's feelings about the subject matter. In English, there is indicative mood, imperative mood, and subjunctive mood.

Indicative mood is used to state facts, ask questions, or state opinions:

Bob will make the trip next week.

When can Bob make the trip?

Imperative mood is used to state a command or make a request:

Wait in the lobby.

Please call me next week.

Subjunctive mood is used to express a wish, an opinion, or a hope that is contrary to fact:

If I were in charge, none of this would have happened.

Allison wished she could take the exam over again when she saw her score.

Adjectives

Adjectives are words used to modify nouns and pronouns. They can be used alone or in a series and are used to further define or describe the nouns they modify.

Mark made us a delicious, four-course meal.

The words *delicious* and *four-course* are adjectives that describe the kind of meal Mark made.

Articles are also considered adjectives because they help to describe nouns. Articles can be general or specific. The three articles in English are: *a, an*, and *the*.

Indefinite articles *(a, an)* are used to refer to nonspecific nouns. The article *a* proceeds words beginning with consonant sounds, and the article *an* proceeds words beginning with vowel sounds.

    A car drove by our house.

    An alligator was loose at the zoo.

    He has always wanted a ukulele. (The first *u* makes a *y* sound.)

Note that *a* and *an* should only proceed nonspecific nouns that are also singular. If a nonspecific noun is plural, it does not need a preceding article.

    Alligators were loose at the zoo.

The **definite article** *(the)* is used to refer to specific nouns:

    The car pulled into our driveway.

Note that *the* should proceed all specific nouns regardless of whether they are singular or plural.

    The cars pulled into our driveway.

Comparative adjectives are used to compare nouns. When they are used in this way, they take on positive, comparative, or superlative form.

    The **positive** form is the normal form of the adjective:

        Alicia is tall.

    The **comparative** form shows a comparison between two things:

        Alicia is taller than Maria.

    Superlative form shows comparison between more than two things:

        Alicia is the tallest girl in her class.

Usually, the comparative and superlative can be made by adding *–er* and *–est* to the positive form, but some verbs call for the helping verbs *more* or *most*. Other exceptions to the rule include adjectives like *bad*, which uses the comparative *worse* and the superlative *worst*.

An **adjective phrase** is not a bunch of adjectives strung together, but a group of words that describes a noun or pronoun and, thus, functions as an adjective. *Very happy* is an adjective phrase; so are *way too hungry* and *passionate about traveling*.

Adverbs
Adverbs have more functions than adjectives because they modify or qualify verbs, adjectives, or other adverbs as well as word groups that express a relation of place, time, circumstance, or cause. Therefore,

adverbs answer any of the following questions: *How, when, where, why, in what way, how much, in what condition,* and/or *to what degree. How good looking is he? He is <u>very</u> handsome.*

Here are some examples of adverbs for different situations:

- how: quickly
- when: daily
- where: there
- in what way: easily
- how often: often
- how much: much
- in what condition: badly
- what degree: hardly

As one can see, for some reason, many adverbs end in *-ly*.

Adverbs do things like emphasize (*really, simply,* and *so*), amplify (*heartily, completely,* and *positively*), and tone down (*almost, somewhat,* and *mildly*).

Adverbs also come in phrases.

The dog ran as <u>though his life depended on it.</u>

Prepositions

Prepositions are connecting words and, while there are only about 150 of them, they are used more often than any other individual groups of words. They describe relationships between other words. They are placed before a noun or pronoun, forming a phrase that modifies another word in the sentence. **Prepositional phrases** begin with a preposition and end with a noun or pronoun, the **object of the preposition.** *A pristine lake is <u>near the store</u> and <u>behind the bank</u>.*

Some commonly used prepositions are *about, after, anti, around, as, at, behind, beside, by, for, from, in, into, of, off, on, to,* and *with*.

Complex prepositions, which also come before a noun or pronoun, consist of two or three words such as *according to, in regard to,* and *because of*.

Conjunctions

Conjunctions are vital words that connect words, phrases, thoughts, and ideas. Conjunctions show relationships between components. There are two types:

Coordinating conjunctions are the primary class of conjunctions placed between words, phrases, clauses, and sentences that are of equal grammatical rank; the coordinating conjunctions are *for, and, nor, but, or, yet,* and *so*. A useful memorization trick is to remember that the first letter of these conjunctions collectively spell the word *fanboys*.

I need to go shopping, *but* I must be careful to leave enough money in the bank.
She wore a black, red, *and* white shirt.

Subordinating conjunctions are the secondary class of conjunctions. They connect two unequal parts, one **main** (or **independent**) and the other *subordinate* (or *dependent*). I must go to the store *even though* I do not have enough money in the bank.

Because I read the review, I do not want to go to the movie.

Notice that the presence of subordinating conjunctions makes clauses dependent. *I read the review* is an independent clause, but *because* makes the clause dependent. Thus, it needs an independent clause to complete the sentence.

Interjections

Interjections are words used to express emotion. Examples include *wow*, *ouch*, and *hooray*. Interjections are often separate from sentences; in those cases, the interjection is directly followed by an exclamation point. In other cases, the interjection is included in a sentence and followed by a comma. The punctuation plays a big role in the intensity of the emotion that the interjection is expressing. Using a comma or semicolon indicates less excitement than using an exclamation mark.

Capitalization Rules

Here's a non-exhaustive list of things that should be capitalized:

- The first word of every sentence
- The first word of every line of poetry
- The first letter of proper nouns (World War II)
- Holidays (Valentine's Day)
- The days of the week and months of the year (Tuesday, March)
- The first word, last word, and all major words in the titles of books, movies, songs, and other creative works (In the novel, *To Kill a Mockingbird*, note that a is lowercase since it's not a major word, but to is capitalized since it's the first word of the title.)
- Titles when preceding a proper noun (President Roberto Gonzales, Aunt Judy)

When simply using a word such as president or secretary, though, the word is not capitalized.

Officers of the new business must include a *president* and *treasurer*.

Seasons—spring, fall, etc.—are not capitalized.

North, *south*, *east*, and *west* are capitalized when referring to regions but are not when being used for directions. In general, if it's preceded by *the* it should be capitalized.

I'm from the South.
I drove south.

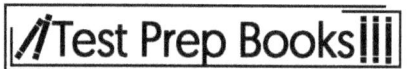

End Punctuation

Periods (.) are used to end a sentence that is a statement (**declarative**) or a command (**imperative**). They should not be used in a sentence that asks a question or is an exclamation. Periods are also used in abbreviations, which are shortened versions of words.

- Declarative: The boys refused to go to sleep.
- Imperative: Walk down to the bus stop.
- Abbreviations: Joan Roberts, M.D., Apple Inc., Mrs. Adamson
- If a sentence ends with an abbreviation, it is inappropriate to use two periods. It should end with a
- single period after the abbreviation.

The chef gathered the ingredients for the pie, which included apples, flour, sugar, etc.

Question marks *(?)* are used with direct questions (**interrogative**). An **indirect question** can use a period:

Interrogative: When does the next bus arrive?

Indirect Question: I wonder when the next bus arrives.

An **exclamation point** *(!)* is used to show strong emotion or can be used as an interjection. This punctuation should be used sparingly in formal writing situations.

What an amazing shot!

Whoa!

Commas

A **comma** (,) is the punctuation mark that signifies a pause—breath—between parts of a sentence. It denotes a break of flow. Proper comma usage helps readers understand the writer's intended emphasis of ideas.

In a complex sentence—one that contains a **subordinate** (dependent) clause or clauses—the use of a comma is dictated by where the subordinate clause is located. If the subordinate clause is located before the main clause, a comma is needed between the two clauses.

I will not pay for the steak, *because I don't have that much money.*

Generally, if the subordinate clause is placed after the main clause, no punctuation is needed.

I did well on my exam because I studied two hours the night before.

Notice how the last clause is dependent because it requires the earlier independent clauses to make sense.

Use a comma on both sides of an interrupting phrase.

I will pay for the ice cream, *chocolate and vanilla,* and then will eat it all myself.

Grammar and Writing Section

The words forming the phrase in italics are nonessential (extra) information. To determine if a phrase is nonessential, try reading the sentence without the phrase and see if it's still coherent.

A comma is not necessary in this next sentence because no interruption—nonessential or extra information—has occurred. Read sentences aloud when uncertain.

> I will pay for his chocolate and vanilla ice cream and then will eat it all myself.

If the nonessential phrase comes at the beginning of a sentence, a comma should only go at the end of the phrase. If the phrase comes at the end of a sentence, a comma should only go at the beginning of the phrase.

Other types of interruptions include the following:

- interjections: Oh no, I am not going.
- abbreviations: Barry Potter, M.D., specializes in heart disorders.
- direct addresses: Yes, Claudia, I am tired and going to bed.
- parenthetical phrases: His wife, lovely as she was, was not helpful.
- transitional phrases: Also, it is not possible.

The second comma in the following sentence is called an **Oxford comma**.

> I will pay for ice cream, syrup, and pop.

It is a comma used after the second-to-last item in a series of three or more items. It comes before the word *or* or *and*. Not everyone uses the Oxford comma; it is optional, but many believe it is needed. The comma functions as a tool to reduce confusion in writing. So, if omitting the Oxford comma would cause confusion, then it's best to include it.

Commas are used in math to mark the place of thousands in numerals, breaking them up so they are easier to read. Other uses for commas are in dates (*March 19, 2016*), letter greetings (*Dear Sally,*), and in between cities and states (*Louisville, KY*).

Semicolons

A **semicolon** *(;)* is used to connect ideas in a sentence in some way. There are three main ways to use semicolons.

Link two independent clauses without the use of a coordinating conjunction:

> I was late for work again; I'm definitely going to get fired.

Link two independent clauses with a transitional word:

> The songs were all easy to play; therefore, he didn't need to spend too much time practicing.

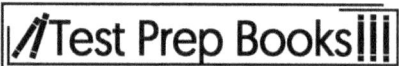

Between items in a series that are already separated by commas or if necessary to separate lengthy items in a list:

> Starbucks has locations in Media, PA; Swarthmore, PA; and Morton, PA.

> Several classroom management issues presented in the study: the advent of a poor teacher persona in the context of voice, dress, and style; teacher follow-through from the beginning of the school year to the end; and the depth of administrative support, including ISS and OSS protocol.

Colons

A **colon** (:) is used after an independent clause to present an explanation or draw attention to what comes next in the sentence. There are several uses.

Explanations of ideas:

> They soon learned the hardest part about having a new baby: sleep deprivation.

Lists of items:

> Shari picked up all the supplies she would need for the party: cups, plates, napkins, balloons, streamers, and party favors.

Time, subtitles, general salutations:

> The time is 7:15.

> I read a book entitled *Pluto: A Planet No More*.

> To whom it may concern:

Parentheses and Dashes

Parentheses are half-round brackets that look like this: ( ). They set off a word, phrase, or sentence that is an afterthought, explanation, or side note relevant to the surrounding text but not essential. A pair of commas is often used to set off this sort of information, but parentheses are generally used for information that would not fit well within a sentence or that the writer deems not important enough to be structurally part of the sentence.

> The picture of the heart (see above) shows the major parts you should memorize.
> Mount Everest is one of three mountains in the world that are over 28,000 feet high (K2 and Kanchenjunga are the other two).

See how the sentences above are complete without the parenthetical statements? In the first example, *see above* would not have fit well within the flow of the sentence. The second parenthetical statement could have been a separate sentence, but the writer deemed the information not pertinent to the topic.

The **em-dash** (—) is a mark longer than a hyphen used as a punctuation mark in sentences and to set apart a relevant thought. Even after plucking out the line separated by the dash marks, the sentence will be intact and make sense.

> Looking out the airplane window at the landmarks—Lake Clarke, Thompson Community College, and the bridge—she couldn't help but feel excited to be home.

The dashes use is similar to that of parentheses or a pair of commas. So, what's the difference? Many believe that using dashes makes the clause within them stand out while using parentheses is subtler. It's advised to not use dashes when commas could be used instead.

Ellipses

An **ellipsi**s (...) is used to show that there is more to the quoted text than is necessary for the current discussion. Writers use them in place of words, lines, phrases, list content, or paragraphs that might just as easily have been omitted from a passage of writing. This can be done to save space or to focus only on the specifically relevant material.

> Exercise is good for some unexpected reasons. Watkins writes, "Exercise has many benefits such as...reducing cancer risk."

In the example above, the ellipsis takes the place of the other benefits of exercise that are more expected.

The ellipsis may also be used to show a pause in sentence flow.

> "I'm wondering...how this could happen," Dylan said in a soft voice.

Quotation Marks

Double quotation marks are used at the beginning and end of a direct quote. They are also used with certain titles and to indicate that a term being used is slang or referenced in the sentence. Quotation marks should not be used with an indirect quote. Single quotation marks are used to indicate a quote within a quote.

> Direct quote: "The weather is supposed to be beautiful this week," she said.

> Indirect quote: One of the customers asked if the sale prices were still in effect.

> Quote within a quote: "My little boy just said 'Mama, I want cookie,'" Maria shared.

Titles: Quotation marks should also be used to indicate titles of short works or sections of larger works, such as chapter titles. Other works that use quotation marks include poems, short stories, newspaper articles, magazine articles, web page titles, and songs.

> "The Road Not Taken" is my favorite poem by Robert Frost.

> "What a Wonderful World" is one of my favorite songs.

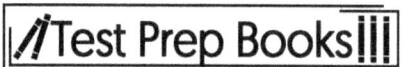

Specific or emphasized terms: Quotation marks can also be used to indicate a technical term or to set off a word that is being discussed in a sentence. Quotation marks can also indicate sarcasm.

The new step, called "levigation," is a very difficult technique.

He said he was "hungry" multiple times, but he only ate two bites.

Use with other punctuation: The use of quotation marks with other punctuation varies, depending on the role of the ending or separating punctuation.

In American English, commas and periods go inside quotation marks:

"This is the last time you are allowed to leave early," his boss stated.

The newscaster said, "We have some breaking news to report."

Question marks or exclamation points go inside the quotation marks when they are part of a direct quote:

The doctor shouted, "Get the crash cart!"

When the question mark or exclamation point is part of the sentence, not the quote, it should be placed outside of the quotation marks:

Was it Jackie that said, "Get some potatoes at the store"?

Apostrophes

This punctuation mark, the **apostrophe** (') is a versatile mark. It has several different functions:

- Quotes: Apostrophes are used when a second quote is needed within a quote.
    - In my letter to my friend, I wrote, "The girl had to get a new purse, and guess what Mary did? She said, 'I'd like to go with you to the store.' I knew Mary would buy it for her."

- Contractions: Another use for an apostrophe in the quote above is a contraction. *I'd is used for I would.*

- Possession: An apostrophe followed by the letter s shows possession (Mary's purse). If the possessive word is plural, the apostrophe generally just follows the word. Not all possessive pronouns require apostrophes.
    - The trees' leaves are all over the ground.

Hyphens

The **hyphen** (-) is a small hash mark that can be used to join words to show that they are linked.

Hyphens can connect two words that work together as a single adjective (a compound adjective).

honey-covered biscuits

Some words always require hyphens even if not serving as an adjective.

    merry-go-round

Hyphens always go after certain prefixes like *anti-* & *all-*.

Hyphens should also be used when the absence of the hyphen would cause a strange vowel combination (*semi-engineer*) or confusion. For example, *re-collect* should be used to describe something being gathered twice rather than being written as *recollect*, which means to remember.

Subjects

Every sentence must include a subject and a verb. The **subject** of a sentence is who or what the sentence is about. It's often directly stated and can be determined by asking "Who?" or "What?" did the action:

Most sentences contain a **direct subject**, in which the subject is mentioned in the sentence.

    Kelly mowed the lawn.

    Who mowed the lawn? *Kelly*

    The air-conditioner ran all night

    What ran all night? *the air-conditioner*

The subject of imperative sentences is the implied *you*, because imperative subjects are commands:

    Go home after the meeting.

    Who should go home after the meeting? *you* (implied)

In **expletive sentences** that start with "there are" or "there is," the subject is found after the predicate. The subject cannot be "there," so it must be another word in the sentence:

    There is a cup sitting on the coffee table.

    What is sitting on the coffee table? *a cup*

Simple and Complete Subjects

A **complete subject** includes the simple subject and all the words modifying it, including articles and adjectives. A **simple subject** is the single noun without its modifiers.

    A warm, chocolate-chip cookie sat on the kitchen table.

    Complete subject: *a warm, chocolate-chip cookie*

    Simple subject: *cookie*

The words *a, warm, chocolate,* and *chip* all modify the simple subject *cookie*.

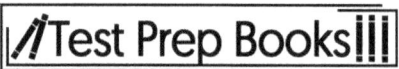

There might also be a **compound subject**, which would be two or more nouns without the modifiers.

    A little girl and her mother walked into the shop.

    Complete subject: *A little girl and her mother*

    Compound subject: *girl, mother*

In this case, *the girl and her mother* are both completing the action of walking into the shop, so this is a compound subject.

Predicates

In addition to the subject, a sentence must also have a predicate. The **predicate** contains a verb and tells something about the subject. In addition to the verb, a predicate can also contain a direct or indirect object, object of a preposition, and other phrases.

    The cats napped on the front porch.

In this sentence, cats is the subject because the sentence is about cats.

The **complete predicate** is everything else in the sentence: *napped on the front porch*. This phrase is the predicate because it tells us what the cats did.

This sentence can be broken down into a simple subject and predicate:

    Cats napped.

In this sentence, *cats* is the simple subject, and *napped* is the **simple predicate**.

Although the sentence is very short and doesn't offer much information, it's still considered a complete sentence because it contains a subject and predicate.

Like a compound subject, a sentence can also have a **compound predicate**. This is when the subject is or does two or more things in the sentence.

    This easy chair reclines and swivels.

In this sentence, *this easy chair* is the complete subject. *Reclines and swivels* shows two actions of the chair, so this is the compound predicate.

Subject-Verb Agreement

The subject of a sentence and its verb must agree. The cornerstone rule of subject-verb agreement is that subject and verb must agree in number. Whether the subject is singular or plural, the verb must follow suit.

    Incorrect: The houses is new.
    Correct: The houses are new.
    Also Correct: The house is new.

In other words, a singular subject requires a singular verb; a plural subject requires a plural verb.

Grammar and Writing Section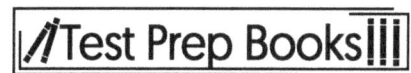

The words or phrases that come between the subject and verb do not alter this rule.

    Incorrect: The houses built of brick is new.
    Correct: The houses built of brick are new.

    Incorrect: The houses with the sturdy porches is new.
    Correct: The houses with the sturdy porches are new.

The subject will always follow the verb when a sentence begins with *here* or *there*. Identify these with care.

    Incorrect: Here *is* the *houses* with sturdy porches.
    Correct: Here *are* the *houses* with sturdy porches.

The subject in the sentences above is not *here*, it is *houses*. Remember, *here* and *there* are never subjects. Be careful that contractions such as *here's* or *there're* do not cause confusion!

Two subjects joined by *and* require a plural verb form, except when the two combine to make one thing:

    Incorrect: Garrett and Jonathan is over there.
    Correct: Garrett and Jonathan are over there.

    Incorrect: Spaghetti and meatballs are a delicious meal!
    Correct: Spaghetti and meatballs is a delicious meal!

In the example above, *spaghetti and meatballs* is a compound noun. However, *Garrett and Jonathan* is not a compound noun.

Two singular subjects joined by *or, either/or,* or *neither/nor* call for a singular verb form.

    Incorrect: Butter or syrup are acceptable.
    Correct: Butter or syrup is acceptable.

Plural subjects joined by *or, either/or,* or *neither/nor* are, indeed, plural.

    The chairs or the boxes are being moved next.

If one subject is singular and the other is plural, the verb should agree with the closest noun.

    Correct: The chair or the boxes are being moved next.
    Correct: The chairs or the box is being moved next.

Some plurals of money, distance, and time call for a singular verb.

    Incorrect: Three dollars *are* enough to buy that.
    Correct: Three dollars *is* enough to buy that.

For words declaring degrees of quantity such as *many of, some of,* or *most of,* let the noun that follows of be the guide:

> Incorrect: Many of the books is in the shelf.
> Correct: Many of the books are in the shelf.
>
> Incorrect: Most of the pie *are* on the table.
> Correct: Most of the pie *is* on the table.

For indefinite pronouns like *anybody* or *everybody*, use singular verbs.

> Everybody *is* going to the store.

However, the pronouns *few, many, several, all, some,* and *both* have their own rules and use plural forms.

> Some *are* ready.

Some nouns like *crowd* and *congress* are called **collective nouns** and they require a singular verb form.

> Congress *is* in session.
> The news *is* over.

Books and movie titles, though, including plural nouns such as *Great Expectations*, also require a singular verb. Remember that only the subject affects the verb. While writing tricky subject-verb arrangements, say them aloud. Listen to them. Once the rules have been learned, one's ear will become sensitive to them, making it easier to pick out what's right and what's wrong.

Direct Objects

The **direct object** is the part of the sentence that receives the action of the verb. It is a noun and can usually be found after the verb. To find the direct object, first find the verb, then ask the question *who* or *what* after it.

> The bear climbed the tree.
>
> What did the bear climb? *The tree.*

Indirect Objects

An **indirect object** receives the direct object. It is usually found between the verb and the direct object. A strategy for identifying the indirect object is to find the verb and ask the questions *to whom/for whom* or *to what/for what*.

> Jane made her daughter a cake.
>
> For whom did Jane make the cake? *Her daughter.*

Cake is the direct object because it is what Jane made, and *daughter* is the indirect object because she receives the cake.

Complements

A **complement** completes the meaning of an expression. A complement can be a pronoun, noun, or adjective. A **verb complement** refers to the direct object or indirect object in the sentence. An **object complement** gives more information about the direct object:

>The magician got the kids excited.

Kids is the direct object, and *excited* is the object complement.

A **subject complement** comes after a linking verb. It is typically an adjective or noun that gives more information about the subject:

>The king was noble and spared the thief's life.

Noble describes the *king* and follows the linking verb *was*.

Predicate Nouns

A **predicate noun** renames the subject:

>John is a carpenter.

The subject is *John*, and the predicate noun is *carpenter*.

Predicate Adjectives

A **predicate adjective** describes the subject:

>Margaret is beautiful.

The subject is *Margaret*, and the predicate adjective is *beautiful*.

Homonyms

Homonyms are words that sound the same but are spelled differently, and they have different meanings. There are several common homonyms that give writers trouble.

There, They're, and *Their*

The word *there* can be used as an adverb, adjective, or pronoun:

>*There* are ten children on the swim team this summer.

>I put my book over *there*, but now I can't find it.

The word *they're* is a contraction of the words *they* and *are*:

>*They're* flying in from Texas on Tuesday.

The word *their* is a possessive pronoun:

>I store *their* winter clothes in the attic.

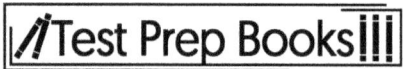

Its and *It's*
Its is a possessive pronoun:

> The cat licked *its* injured paw.

It's is the contraction for the words *it* and *is*:

> *It's* unbelievable how many people opted not to vote in the last election.

Your and *You're*
Your is a possessive pronoun:

> Can I borrow *your* lawnmower this weekend?

You're is a contraction for the words *you* and *are*:

> *You're* about to embark on a fantastic journey.

To, Too, and *Two*
To is an adverb or a preposition used to show direction, relationship, or purpose:

> We are going *to* New York.

> They are going *to* see a show.

Too is an adverb that means more than enough, also, and very:

> You have had *too* much candy.

> We are on vacation that week, *too*.

Two is the written-out form of the numeral 2:

> *Two* of the shirts didn't fit, so I will have to return them.

New and *Knew*
New is an adjective that means recent:

> There's a *new* customer on the phone.

Knew is the past tense of the verb *know*:

> I *knew* you'd have fun on this ride.

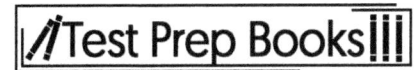

Affect and *Effect*

Affect and *effect* are complicated because they are used as both nouns and verbs, have similar meanings, and are pronounced the same.

	Affect	Effect
Noun Definition	emotional state	result
Noun Example	The patient's affect was flat.	The effects of smoking are well documented.
Verb Definition	to influence	to bring about
Verb Example	The pollen count affects my allergies.	The new candidate hopes to effect change.

Independent and Dependent Clauses

Independent and **dependent** clauses are strings of words that contain both a subject and a verb. An independent clause *can* stand alone as complete thought, but a dependent clause *cannot*. A dependent clause relies on other words to be a complete sentence.

    Independent clause: The keys are on the counter.
    Dependent clause: If the keys are on the counter

Notice that both clauses have a subject (*keys*) and a verb (*are*). The independent clause expresses a complete thought, but the word *if* at the beginning of the dependent clause makes it *dependent* on other words to be a complete thought.

    Independent clause: If the keys are on the counter, please give them to me.

This example constitutes a complete sentence since it includes at least one verb and one subject and is a complete thought. In this case, the independent clause has two subjects (*keys* & an implied *you*) and two verbs (*are* & *give*).

    Independent clause: I went to the store.
    Dependent clause: Because we are out of milk,

    Complete Sentence: Because we are out of milk, I went to the store.
    Complete Sentence: I went to the store because we are out of milk.

Phrases

A **phrase** is a group of words that do not make a complete thought or a clause. They are parts of sentences or clauses. Phrases can be used as nouns, adjectives, or adverbs. A phrase does not contain both a subject and a verb.

Prepositional Phrases

A **prepositional phrase** shows the relationship between a word in the sentence and the object of the preposition. The **object of the preposition** is a noun that follows the preposition.

    The orange pillows are on the couch.

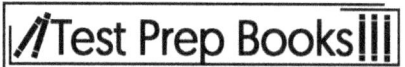

On is the preposition, and *couch* is the object of the preposition.

She brought her friend with the nice car.

With is the preposition, and *car* is the object of the preposition. Here are some common prepositions:

about	as	at	after
by	for	from	in
of	on	to	with

Verbals and Verbal Phrases

Verbals are forms of verbs that act as other parts of speech. They can be used as nouns, adjectives, or adverbs. Though they are verb forms, they are not to be used as the verb in the sentence. A word group that is based on a verbal is considered a **verbal phrase**. There are three major types of verbals: participles, gerunds, and infinitives.

Participles are verbals that act as adjectives. The present participle ends in –*ing*, and the past participle ends in –*d*, -*ed*, -*n*, or-*t*.

Verb	Present Participle	Past Participle
walk	walking	walked
share	sharing	shared

Participial phrases are made up of the participle and modifiers, complements, or objects.

Crying for most of an hour, the baby didn't seem to want to nap.

Having already taken this course, the student was bored during class.

Crying for most of an hour and *Having already taken this course* are the participial phrases.

Gerunds are verbals that are used as nouns and end in –*ing*. A gerund can be the subject or object of the sentence like a noun. Note that a present participle can also end in –*ing*, so it is important to distinguish between the two. The gerund is used as a noun, while the participle is used as an adjective.

Swimming is my favorite sport.

I wish I were sleeping.

A **gerund phrase** includes the gerund and any modifiers or complements, direct objects, indirect objects, or pronouns.

Cleaning the house is my least favorite weekend activity.

Cleaning the house is the gerund phrase acting as the subject of the sentence.

The most important goal this year is raising money for charity.

Raising money for charity is the gerund phrase acting as the direct object.

The police accused the woman of stealing the car.

The gerund phrase *stealing the car* is the object of the preposition in this sentence.

An **infinitive** is a verbal made up of the word *to* and a verb. Infinitives can be used as nouns, adjectives, or adverbs.

Examples: To eat, to jump, to swim, to lie, to call, to work

An *infinitive phrase* is made up of the infinitive plus any complements or modifiers. The infinitive phrase *to wait* is used as the subject in this sentence:

To wait was not what I had in mind.

The infinitive phrase *to sing* is used as the subject complement in this sentence:

Her dream is to sing.

The infinitive phrase *to grow* is used as an adverb in this sentence:

Children must eat to grow.

Appositive Phrases

An **appositive** is a noun or noun phrase that renames a noun that comes immediately before it in the sentence. An appositive can be a single word or several words. These phrases can be **essential** or **nonessential**. An essential appositive phrase is necessary to the meaning of the sentence and a nonessential appositive phrase is not. It is important to be able to distinguish these for purposes of comma use.

Essential: My sister Christina works at a school.

Naming which sister is essential to the meaning of the sentence, so no commas are needed.

Nonessential: My sister, who is a teacher, is coming over for dinner tonight.

Who is a teacher is not essential to the meaning of the sentence, so commas are required.

Absolute Phrases

An **absolute phrase** modifies a noun without using a conjunction. It is not the subject of the sentence and is not a complete thought on its own. Absolute phrases are set off from the independent clause with a comma.

Arms outstretched, she yelled at the sky.

All things considered, this has been a great day.

The Four Types of Sentence Structures

A **simple sentence** has one independent clause.

I am going to win.

A **compound sentence** has two independent clauses. A conjunction—*for, and, nor, but, or, yet, so*—links them together. Note that each of the independent clauses has a subject and a verb.

I am going to win, but the odds are against me.

A **complex sentence** has one independent clause and one or more dependent clauses.

I am going to win, even though I don't deserve it.

Even though I don't deserve it is a dependent clause. It does not stand on its own. Some conjunctions that link an independent and a dependent clause are *although, because, before, after, that, when, which*, and *while*.

A **compound-complex sentence** has at least three clauses, two of which are independent and at least one that is a dependent clause.

While trying to dance, I tripped over my partner's feet, but I regained my balance quickly.

The dependent clause is *While trying to dance*.

Sentence Fragments

A **sentence fragment** is an incomplete sentence. An independent clause is made up of a subject and a predicate, and both are needed to make a complete sentence.

Sentence fragments often begin with relative pronouns (when, which), subordinating conjunctions (because, although) or gerunds (trying, being, seeing). They might be missing the subject or the predicate.

The most common type of fragment is the isolated dependent clause, which can be corrected by joining it to the independent clause that appears before or after the fragment:

Fragment: While the cookies baked.

Correction: While the cookies baked, we played cards. (We played cards while the cookies baked.)

Run-on Sentences

A **run-on sentence** is created when two independent clauses (complete thoughts) are joined without correct punctuation or a conjunction. Run-on sentences can be corrected in the following ways:

- Join the independent clauses with a comma and coordinating conjunction.

    Run-on: We forgot to return the library books we had to pay a fine.

    Correction: We forgot to return the library books, so we had to pay a fine.

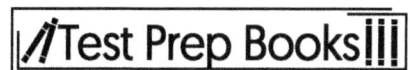

Grammar and Writing Section

- Join the independent clauses with a semicolon, dash, or colon when the clauses are closely related in meaning.

    Run-on: I had a salad for lunch every day this week I feel healthier already.

    Correction: I had a salad for lunch every day this week; I feel healthier already.

- Join the independent clauses with a semicolon and a conjunctive adverb.

    Run-on: We arrived at the animal shelter on time however the dog had already been adopted.

    Correction: We arrived at the animal shelter on time; however, the dog had already been adopted.

- Separate the independent clauses into two sentences with a period.

    Run-on: He tapes his favorite television show he never misses an episode.

    Correction: He tapes his favorite television show. He never misses an episode.

- Rearrange the wording of the sentence to create an independent clause and a dependent clause.

    Run-on: My wedding date is coming up I am getting more excited to walk down the aisle.

    Correction: As my wedding date approaches, I am getting more excited to walk down the aisle.

Dangling and Misplaced Modifiers

A **modifier** is a phrase that describes, alters, limits, or gives more information about a word in the sentence. The two most common issues are dangling and misplaced modifiers.

A **dangling modifier** is created when the phrase modifies a word that is not clearly stated in the sentence.

   Dangling modifier: Having finished dinner, the dishes were cleared from the table.

   Correction: Having finished dinner, Amy cleared the dishes from the table.

In the first sentence, *having finished dinner* appears to modify *the dishes*, which obviously can't finish dinner. The second sentence adds the subject *Amy*, to make it clear who has finished dinner.

   Dangling modifier: Hoping to improve test scores, all new books were ordered for the school.

   Correction: Hoping to improve test scores, administrators ordered all new books for the school.

   Without the subject *administrators*, it appears the books are hoping to improve test scores, which doesn't make sense.

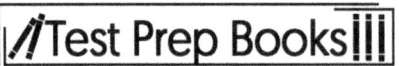

Misplaced modifiers are placed incorrectly in the sentence, which can cause confusion. Compare these examples:

> Misplaced modifier: Rory purchased a new flat screen television and placed it on the wall above the fireplace, with all the bells and whistles.

> Revised: Rory purchased a new flat screen television, with all the bells and whistles, and placed it on the wall above the fireplace.

The bells and whistles should modify the television, not the fireplace.

> Misplaced modifier: The delivery driver arrived late with the pizza, who was usually on time.

> Revised: The delivery driver, who usually was on time, arrived late with the pizza.

This suggests that the delivery driver was usually on time, instead of the pizza.

> Misplaced modifier: We saw a family of ducks on the way to church.

> Revised: On the way to church, we saw a family of ducks.

The misplaced modifier, here, suggests the *ducks* were on their way to church, instead of the pronoun *we*.

Split Infinitives

An **infinitive** is made up of the word *to* and a verb, such as: to run, to jump, to ask. A **split infinitive** is created when a word comes between *to* and the verb.

> Split infinitive: To quickly run

> Correction: To run quickly

> Split infinitive: To quietly ask

> Correction: To ask quietly

Double Negatives

A **double negative** is a negative statement that includes two negative elements. This is incorrect in Standard English.

> Incorrect: She hasn't never come to my house to visit.

> Correct: She has never come to my house to visit.

The intended meaning is that she has never come to the house, so the double negative is incorrect. However, it is possible to use two negatives to create a positive statement.

> Correct: She was not unhappy with her performance on the quiz.

In this case, the double negative, *was not unhappy*, is intended to show a positive, so it is correct. This means that she was somewhat happy with her performance.

Faulty Parallelism

It is necessary to use parallel construction in sentences that have multiple similar ideas. Using parallel structure provides clarity in writing. **Faulty parallelism** is created when multiple ideas are joined using different sentence structures. Compare these examples:

Incorrect: We start each practice with stretches, a run, and fielding grounders.
Correct: We start each practice with stretching, running, and fielding grounders.

Incorrect: I watched some television, reading my book, and fell asleep.
Correct: I watched some television, read my book, and fell asleep.

Incorrect: Some of the readiness skills for kindergarten are to cut with scissors, to tie shoes, and dressing independently.
Correct: Some of the readiness skills for kindergarten are being able to cut with scissors, to tie shoes, and to dress independently.

Subordination

If multiple pieces of information in a sentence are not equal, they can be joined by creating an independent clause and a dependent clause. The less important information becomes the **subordinate clause:**

Draft: The hotel was acceptable. We wouldn't stay at the hotel again.

Revised: Though the hotel was acceptable, we wouldn't stay there again.

The more important information (*we wouldn't stay there again*) becomes the main clause, and the less important information (*the hotel was acceptable*) becomes the subordinate clause.

Practice Quiz

Passage

This passage is adapted from The Social Contract *by Jean-Jacques Rousseau.*

Each member of the community gives himself to it, at the moment of its foundation, just as he is, with all the resources at his command, including the politicians he supports. This act does not make possession, in changing hands, change its nature, and becomes property in the hands of the Sovereign; but, as the forces of the city are incomparably greater than those of an individual, public possession is also, in fact, stronger and more [1] <u>irrevocable</u>, without being any more legitimate, at any rate from the point of view of foreigners. For the State, in relation to its members, is master of all their goods by the social contract, which, within the State, is the basis of all rights; but, in relation to other powers, it is so only by the right of the first occupier, which it holds from its members.

The right of the first occupier, though more real than the right of the strongest, becomes a real right only when the right of property has already been established. Every man has naturally a right to everything [2] <u>he needs: but the</u> positive act which makes him proprietor of one thing excludes him from everything else. Having his share, he ought to keep to it, and can have no further right against the community. This is why the right of the first occupier, which in the state of nature is so weak, claims the respect of every man in civil society. In this right we are respecting not so much what belongs to another as what does not belong to ourselves.

In general, to establish the right of the first occupier over a plot of ground, the following conditions are necessary: first, the land must not yet be inhabited; secondly, a man must occupy only the amount he needs for his subsistence; and, in the third place, possession must be taken, not by an empty ceremony, but by labor and cultivation, the only sign of proprietorship that should be respected by others, in default of a legal title.

In granting the right of first occupancy to necessity and labor, are we not really stretching it as far as it can go? Is it possible to leave such a right unlimited? Is it to be enough to set foot on a plot of common ground, in order to be able to call yourself at once the master of it? Is it to be enough that a man has the strength to expel others for a moment, in order to establish his right to prevent them from ever returning? [3] <u>How can a man or a people seize an immense territory and keep it from the rest of the world except by a punishable usurpation, since all others are being robbed, by such an act, of the place of habitation and the means of subsistence which nature gave them in common?</u> When Nuñez Balbao, standing on the seashore, took possession of the South Seas and the whole of South America in the name of the crown of Castille, was that enough to dispossess all their actual inhabitants, and to shut out from them all the princes of the world? On such a showing, [4] <u>these ceremonies is idly multiplied</u>, and the Catholic King need only take possession all at once, from his apartment, of the whole universe, merely making a subsequent reservation about what was already in the possession of other princes.

We can imagine how the lands of individuals, where they were contiguous and came to be united, became the public territory, and how the right of Sovereignty, extending from the subjects over the lands they held, became at once real and personal. The possessors were thus made more dependent, and the forces at their command used to guarantee their fidelity. The advantage of this does not seem to have been felt by ancient monarchs, who called themselves King of the Persians, Scythians, or Macedonians, and seemed to regard themselves more as rulers of men than as masters of a country. Those of the present day more cleverly call themselves Kings of France, Spain, England, etc.; thus holding the land, they are quite confident of [5] <u>aiding the inhabitants</u>.

1. irrevocable
    a. NO CHANGE
    b. irreverent
    c. infectious
    d. impressive

2. he needs: but the
    a. NO CHANGE
    b. he needs. But the
    c. he needs, but the
    d. he needs... but the

3. Which of the following choices represents the clearest and most concise way to convey all the information in the sentence?

    How can a man or a people seize an immense territory and keep it from the rest of the world except by a punishable usurpation, since all others are being robbed, by such an act, of the place of habitation and the means of subsistence which nature gave them in common?

    a. NO CHANGE
    b. How can an immense territory be seized and kept from the rest of the world except by a punishable usurpation, since all others are being robbed, by such an act, of the place of habitation and the means of subsistence which nature gave them instead of those seizing it?
    c. How can a man or a people seize an immense territory and keep it from the rest of the world except by a punishable usurpation, since all others are being given, by such an act, a place of habitation and the means of subsistence which nature gave their conqueror?
    d. How can a man or a people seize an immense territory and keep it from the rest of the world except by a punishable usurpation, since all others are being robbed, by such an act, of the livable land which nature gave them as well?

4. these ceremonies <u>is</u> idly multiplied
    a. NO CHANGE
    b. are
    c. of
    d. at

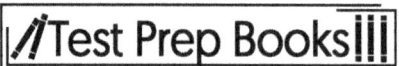

Grammar and Writing Section

5. Which of the examples fits best in the paragraph?

> Those of the present day more cleverly call themselves Kings of France, Spain, England, etc.: thus holding the land, they are quite confident of <u>aiding the inhabitants</u>.

a. NO CHANGE
b. enslaving the inhabitants
c. keeping the inhabitants
d. inspiring the inhabitants

See answers on the next page.

Answer Explanations

1. A: Choice *A* is the correct answer because the word *irrevocable* fits perfectly within the text. The text discusses the topic of possessions being taken away and claims that public possession is *irrevocable* or cannot be taken away. Choice *B* is incorrect because public possession is unrelated to having a disrespectful demeanor, which is the meaning of *irreverent*. Choice *C* is incorrect because the word *infectious* describes the spread of something. That does not apply in this situation. Choice *D* is incorrect because, although public possession may be *impressive*, the word *irrevocable* better fits what the author is saying.

2. C: Choice *C* is the correct answer because the text includes a coordinating conjunction, which requires a comma. Choice *A* is incorrect because the original text uses a colon in the wrong situation. Choices *B* and *D* are incorrect because they do not conform to the standard use of punctuation or the needs of this sentence.

3. D: Choice *D* is the correct answer because it is the option that most concisely states what the author is conveying while still maintaining all of the information from the original sentence. Choice *A* is incorrect because Choice *D* is a more concise version of the sentence, and therefore, a change is warranted. Choice *B* is incorrect because the original sentence states that nature gives everyone, regardless of status, the same place of habituation and means to survive. Choice *B* changes this sentiment to say that nature only gave those things to the conquered. Choice *C* is incorrect for the same reason, except that it is stating that nature only gave its gifts to the conqueror and not those who are having their land taken from them.

4. B: Choice *B* selects the right word for the needs of the sentence. "These ceremonies are idly multiplied" makes sense, with *are multiplied* being a passive-voice form of *multiply*, constructed with a *to be* verb, and the plural *are* agreeing with the plural noun *ceremonies*. Choice *A* is incorrect because the singular *is* does not agree with *ceremonies*. Choices *C* and *D* are prepositions, which do not fit the sentence.

5. C: The sentence states that because the kings hold the land, they can also hold the inhabitants. In this case, the word *keeping* is synonymous with holding. Choice *A* is incorrect because there is nothing in the text suggesting that the kings are aiding the inhabitants because they hold the land. Choice *B* is incorrect because the text does not suggest that the kings want to enslave the inhabitants of the land they own. Choice *D* is incorrect because there is nothing to suggest that the kings are inspiring their inhabitants by owning the land.

Quantitative Reasoning Section

The Quantitative Reasoning portion of the exam tests a number of related mathematical disciplines. While a series of basic formulas are provided for reference, calculators are not permitted. Some questions are related to general algebra, some feature geometry (including trigonometry), and some questions examine general mathematical reasoning through logic and word problems.

General Mathematics

Place Value of Digits

The number system that is used consists of only ten different digits or characters. However, this system is used to represent an infinite number of values. The place value system makes this infinite number of values possible. The position in which a digit is written corresponds to a given value. Starting from the decimal point (which is implied, if not physically present), each subsequent place value to the left represents a value greater than the one before it. Conversely, starting from the decimal point, each subsequent place value to the right represents a value less than the one before it.

The names for the place values to the left of the decimal point are as follows:

...	Billions	Hundred-Millions	Ten-Millions	Millions	Hundred-Thousands	Ten-Thousands	Thousands	Hundreds	Tens	Ones

Note that this table can be extended infinitely further to the left.

The names for the place values to the right of the decimal point are as follows:

Decimal Point (.)	Tenths	Hundredths	Thousandths	Ten-Thousandths	...

Note that this table can be extended infinitely further to the right.

When given a multi-digit number, the value of each digit depends on its place value. Consider the number 682,174.953. Referring to the chart above, it can be determined that the digit 8 is in the ten-thousands place. It is in the fifth place to the left of the decimal point. Its value is 8 ten-thousands or 80,000. The digit 5 is two places to the right of the decimal point. Therefore, the digit 5 is in the hundredths place. Its value is 5 hundredths or $\frac{5}{100}$ (equivalent to .05).

Base-10 System

Value of Digits

In accordance with the base-10 system, the value of a digit increases by a factor of ten each place it moves to the left. For example, consider the number 7. Moving the digit one place to the left (70), increases its value by a factor of 10 ($7 \times 10 = 70$). Moving the digit two places to the left (700) increases its value by a factor of 10 twice ($7 \times 10 \times 10 = 700$). Moving the digit three places to the left (7,000) increases its value by a factor of 10 three times ($7 \times 10 \times 10 \times 10 = 7,000$), and so on.

Conversely, the value of a digit decreases by a factor of ten each place it moves to the right. (Note that multiplying by $\frac{1}{10}$ is equivalent to dividing by 10). For example, consider the number 40. Moving the digit one place to the right (4) decreases its value by a factor of 10 ($40 \div 10 = 4$). Moving the digit two places to the right (0.4), decreases its value by a factor of 10 twice ($40 \div 10 \div 10 = 0.4$) or ($40 \times \frac{1}{10} \times \frac{1}{10} = 0.4$). Moving the digit three places to the right (0.04) decreases its value by a factor of 10 three times ($40 \div 10 \div 10 \div 10 = 0.04$) or ($40 \times \frac{1}{10} \times \frac{1}{10} \times \frac{1}{10} = 0.04$), and so on.

Exponents to Denote Powers of 10

The value of a given digit of a number in the base-10 system can be expressed utilizing powers of 10. A power of 10 refers to 10 raised to a given exponent such as $10^0, 10^1, 10^2, 10^3$, etc. For the number 10^3, 10 is the base and 3 is the exponent. A base raised by an exponent represents how many times the base is multiplied by itself. Therefore:

$$10^1 = 10$$

$$10^2 = 10 \times 10 = 100$$

$$10^3 = 10 \times 10 \times 10 = 1,000$$

$10^4 = 10 \times 10 \times 10 \times 10 = 10,000$ etc.

Any base with a zero exponent equals one.

Powers of 10 are utilized to decompose a multi-digit number without writing all the zeroes. Consider the number 872,349. This number is decomposed to:

$$800,000 + 70,000 + 2,000 + 300 + 40 + 9$$

When utilizing powers of 10, the number 872,349 is decomposed to:

$$(8 \times 10^5) + (7 \times 10^4) + (2 \times 10^3) + (3 \times 10^2) + (4 \times 10^1) + (9 \times 10^0)$$

The power of 10 by which the digit is multiplied corresponds to the number of zeroes following the digit when expressing its value in standard form. For example, 7×10^4 is equivalent to 70,000 or 7 followed by four zeros.

Structure of the Number System

The mathematical number system is made up of two general types of numbers: real and complex. **Real numbers** are both irrational and rational numbers. **Complex numbers** are those composed of both a real number and an imaginary one. Imaginary numbers are the result of taking the square root of -1, and $\sqrt{-1} = i$.

The real number system is often explained using a Venn diagram similar to the one below. After a number has been labeled as a real number, further classification occurs when considering the other groups in this diagram. If a number is a never-ending, non-repeating decimal, it falls in the irrational category. Otherwise, it is rational. More information on these types of numbers is provided in the previous section. Furthermore, if a number does not have a fractional part, it is classified as an integer, such as -2, 75, or zero. Whole numbers are an even smaller group that only includes positive integers and zero. The last group of natural numbers is made up of only positive integers, such as 2, 56, or 12.

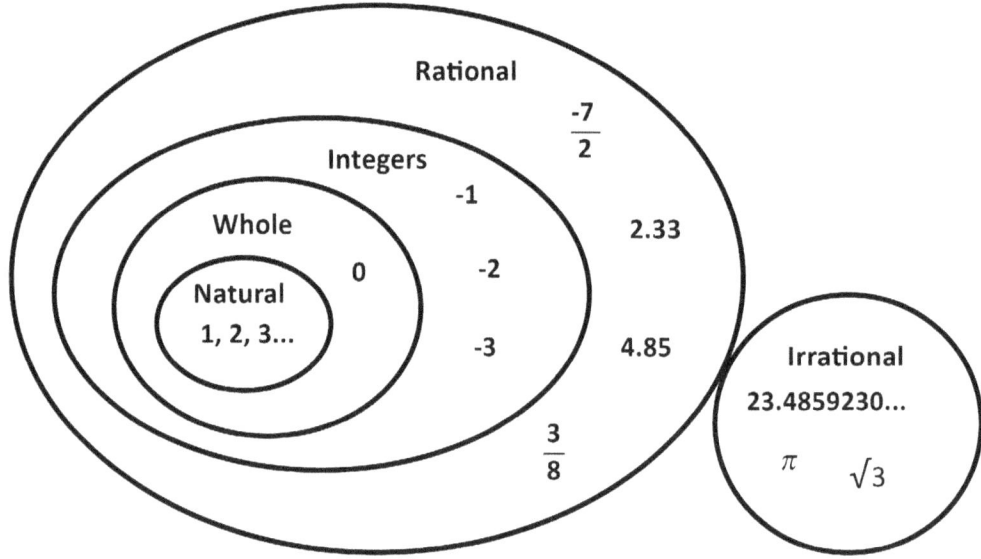

Real numbers can be compared and ordered using the number line. If a number falls to the left on the real number line, it is less than a number on the right. For example, $-2 < 5$ because -2 falls to the left of zero, and 5 falls to the right. Numbers to the left of zero are negative while those to the right are positive.

Complex numbers are made up of the sum of a real number and an imaginary number. Some examples of complex numbers include $6 + 2i, 5 - 7i$, and $-3 + 12i$. Adding and subtracting complex numbers is similar to collecting like terms. The real numbers are added together, and the imaginary numbers are added together.

For example, if the problem asks to simplify the expression $6 + 2i - 3 + 7i$, the 6 and -3 are combined to make 3, and the $2i$ and $7i$ combine to make $9i$. Multiplying and dividing complex numbers is similar to working with exponents. One rule to remember when multiplying is that $i * i = -1$. For example, if a problem asks to simplify the expression $4i(3 + 7i)$, the $4i$ should be distributed throughout the 3 and the $7i$. This leaves the final expression $12i - 28$. The 28 is negative because $i * i$ results in a negative number. The last type of operation to consider with complex numbers is the conjugate. The **conjugate** of a complex number is a technique used to change the complex number into a real number. For example, the conjugate of $4 - 3i$ is $4 + 3i$. Multiplying $(4 - 3i)(4 + 3i)$ results in $16 + 12i - 12i + 9$, which has a final answer of $16 + 9 = 25$.

The order of operations—PEMDAS—simplifies longer expressions with real or imaginary numbers. Each operation is listed in the order of how they should be completed in a problem containing more than one operation. Parentheses can also mean grouping symbols, such as brackets and absolute value. Then, exponents are calculated. Multiplication and division should be completed from left to right, and addition and subtraction should be completed from left to right.

Simplification of another type of expression occurs when radicals are involved. As explained previously, root is another word for radical. For example, the following expression is a radical that can be simplified: $\sqrt{24x^2}$.

First, the number must be factored out to the highest perfect square. Any perfect square can be taken out of a radical. Twenty-four can be factored into 4 and 6, and 4 can be taken out of the radical. $\sqrt{4} = 2$ can be taken out, and 6 stays underneath. If $x > 0$, x can be taken out of the radical because it is a perfect square. The simplified radical is $2x\sqrt{6}$. An approximation can be found using a calculator.

There are also properties of numbers that are true for certain operations. The **commutative** property allows the order of the terms in an expression to change while keeping the same final answer. Both addition and multiplication can be completed in any order and still obtain the same result. However, order does matter in subtraction and division. The **associative** property allows any terms to be "associated" by parentheses and retain the same final answer.

For example, $(4 + 3) + 5 = 4 + (3 + 5)$. Both addition and multiplication are associative; however, subtraction and division do not hold this property. The **distributive** property states that $a(b + c) = ab + ac$. It is a property that involves both addition and multiplication, and the a is distributed onto each term inside the parentheses.

Integers can be factored into prime numbers. To **factor** is to express as a product. For example, $6 = 3 \cdot 2$, and $6 = 6 \cdot 1$. Both are factorizations, but the expression involving the factors of 3 and 2 is known as a **prime factorization** because it is factored into a product of two **prime numbers**—integers which do not have any factors other than themselves and 1. A **composite number** is a positive integer that can be divided into at least one other integer other than itself and 1, such as 6. Integers that have a factor of 2 are even, and if they are not divisible by 2, they are odd. Finally, a **multiple** of a number is the product of that number and a counting number—also known as a **natural number**. For example, some multiples of 4 are 4, 8, 12, 16, etc.

Positive and Negative Numbers

Signs
Aside from 0, numbers can be either positive or negative. The sign for a positive number is the plus sign or the + symbol, while the sign for a negative number is the minus sign or the – symbol. If a number has no designation, then it's assumed to be positive.

Absolute Values
Both positive and negative numbers are valued according to their distance from 0. Look at this number line for +3 and -3:

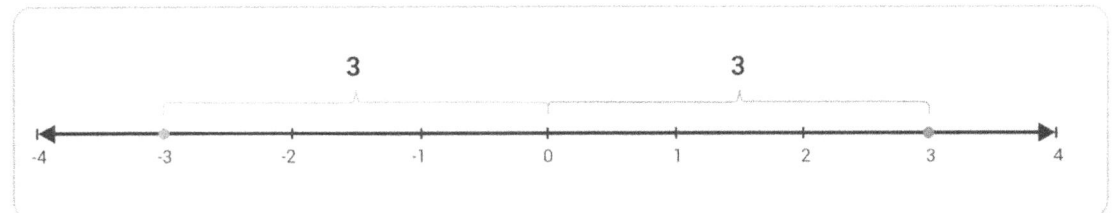

Both 3 and -3 are three spaces from 0. The distance from 0 is called its absolute value. Thus, both -3 and 3 have an absolute value of 3 since they're both three spaces away from 0.

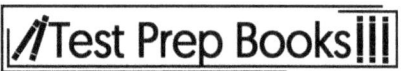

An absolute number is written by placing | | around the number. So, |3| and |−3| both equal 3, as that's their common absolute value.

Rational Numbers on a Number Line

A number line typically consists of integers (...3, 2, 1, 0, -1, -2, -3...), and is used to visually represent the value of a rational number. Each rational number has a distinct position on the line determined by comparing its value with the displayed values on the line. For example, if plotting -1.5 on the number line below, it is necessary to recognize that the value of -1.5 is .5 less than -1 and .5 greater than -2. Therefore, -1.5 is plotted halfway between -1 and -2.

Number lines can also be useful for visualizing sums and differences of rational numbers. Adding a value indicates moving to the right (values increase to the right), and subtracting a value indicates moving to the left (numbers decrease to the left). For example, $5 - 7$ is displayed by starting at 5 and moving to the left 7 spaces, if the number line is in increments of 1. This will result in an answer of -2.

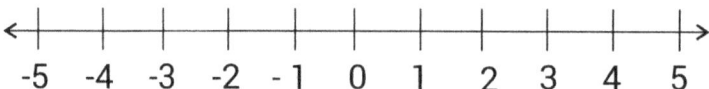

Comparing, Classifying, and Ordering Rational Numbers

A **rational number** is any number that can be written as a fraction or ratio. Within the set of rational numbers, several subsets exist that are referenced throughout the mathematics topics. Counting numbers are the first numbers learned as a child. Counting numbers consist of 1,2,3,4, and so on.

Whole numbers include all counting numbers and zero (0,1,2,3,4,...). Integers include counting numbers, their opposites, and zero (..., -3, -2, -1, 0, 1, 2, 3, ...). Rational numbers are inclusive of integers, fractions, and decimals that terminate, or end (1.7, 0.04213) or repeat (0.136$\underline{5}$).

When comparing or ordering numbers, the numbers should be written in the same format (decimal or fraction), if possible. For example, $\sqrt{49}$, 7.3, and $\frac{15}{2}$ are easier to order if each one is converted to a decimal, such as 7, 7.3, and 7.5. A number line is used to order and compare the numbers. Any number that is to the right of another number is greater than that number. Conversely, a number positioned to the left of a given number is less than that number.

Factors and Multiples of Numbers

The factors of a number are all integers that can be multiplied by another integer to produce the given number. For example, 2 is multiplied by 3 to produce 6. Therefore, 2 and 3 are both factors of 6. Similarly, $1 \times 6 = 6$ and $2 \times 3 = 6$, so 1, 2, 3, and 6 are all factors of 6. Another way to explain a factor is to say that a given number divides evenly by each of its factors to produce an integer. For example, 6 does not divide evenly by 5. Therefore, 5 is not a factor of 6.

Multiples of a given number are found by taking that number and multiplying it by any other whole number. For example, 3 is a factor of 6, 9, and 12. Therefore, 6, 9, and 12 are multiples of 3. The multiples of any number are an infinite list. For example, the multiples of 5 are 5, 10, 15, 20, and so on. This list continues without end. A list of multiples is used in finding the least common multiple, or LCM,

Quantitative Reasoning Section

for fractions when a common denominator is needed. The denominators are written down and their multiples listed until a common number is found in both lists. This common number is the LCM.

Prime factorization breaks down each factor of a whole number until only prime numbers remain. All composite numbers can be factored into prime numbers. For example, the prime factors of 12 are 2, 2, and 3 ($2 \times 2 \times 3 = 12$). To produce the prime factors of a number, the number is factored, and any composite numbers are continuously factored until the result is the product of prime factors only. A factor tree, such as the one below, is helpful when exploring this concept.

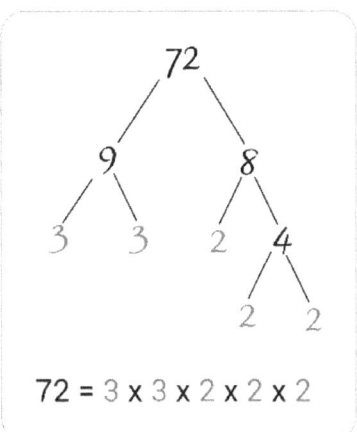

$72 = 3 \times 3 \times 2 \times 2 \times 2$

Properties of Exponents

Exponents are used in mathematics to express a number or variable multiplied by itself a certain number of times. For example, x^3 means x is multiplied by itself three times. In this expression, x is called the **base**, and 3 is the **exponent**. Exponents can be used in more complex problems when they contain fractions and negative numbers.

Fractional exponents can be explained by looking first at the inverse of exponents, which are **roots**. Given the expression x^2, the square root can be taken, $\sqrt{x^2}$, cancelling out the 2 and leaving x by itself, if x is positive. Cancellation occurs because $\sqrt{x}$ can be written with exponents, instead of roots, as $x^{\frac{1}{2}}$. The numerator of 1 is the exponent, and the denominator of 2 is called the root (which is why it's referred to as **square root**). Taking the square root of x^2 is the same as raising it to the $\frac{1}{2}$ power.

Written out in mathematical form, it takes the following progression:

$$\sqrt{x^2} = (x^2)^{\frac{1}{2}} = x$$

From properties of exponents, $2 \cdot \frac{1}{2} = 1$ is the actual exponent of x. Another example can be seen with $x^{\frac{4}{7}}$. The variable x, raised to four-sevenths, is equal to the seventh root of x to the fourth power: $\sqrt[7]{x^4}$. In general, $x^{\frac{1}{n}} = \sqrt[n]{x}$ and $x^{\frac{m}{n}} = \sqrt[n]{x^m}$.

Negative exponents also involve fractions. Whereas y^3 can also be rewritten as $\frac{y^3}{1}$, y^{-3} can be rewritten as $\frac{1}{y^3}$. A negative exponent means the exponential expression must be moved to the opposite spot in a

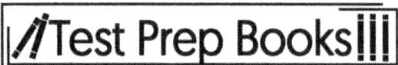

fraction to make the exponent positive. If the negative appears in the numerator, it moves to the denominator. If the negative appears in the denominator, it is moved to the numerator. In general, $a^{-n} = \frac{1}{a^n}$, and a^{-n} and a^n are reciprocals.

Take, for example, the following expression: $\frac{a^{-4}b^2}{c^{-5}}$. Since a is raised to the negative fourth power, it can be moved to the denominator. Since c is raised to the negative fifth power, it can be moved to the numerator. The b variable is raised to the positive second power, so it does not move. The simplified expression is as follows: $\frac{b^2 c^5}{a^4}$.

In mathematical expressions containing exponents and other operations, the order of operations must be followed. *PEMDAS* states that exponents are calculated after any parentheses and grouping symbols but before any multiplication, division, addition, and subtraction.

Scientific Notation

Scientific Notation is used to represent numbers that are either very small or very large. For example, the distance to the sun is approximately 150,000,000,000 meters. Instead of writing this number with so many zeros, it can be written in scientific notation as $1.5 * 10^{11}$ meters.

The same is true for very small numbers, but the exponent becomes negative. If the mass of a human cell is 0.000000000001 kilograms, that measurement can be easily represented by $1.0 * 10^{-12}$ kilograms. In both situations, scientific notation makes the measurement easier to read and understand. Each number is translated to an expression with one digit in the tens place times an expression corresponding to the zeros.

When two measurements are given and both involve scientific notation, it is important to know how these interact with each other:

- In addition and subtraction, the exponent on the ten must be the same before any operations are performed on the numbers. For example, $(1.3 * 10^4) + (3.0 * 10^3)$ cannot be added until one of the exponents on the ten is changed. The $3.0 * 10^3$ can be changed to $0.3 * 10^4$, then the 1.3 and 0.3 can be added. The answer comes out to be $1.6 * 10^4$.

- For multiplication, the first numbers can be multiplied and then the exponents on the tens can be added. Once an answer is formed, it may have to be converted into scientific notation again depending on the change that occurred.

  o The following is an example of multiplication with scientific notation: $(4.5 * 10^3) * (3.0 * 10^{-5}) = 13.5 * 10^{-2}$. Since this answer is not in scientific notation, the decimal is moved over to the left one unit, and 1 is added to the ten's exponent. This results in the final answer: $1.35 * 10^{-1}$.

- For division, the first numbers are divided, and the exponents on the tens are subtracted. Again, the answer may need to be converted into scientific notation form, depending on the type of changes that occurred during the problem.

- **Order of magnitude** relates to scientific notation and is the total count of powers of 10 in a number. For example, there are 6 orders of magnitude in 1,000,000. If a number is raised by an order of magnitude, it is multiplied times 10. Order of magnitude can be helpful in estimating results using very large or small numbers. An answer should make sense in terms of its order of magnitude.

- o For example, if area is calculated using two dimensions with 6 orders of magnitude, because area involves multiplication, the answer should have around 12 orders of magnitude. Also, answers can be estimated by rounding to the largest place value in each number. For example, 5,493,302 * 2,523,100 can be estimated by 5 * 3 = 15 with 12 orders of magnitude.

Implications for Addition and Subtraction

For addition, if all numbers are either positive or negative, simply add them together. For example, 4 + 4 = 8 and -4 + -4 = -8. However, things get tricky when some of the numbers are negative, and some are positive.

Take 6 + (-4) as an example. First, take the absolute values of the numbers, which are 6 and 4. Second, subtract the smaller value from the larger. The equation becomes 6– 4 = 2. Third, place the sign of the original larger number on the sum. Here, 6 is the larger number, and it's positive, so the sum is 2.

Here's an example where the negative number has a larger absolute value: (-6) + 4. The first two steps are the same as the example above. However, on the third step, the negative sign must be placed on the sum, as the absolute value of (-6) is greater than 4. Thus, -6 + 4 = -2.

The absolute value of numbers implies that subtraction can be thought of as flipping the sign of the number following the subtraction sign and simply adding the two numbers. This means that subtracting a negative number will in fact be adding the positive absolute value of the negative number. Here are some examples:

$$-6 - 4 = -6 + -4 = -10$$

$$3 - -6 = 3 + 6 = 9$$

$$-3 - 2 = -3 + -2 = -5$$

Implications for Multiplication and Division

For multiplication and division, if both numbers are positive, then the product or quotient is always positive. If both numbers are negative, then the product or quotient is also positive. However, if the numbers have opposite signs, the product or quotient is always negative.

Simply put, the product in multiplication and quotient in division is always positive, unless the numbers have opposing signs, in which case it's negative. Here are some examples:

$$(-6) \times (-5) = 30$$

$$(-50) \div 10 = -5$$

$$8 \times |-7| = 56$$

$$(-48) \div (-6) = 8$$

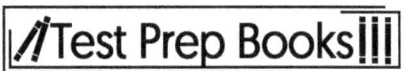

If there are more than two numbers in a multiplication or division problem, then whether the product or quotient is positive or negative depends on the number of negative numbers in the problem. If there is an odd number of negatives, then the product or quotient is negative. If there is an even number of negative numbers, then the result is positive.

Here are some examples:

$$(-6) \times 5 \times (-2) \times (-4) = -240$$

$$(-6) \times 5 \times 2 \times (-4) = 240$$

Arithmetic and Operations

Order of Operations

When solving equations with multiple operations, special rules apply. These rules are known as the Order of Operations. The order is as follows: Parentheses, Exponents, Multiplication and Division from left to right, and Addition and Subtraction from left to right. A popular mnemonic device to help remember the order is Please Excuse My Dear Aunt Sally (PEMDAS). Evaluate the following two problems to understand the Order of Operations:

1) $4 + (3 \times 2)^2 \div 4$

    First, solve the operation within the parentheses: $4 + 6^2 \div 4$.

    Second, solve the exponent: $4 + 36 \div 4$.

    Third, solve the division operation: $4 + 9$.

    Fourth, finish the operation with addition for the answer, 13.

2) $2 \times (6 + 3) \div (2 + 1)^2$

    $2 \times 9 \div (3)^2$

    $2 \times 9 \div 9$

    $18 \div 9$

    2

Strategies and Algorithms to Perform Operations on Rational Numbers

A rational number is any number that can be written in the form of a ratio or fraction. Integers can be written as fractions with a denominator of 1 ($5 = \frac{5}{1}$; $-342 = \frac{-342}{1}$; etc.). Decimals that terminate and/or repeat can also be written as fractions ($47 = \frac{47}{100}$; $.\overline{33} = \frac{1}{3}$). For more on converting decimals to fractions, see the section *Converting Between Fractions, Decimals,* and *Percent*.

When adding or subtracting fractions, the numbers must have the same denominators. In these cases, numerators are added or subtracted, and denominators are kept the same.

Quantitative Reasoning Section

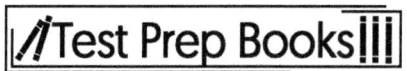

For example, $\frac{2}{7} + \frac{3}{7} = \frac{5}{7}$ and $\frac{4}{5} - \frac{3}{5} = \frac{1}{5}$. If the fractions to be added or subtracted do not have the same denominator, a common denominator must be found. This is accomplished by changing one or both fractions to a different but equivalent fraction.

Consider the example $\frac{1}{6} + \frac{4}{9}$. First, a common denominator must be found. One method is to find the least common multiple (LCM) of the denominators 6 and 9. This is the lowest number that both 6 and 9 will divide into evenly. In this case the LCM is 18. Both fractions should be changed to equivalent fractions with a denominator of 18. To obtain the numerator of the new fraction, the old numerator is multiplied by the same number by which the old denominator is multiplied. For the fraction $\frac{1}{6}$, 6 multiplied by 3 will produce a denominator of 18.

Therefore, the numerator is multiplied by 3 to produce the new numerator $\left(\frac{1 \times 3}{6 \times 3} = \frac{3}{18}\right)$.

For the fraction $\frac{4}{9}$, multiplying both the numerator and denominator by 2 produces $\frac{8}{18}$. Since the two new fractions have common denominators, they can be added $\left(\frac{3}{18} + \frac{8}{18} = \frac{11}{18}\right)$.

When multiplying or dividing rational numbers, these numbers may be converted to fractions and multiplied or divided accordingly. When multiplying fractions, all numerators are multiplied by each other and all denominators are multiplied by each other. For example:

$$\frac{1}{3} \times \frac{6}{5} = \frac{1 \times 6}{3 \times 5} = \frac{6}{15}$$

and

$$\frac{-1}{2} \times \frac{3}{1} \times \frac{11}{100} = \frac{-1 \times 3 \times 11}{2 \times 1 \times 100} = \frac{-33}{200}$$

When dividing fractions, the problem is converted by multiplying by the reciprocal of the divisor. This is done by changing division to multiplication and "flipping" the second fraction, or divisor. For example:

$$\frac{1}{2} \div \frac{3}{5} \rightarrow \frac{1}{2} \times \frac{5}{3}$$

and

$$\frac{5}{1} \div \frac{1}{3} \rightarrow \frac{5}{1} \times \frac{3}{1}$$

To complete the problem, the rules for multiplying fractions should be followed.

Note that when adding, subtracting, multiplying, and dividing mixed numbers (ex. $4\frac{1}{2}$), it is easiest to convert these to improper fractions (larger numerator than denominator). To do so, the denominator is kept the same. To obtain the numerator, the whole number is multiplied by the denominator and added to the numerator. For example:

$$4\frac{1}{2} = \frac{9}{2}$$

and

$$7\frac{2}{3} = \frac{23}{3}$$

Also, note that answers involving fractions should be converted to the simplest form.

Converting Between Fractions, Decimals, and Percent

To convert a fraction to a decimal, the numerator is divided by the denominator. For example, $\frac{3}{8}$ can be converted to a decimal by dividing 3 by 8 ($\frac{3}{8} = 0.375$).

To convert a decimal to a fraction, the decimal point is dropped, and the value is written as the numerator. The denominator is the place value farthest to the right with a digit other than zero. For example, to convert .48 to a fraction, the numerator is 48, and the denominator is 100 (the digit 8 is in the hundredths place).

Therefore, .48 = $\frac{48}{100}$. Fractions should be written in the simplest form, or reduced. To reduce a fraction, the numerator and denominator are divided by the largest common factor. In the previous example, 48 and 100 are both divisible by 4. Dividing the numerator and denominator by 4 results in a reduced fraction of $\frac{12}{25}$.

To convert a decimal to a percent, the number is multiplied by 100. To convert .13 to a percent, .13 is multiplied by 100 to get 13 percent. To convert a fraction to a percent, the fraction is converted to a decimal and then multiplied by 100. For example, $\frac{1}{5}$ = .20 and .20 multiplied by 100 produces 20 percent.

To convert a percent to a decimal, the value is divided by 100. For example, 125 percent is equal to 1.25 ($\frac{125}{100}$). To convert a percent to a fraction, the percent sign is dropped, and the value is written as the numerator with a denominator of 100. For example, 80% = $\frac{80}{100}$. This fraction can be reduced ($\frac{80}{100} = \frac{4}{5}$).

Representing Rational Numbers and Their Operations

Concrete Models

Concrete objects are used to develop a tangible understanding of operations of rational numbers. Tools such as tiles, blocks, beads, and hundred charts are used to model problems. For example, a hundred chart (10 × 10) and beads can be used to model multiplication. If multiplying 5 by 4, beads are placed across 5 rows and down 4 columns producing a product of 20. Similarly, tiles can be used to model division by splitting the total into equal groups. If dividing 12 by 4, 12 tiles are placed one at a time into 4 groups. The result is 4 groups of 3. This is also an effective method for visualizing the concept of remainders.

Representations of objects can be used to expand on the concrete models of operations. Pictures, dots, and tallies can help model these concepts. Utilizing concrete models and representations creates a foundation upon which to build an abstract understanding of the operations.

Multiplication and Division Problems

Multiplication and division are inverse operations that can be represented by using rectangular arrays, area models, and equations. Rectangular arrays include an arrangement of rows and columns that correspond to the factors and display product totals.

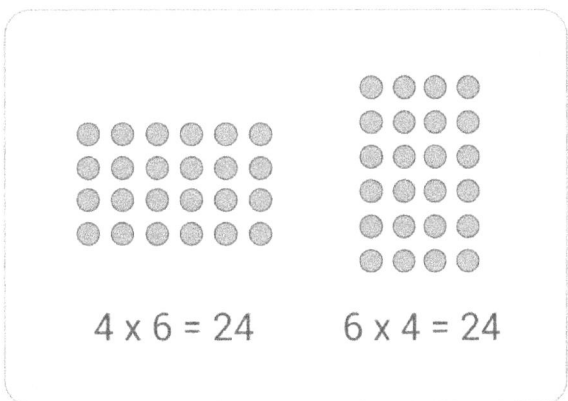

Another method of multiplication can be done with the use of an *area model*. An area model is a rectangle that is divided into rows and columns that match up to the number of place values within each number. Take the example 29×65. These two numbers can be split into simpler numbers: $29 = 25 + 4$ and $65 = 60 + 5$. The products of those 4 numbers are found within the rectangle and then summed up to get the answer. The entire process is:

$$(60 \times 25) + (5 \times 25) + (60 \times 4) + (5 \times 4)$$

$$1,500 + 240 + 125 + 20 = 1,885$$

Here is the actual area model:

	25	4
60	60x25 1,500	60x4 240
5	5x25 125	5x4 20

```
   1,500
     240
     125
+     20
   1,885
```

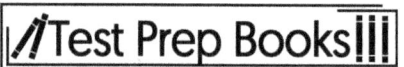

Dividing a number by a single digit or two digits can be turned into repeated subtraction problems. An area model can be used throughout the problem that represents multiples of the divisor. For example, the answer to $8580 \div 55$ can be found by subtracting 55 from 8580 one at a time and counting the total number of subtractions necessary.

However, a simpler process involves using larger multiples of 55. First, $100 \times 55 = 5,500$ is subtracted from 8,580, and 3,080 is leftover. Next, $50 \times 55 = 2,750$ is subtracted from 3,080 to obtain 380. $5 \times 55 = 275$ is subtracted from 330 to obtain 55, and finally, $1 \times 55 = 55$ is subtracted from 55 to obtain zero. Therefore, there is no remainder, and the answer is $100 + 50 + 5 + 1 = 156$.

Here is a picture of the area model and the repeated subtraction process:

$$8580 \div 55$$

	55
100	5500
50	2750
5	275
1	55

```
  55 | 8580
      -5500  (100 x 55)
       3080
      -2750  (50 x 55)
        330
       -275  (5 x 55)
         55
        -55  (1 x 55)
          0
```

Determining Reasonableness of Results

When solving math word problems, the solution obtained should make sense within the given scenario. The step of checking the solution will reduce the possibility of a calculation error or a solution that may be **mathematically** correct but not applicable in the real world. Consider the following scenarios:

A problem states that Lisa got 24 out of 32 questions correct on a test and asks to find the percentage of correct answers. To solve the problem, a student divided 32 by 24 to get 1.33, and then multiplied by 100 to get 133 percent. By examining the solution within the context of the problem, the student should recognize that getting all 32 questions correct will produce a perfect score of 100 percent. Therefore, a score of 133 percent with 8 incorrect answers does not make sense, and the calculations should be checked.

A problem states that the maximum weight on a bridge cannot exceed 22,000 pounds. The problem asks to find the maximum number of cars that can be on the bridge at one time if each car weighs 4,000 pounds. To solve this problem, a student divided 22,000 by 4,000 to get an answer of 5.5. By examining the solution within the context of the problem, the student should recognize that although the calculations are mathematically correct, the solution does not make sense. Half of a car on a bridge is not possible, so the student should determine that a maximum of 5 cars can be on the bridge at the same time.

Quantitative Reasoning Section

Mental Math Estimation

Once a result is determined to be logical within the context of a given problem, the result should be evaluated by its nearness to the expected answer. This is performed by approximating given values to perform mental math. Numbers should be rounded to the nearest value possible to check the initial results.

Consider the following example: A problem states that a customer is buying a new sound system for their home. The customer purchases a stereo for $435, 2 speakers for $67 each, and the necessary cables for $12. The customer chooses an option that allows him to spread the costs over equal payments for 4 months. How much will the monthly payments be?

After making calculations for the problem, a student determines that the monthly payment will be $145.25. To check the accuracy of the results, the student rounds each cost to the nearest ten $(440 + 70 + 70 + 10)$ and determines that the total is approximately $590. Dividing by 4 months gives an approximate monthly payment of $147.50. Therefore, the student can conclude that the solution of $145.25 is very close to what should be expected.

When rounding, the place-value that is used in rounding can make a difference. Suppose the student had rounded to the nearest hundred for the estimation. The result:

$$(400 + 100 + 100 + 0 = 600;\ 600 \div 4 = 150)$$

will show that the answer is reasonable but not as close to the actual value as rounding to the nearest ten.

Number Patterns

Given a sequence of numbers, a mathematical rule can be defined that represents the numbers if a pattern exists within the set. For example, consider the sequence of numbers 1, 4, 9, 16, 25, etc. This set of numbers represents the positive integers squared, and an explicitly defined sequence that represents this set is $f_n = n^2$. An important mathematical concept is recognizing patterns in sequences and translating the patterns into an explicit formula. Once the pattern is recognized and the formula is defined, the sequence can be extended easily. For example, the next three numbers in the sequence are 36, 49, and 64.

Predicting Values

In a similar sense, patterns can be used to make conjectures, predictions, and generalizations. If a pattern is recognized in a set of numbers, values can be predicted that aren't originally provided. For example, if an experiment results in the sequence of numbers 1, 4, 9, 16, and 25, where 1 represents the first trial, 2 represents the second trial, etc., one expects the tenth trial to result in a value of 100 because that value is equal to the square of the trial number.

Recursively Defined Functions

Similar to recursively defined sequences, recursively defined functions are not explicitly defined in terms of a variable. A recursive function builds on itself and consists of a smaller argument, such as $f(0)$ or

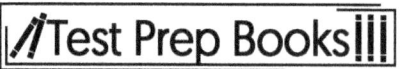

$f(1)$ and the actual definition of the function. For example, a recursively defined function is the following:

$$f(0) = 3$$

$$f(n) = f(n-1) + 2n$$

Contrasting an explicitly defined function, a recursively defined function must be evaluated in order. The first five terms of this function are:

$$f(0) = 3, f(1) = 5, f(2) = 9, f(3) = 15, and\ f(4) = 23$$

Some recursively defined functions have an explicit counterpart and, like sequences, they can be used to model real-life applications. The Fibonacci numbers can also be thought of as a recursively defined function if $f(n) = f_n$.

Closed-Form Functions

A **closed-form function** can be evaluated using a finite number of operations such as addition, subtraction, multiplication, and division. An example of a function that's not a closed-form function is one involving an infinite sum.

For example, $y = \sum_{n=1}^{\infty} x$ isn't a closed-form function because it consists of a sum of infinitely many terms. Many recursively defined functions can be expressed as a closed-form expression. To convert to a closed-form expression, a formula must be found for the nth term. This means that the recursively defined sequence must be converted to its explicit formula.

Algebraic Expressions and Equations

Translating Between Verbal and Symbolic Forms

Being able to translate verbal scenarios into symbolic forms is a critical skill in mathematics. This idea is seen mostly when solving word problems. First, the problem needs to be read carefully several times until one can state clearly what is being sought. Then, variables that represent the unknown quantities need to be defined. Equations can be defined using those variables that model the verbal conditions of the given problem. The equations then need to be solved to answer the problem's questions. The problem-solving skills learned in these types of problems is an invaluable skill, and is ultimately more important than finding the answer to each individual problem.

Ratios and Proportions

Ratios are used to show the relationship between two quantities. The ratio of oranges to apples in the grocery store may be 3 to 2. That means that for every 3 oranges, there are 2 apples. This comparison can be expanded to represent the actual number of oranges and apples. Another example may be the number of boys to girls in a math class. If the ratio of boys to girls is given as 2 to 5, that means there are 2 boys to every 5 girls in the class. Ratios can also be compared if the units in each ratio are the same. The ratio of boys to girls in the math class can be compared to the ratio of boys to girls in a science class by stating which ratio is higher and which is lower.

Rates are used to compare two quantities with different units. **Unit rates** are the simplest form of rate. With unit rates, the denominator in the comparison of two units is one. For example, if someone can

Quantitative Reasoning Section

type at a rate of 1000 words in 5 minutes, then their unit rate for typing is $\frac{1000}{5} = 200$ words in one minute or 200 words per minute. Any rate can be converted into a unit rate by dividing to make the denominator one. 1000 words in 5 minutes has been converted into the unit rate of 200 words per minute.

Ratios and rates can be used together to convert rates into different units. For example, if someone is driving 50 kilometers per hour, that rate can be converted into miles per hour by using a ratio known as the **conversion factor**. Since the given value contains kilometers and the final answer needs to be in miles, the ratio relating miles to kilometers needs to be used. There are 0.62 miles in 1 kilometer. This, written as a ratio and in fraction form, is $\frac{0.62\ miles}{1\ km}$.

To convert 50km/hour into miles per hour, the following conversion needs to be set up:

$$\frac{50\ km}{hour} * \frac{0.62\ miles}{1\ km} = 31\ miles\ per\ hour$$

The ratio between two similar geometric figures is called the **scale factor**. For example, a problem may depict two similar triangles, A and B. The scale factor from the smaller triangle A to the larger triangle B is given as 2 because the length of the corresponding side of the larger triangle, 16, is twice the corresponding side on the smaller triangle, 8. This scale factor can also be used to find the value of a missing side, x, in triangle A. Since the scale factor from the smaller triangle (A) to larger one (B) is 2, the larger corresponding side in triangle B (given as 25) can be divided by 2 to find the missing side in A ($x=$ 12.5). The scale factor can also be represented in the equation $2A = B$ because two times the lengths of A gives the corresponding lengths of B. This is the idea behind similar triangles.

Much like a scale factor can be written using an equation like $2A = B$, a **relationship** is represented by the equation $Y = kX$. X and Y are proportional because as values of X increase, the values of Y also increase. A relationship that is inversely proportional can be represented by the equation $Y = \frac{k}{x}$, where the value of Y decreases as the value of x increases and vice versa.

Proportional reasoning can be used to solve problems involving ratios, percentages, and averages. Ratios can be used in setting up proportions and solving them to find unknowns. For example, if a student completes an average of 10 pages of math homework in 3 nights, how long would it take the student to complete 22 pages? Both ratios can be written as fractions. The second ratio would contain the unknown. The following proportion represents this problem, where x is the unknown number of nights:

$$\frac{10\ pages}{3\ nights} = \frac{22\ pages}{x\ nights}$$

Solving this proportion entails cross-multiplying and results in the following equation: $10x = 22 * 3$. Simplifying and solving for x results in the exact solution: $x = 6.6\ nights$. The result would be rounded up to 7 because the homework would actually be completed on the 7th night.

The following problem uses ratios involving percentages:

> If 20% of the class is girls and 30 students are in the class, how many girls are in the class?

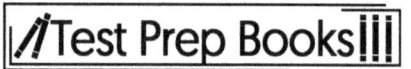

To set up this problem, it is helpful to use the common proportion: $\frac{\%}{100} = \frac{is}{of}$. Within the proportion, % is the percentage of girls, 100 is the total percentage of the class, *is* is the number of girls, and *of* is the total number of students in the class.

Most percentage problems can be written using this language. To solve this problem, the proportion should be set up as $\frac{20}{100} = \frac{x}{30}$, and then solved for x. Cross-multiplying results in the equation $20 * 30 = 100x$, which results in the solution $x = 6$. There are 6 girls in the class.

Ratios can be used to solve problems that concern length, volume, and other units. For example, a problem may ask for the volume of a cone to be found that has a radius, $r = 7m$ and a height, $h = 16m$. Referring to the formulas provided on the test, the volume of a cone is given as: $V = \pi r^2 \frac{h}{3}$, where r is the radius, and h is the height.

Plugging $r = 7$ and $h = 16$ into the formula, the following is obtained:

$$V = \pi (7^2) \frac{16}{3}$$

Therefore, the volume of the cone is found to be approximately 821m³. Sometimes, answers in different units are sought. If this problem wanted the answer in liters, 821m³ would need to be converted. Using the equivalence statement 1m³ = 1000L, the following ratio would be used to solve for liters:

$$821m^3 * \frac{1000L}{1m^3}$$

Cubic meters in the numerator and denominator cancel each other out, and the answer is converted to 821,000 liters, or $8.21 * 10^5$ L.

Other conversions can also be made between different given and final units. If the temperature in a pool is 30°C, what is the temperature of the pool in degrees Fahrenheit? To convert these units, an equation is used relating Celsius to Fahrenheit. The following equation is used:

$$T_{°F} = 1.8 T_{°C} + 32$$

Plugging in the given temperature and solving the equation for T yields the result:

$$T_{°F} = 1.8(30) + 32 = 86°F$$

Units in both the metric system and US customary system are widely used.

Solving Problems by Quantitative Reasoning

Dimensional analysis is the process of converting between different units using equivalent measurement statements. For instance, running 5 kilometers is approximately the same as running 3.1 miles. This conversion can be found by knowing that 1 kilometer is equal to approximately 0.62 miles.

When setting up the dimensional analysis calculations, the original units need to be opposite one another in each of the two fractions: one in the original amount (essentially in the numerator) and one in the denominator of the conversion factor. This enables them to cancel after multiplying, leaving the converted result.

Calculations involving formulas, such as determining volume and area, are a common situation in which units need to be interpreted and used. However, graphs can also carry meaning through units. The graph below is an example. It represents a graph of the position of an object over time. The y-axis represents the position or the number of meters the object is from the starting point at time s, in seconds. Interpreting this graph, the origin shows that at time zero seconds, the object is zero meters away from the starting point. As the time increases to one second, the position increases to five meters away. This trend continues until 6 seconds, where the object is 30 meters away from the starting position. After this point in time—since the graph remains horizontal from 6 to 10 seconds—the object must have stopped moving.

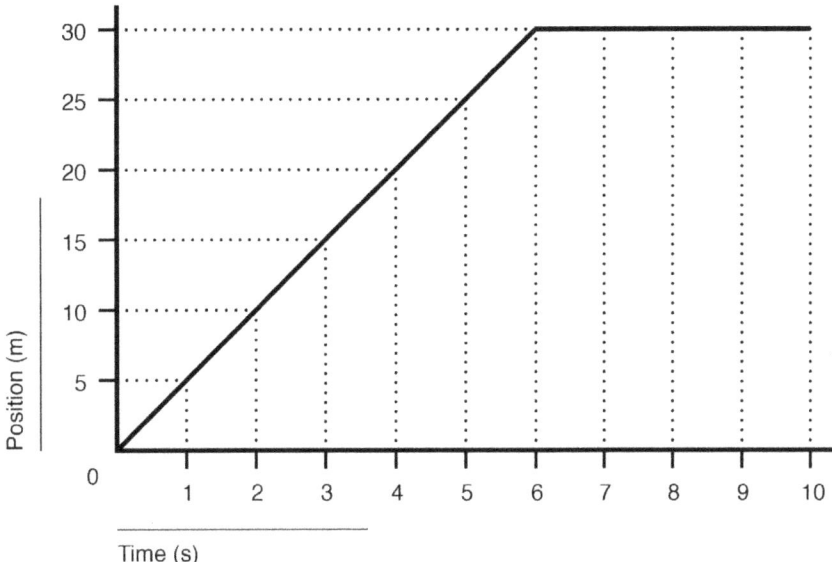

When solving problems with units, it's important to consider the reasonableness of the answer. If conversions are used, it's helpful to have an estimated value to compare the final answer to. This way, if the final answer is too distant from the estimate, it will be obvious that a mistake was made.

Functions

A **function** is defined as a relationship between inputs and outputs where there is only one output value for a given input. As an example, the following function is in function notation:

$$f(x) = 3x - 4$$

The $f(x)$ represents the output value for an input of x. If $x = 2$, the equation becomes:

$$f(2) = 3(2) - 4 = 6 - 4 = 2$$

The input of 2 yields an output of 2, forming the ordered pair $(2, 2)$.

The following set of ordered pairs corresponds to the given function: $(2, 2), (0, -4), (-2, -10)$. The set of all possible inputs of a function is its **domain**, and all possible outputs is called the **range**. By definition, each member of the domain is paired with only one member of the range.

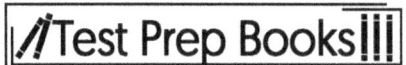

Functions can also be defined recursively. In this form, they are not defined explicitly in terms of variables. Instead, they are defined using previously evaluated function outputs, starting with either $f(0)$ or $f(1)$. An example of a recursively defined function is:

$$f(1) = 2, f(n) = 2f(n-1) + 2n, n > 1$$

The domain of this function is the set of all integers.

Domain and Range

The domain and range of a function can be found visually by its plot on the coordinate plane. In the function $f(x) = x^2 - 3$, for example, the domain is all real numbers because the parabola stretches as far left and as far right as it can go, with no restrictions. This means that any input value from the real number system will yield an answer in the real number system. For the range, the inequality $y \geq -3$ would be used to describe the possible output values because the parabola has a minimum at $y = -3$. This means there will not be any real output values less than -3 because -3 is the lowest value it reaches on the y-axis.

These same answers for domain and range can be found by observing a table. The table below shows that from input values $x = -1$ to $x = 1$, the output results in a minimum of -3. On each side of $x = 0$, the numbers increase, showing that the range is all real numbers greater than or equal to -3.

x (domain/input)	y (range/output)
-2	1
-1	-2
0	-3
-1	-2
2	1

Finding Zeros of Functions

The zeros of a function are the points where its graph crosses the x-axis. At these points, $y = 0$. One way to find the zeros is to analyze the graph. If given the graph, the x-coordinates can be found where the line crosses the x-axis. Another way to find the zeros is to set $y = 0$ in the equation and solve for x. Depending on the type of equation, this could be done by using opposite operations, by factoring the equation, by completing the square, or by using the quadratic formula. If a graph does not cross the x-axis, then the function may have complex roots.

Translating Functions

A function can be translated in many ways. Typical translations involve shifting, reflecting, and scaling graphs. A shift is a translation that does not change the original shape of the function. A vertical shift adds or subtracts a constant from every y-coordinate, and is represented as $y = f(x) \pm c$. A horizontal shift adds or subtracts a constant from every x-coordinate, and is represented as $y = f(x \pm c)$.

A reflection involves flipping a function over an axis. To reflect about the y-axis, every x-coordinate needs to be multiplied times -1. This reflection is represented as $y = f(-x)$. To reflect about the x-axis, every y-coordinate needs to be multiplied times -1. This reflection is represented as $y = -f(x)$.

Finally, a scale involves changing the shape of the graph through either a shrink or stretch. A scale either multiplies or divides each coordinate by a constant. A vertical scale involves multiplying or dividing every y-coordinate by a constant. This scaling is represented by $y = kf(x)$ and is a vertical stretch if $k > 1$ and vertical shrink if $0 < k < 1$. A horizontal scale involves multiplying or dividing every x-coordinate by a constant. This scaling is represented by $y = f(kx)$ and is a horizontal stretch if $0 < k < 1$ and horizontal shrink if $k > 1$.

Graphing Functions

Typically, a function can be graphed using a graphing calculator. However, some characteristics can be found that allow for enough information to be compounded to graph a very good sketch without technology. Such information includes significant points such as zeros, local extrema, and points where a function is not continuous and not differentiable. Zeros are points in which a function crosses the y-axis. These points are found by plugging 0 into the independent variable x and solving for the dependent variable y.

Local extrema are points in which a function is either a local maxima or minima. These points occur where the derivative of the function is either equal to zero or undefined, and those points are known as critical values. The first derivative test can be used to decide whether a critical value is a maximum or minimum. If a function increases to a point, showing that the first derivative is positive over that interval, and if a function decreases after that same point, showing that the derivative is negative over that interval, then the point is a local maximum. The opposite occurs at a local minimum. Finally, points in which a function is not continuous or not differentiable are also important points. A function is continuous over its domain. A function is not differentiable at a point if there exists a vertical tangent at that point, if there is a corner or a cusp at that point, or if the function is not defined at that point.

Asymptotes

An **asymptote** is a line that approaches the graph of a given function, but never meets it. Vertical asymptotes correspond to denominators of zero for a rational function. They also exist in logarithmic functions and trigonometric functions, such as tangent and cotangent. In rational functions and trigonometric functions, the asymptotes exist at x-values that cause a denominator equal to zero. For example, vertical asymptotes exist at $x = \pm 2$ for the function:

$$f(x) = \frac{x+1}{(x-2)(x+2)}$$

Horizontal and oblique asymptotes correspond to the behavior of a curve as the x-values approach either positive or negative infinity. For example, the graph of $f(x) = e^x$ has a horizontal asymptote of $y = 0$ as x approaches negative infinity. In regard to rational functions, there is a rule to follow. Consider the following rational function:

$$f(x) = \frac{ax^n + \cdots}{bx^m + \cdots}$$

The numerator is an nth degree polynomial and the denominator is an mth degree polynomial. If $m < n$, the line $y = 0$ is a horizontal asymptote. If $n = m$, the line $y = \frac{a}{b}$ is a horizontal asymptote. If $m > n$, then there is an oblique asymptote. In order to find the equation of the oblique asymptote, the denominator is divided into the numerator using long division. The result, minus the remainder, gives the equation of the oblique asymptote.

Here is a graph that shows an example of both a slant and a vertical asymptote:

Graphed Asymptotes

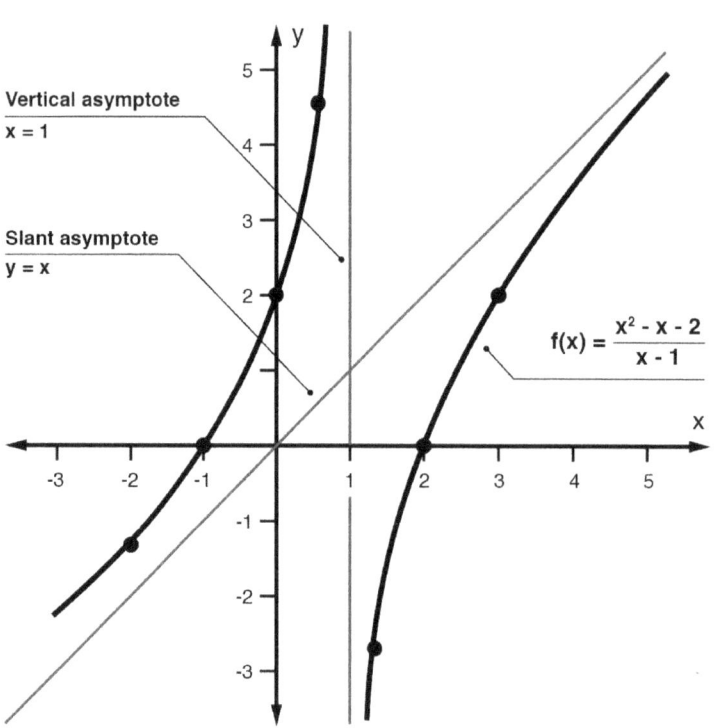

Inverse Variation and Rational Functions

The variable y varies inversely with respect to x if $y = \frac{k}{x}$, where k is the constant of variation. This means that as x decreases, y increases, and y is said to be inversely proportional to x. Also, this can be written as $k = xy$, and this specific example is known as inverse linear variation. The function $f(x) = \frac{k}{x}$ is a rational function because it is a rational fraction in which both the numerator and denominator are polynomials. Other types of inverse variation exist with nonlinear factors. The variable y can vary inversely with respect to x^2, and in this case: $y = \frac{k}{x^2}$. The exponent on the variable x can be any positive real number. In any case, the function will always be a rational function.

Rate of Change

Rate of change for any line calculates the steepness of the line over a given interval. Rate of change is also known as the slope or rise/run. The rates of change for nonlinear functions vary depending on the interval being used for the function. The rate of change over one interval may be zero, while the next interval may have a positive rate of change. The equation plotted on the graph below, $y = x^2$, is a quadratic function and non-linear.

The average rate of change from points $(0, 0)$ to $(1, 1)$ is 1 because the vertical change is 1 over the horizontal change of 1. For the next interval, $(1, 1)$ to $(2, 4)$, the average rate of change is 3 because the slope is $\frac{3}{1}$.

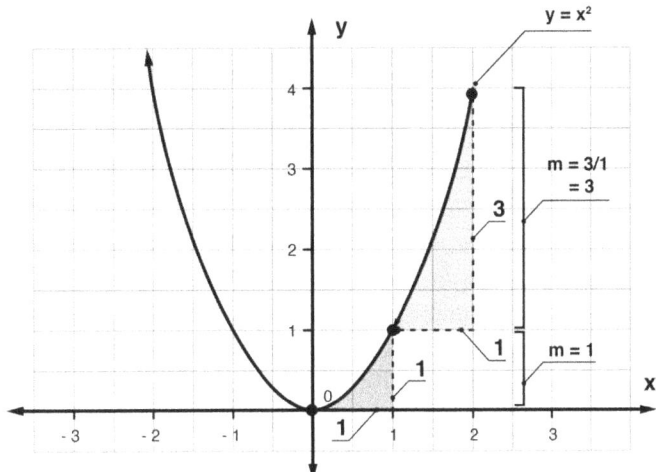

The rate of change for a linear function is constant and can be determined based on a few representations. One method is to place the equation in slope-intercept form: $y = mx + b$. Thus, m is the slope, and b is the y-intercept. In the graph below, the equation is $y = x + 1$, where the slope is 1 and the y-intercept is 1. For every vertical change of 1 unit, there is a horizontal change of 1 unit. The x-intercept is -1, which is the point where the line crosses the x-axis.

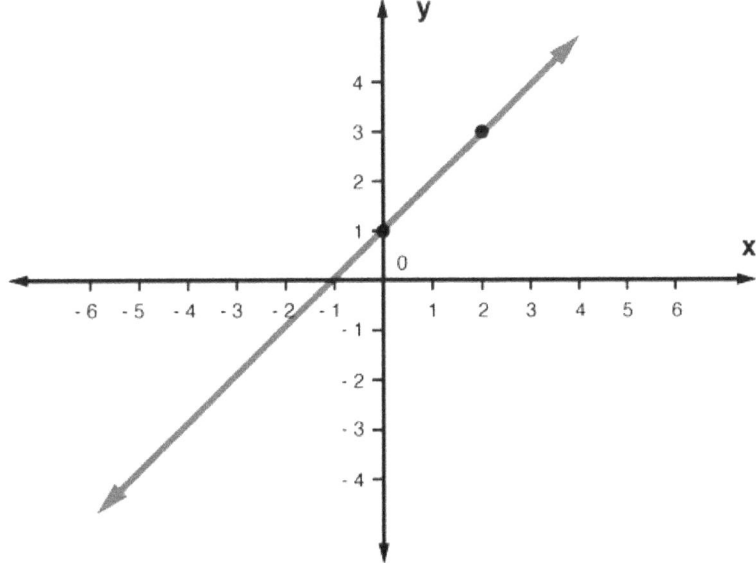

Solving Line Problems

Two lines are parallel if they have the same slope and a different intercept. Two lines are perpendicular if the product of their slope equals -1. Parallel lines never intersect unless they are the same line, and perpendicular lines intersect at a right angle. If two lines aren't parallel, they must intersect at one

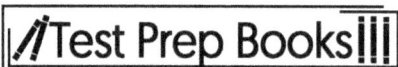

point. Determining equations of lines based on properties of parallel and perpendicular lines appears in word problems. To find an equation of a line, both the slope and a point the line goes through are necessary. Therefore, if an equation of a line is needed that's parallel to a given line and runs through a specified point, the slope of the given line and the point are plugged into the point-slope form of an equation of a line. Secondly, if an equation of a line is needed that's perpendicular to a given line running through a specified point, the negative reciprocal of the slope of the given line and the point are plugged into the point-slope form. Also, if the point of intersection of two lines is known, that point will be used to solve the set of equations. Therefore, to solve a system of equations, the point of intersection must be found. If a set of two equations with two unknown variables has no solution, the lines are parallel.

Modeling Functions

Mathematical functions such as polynomials, rational functions, radical functions, absolute value functions, and piecewise-defined functions can be utilized to approximate, or model, real-life phenomena. For example, a function can be built that approximates the average amount of snowfall on a given day of the year in Chicago. This example could be as simple as a polynomial. Modeling situations using such functions has limitations; the most significant issue is the error that exists between the exact amount and the approximate amount. Typically, the model will not give exact values as outputs. However, choosing the type of function that provides the best fit of the data will reduce this error. Technology can be used to model situations. For example, given a set of data, the data can be inputted into tools such as graphing calculators or spreadsheet software that output a function with a good fit. Some examples of polynomial modeling are linear, quadratic, and cubic regression.

Representing Exponential and Logarithmic Functions

The logarithmic function with base b is denoted $y = x$. Its base must be greater than 0 and not equal to 1, and the domain is all $x > 0$. The exponential function with base b is denoted $y = b^x$. Exponential and logarithmic functions with base b are inverses. By definition, if $y = x$, $x = b^y$. Because exponential and logarithmic functions are inverses, the graph of one is obtained by reflecting the other over the line $y = x$. A common base used is e, and in this case $y = e^x$ and its inverse $y = x$ is commonly written as the natural logarithmic function $y = \ln \ln x$.

Here is the graph of both functions:

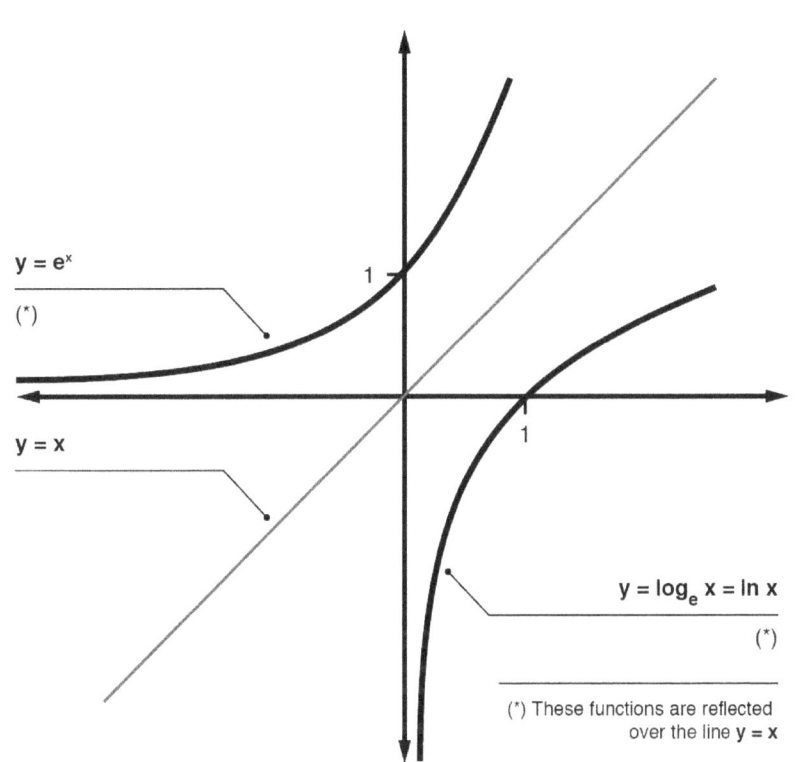

Graphing Functions
The x-intercept of the logarithmic function $y = x$ with any base is always the ordered pair $(1, 0)$. By the definition of inverse, the point $(0, 1)$ always lies on the exponential function $y = b^x$. This is true because any real number raised to the power of 0 equals 1. Therefore, the exponential function only has a y-intercept. The exponential function also has a horizontal asymptote of the x-axis as x approaches negative infinity. Because the graph is reflected over the line $y = x$, to obtain the graph of the logarithmic function, the asymptote is also reflected. Therefore, the logarithmic function has a one-sided vertical asymptote at $y = 0$. These asymptotes can be seen in the above graphs of $y = e^x$ and $y = \ln \ln x$.

Solving Logarithmic and Exponential Functions
To solve an equation involving exponential expressions, the goal is to isolate the exponential expression. Once this process is completed, the logarithm—with the base equaling the base of the exponent of both sides—needs to be taken to get an expression for the variable. If the base is e, the natural log of both sides needs to be taken.

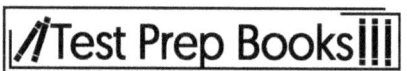

To solve an equation with logarithms, the given equation needs to be written in exponential form, using the fact that $y = x$ means $b^x = y$, and then solved for the given variable. Lastly, properties of logarithms can be used to simplify more than one logarithmic expression into one.

Some equations involving exponential and logarithmic functions can be solved algebraically, or analytically. To solve an equation involving exponential functions, the goal is to isolate the exponential expression. Then, the logarithm of both sides is found in order to yield an expression for the variable. Laws of Logarithms will be helpful at this point.

To solve an equation with logarithms, the equation needs to be rewritten in exponential form. The definition that $x = y$ means $b^y = x$ needs to be used. Then, one needs to solve for the given variable. Properties of logarithms can be used to simplify multiple logarithmic expressions into one.

Other methods can be used to solve equations containing logarithmic and exponential functions. Graphs and graphing calculators can be used to see points of intersection. In a similar manner, tables can be used to find points of intersection. Also, numerical methods can be utilized to find approximate solutions.

Exponential Growth and Decay

Exponential growth and decay are important concepts in modeling real-world phenomena. The growth and decay formula is $A(t) = Pe^{rt}$, where the independent variable t represents temperature, P represents an initial quantity, r represents the rate of increase or decrease, and $A(t)$ represents the amount of the quantity at time t. If $r > 0$, the equation models exponential growth and a common application is population growth. If $r < 0$, the equation models exponential decay and a common application is radioactive decay. Exponential and logarithmic solving techniques are necessary to work with the growth and decay formula.

Logarithmic Scales

A logarithmic scale is a scale of measurement that uses the logarithm of the given units instead of the actual given units. Each tick mark on such a scale is the product of the previous tick mark multiplied by a number. The advantage of using such a scale is that if one is working with large measurements, this technique reduces the scale into manageable quantities that are easier to read. The Richter magnitude scale is the famous logarithmic scale used to measure the intensity of earthquakes, and the decibel scale is commonly used to measure sound level in electronics.

Using Exponential and Logarithmic Functions in Finance Problems

Modeling within finance also involves exponential and logarithmic functions. Compound interest results when the bank pays interest on the original amount of money – the principal – and the interest that has accrued. The compound interest equation is:

$$A(t) = P\left(1 + \frac{r}{n}\right)^{nt}$$

where P is the principal, r is the interest rate, n is the number of times per year the interest is compounded, and t is the time in years. The result, $A(t)$, is the final amount after t years. Mathematical problems of this type that are frequently encountered involve receiving all but one of these quantities and solving for the missing quantity. The solving process then involves employing properties of logarithmic and exponential functions. Interest can also be compounded continuously. This formula is given as $A(t) = Pe^{rt}$.

If $1,000 was compounded continuously at a rate of 2% for 4 years, the result would be $A(4) = 1000e^{0.02 \cdot 4} = \$1,083$.

Rate of Change Proportional to Current Quantity

Many quantities grow or decay as fast as exponential functions. Specifically, if such a quantity grows or decays at a rate proportional to the quantity itself, it shows exponential behavior. If a data set is given with such specific characteristics, the initial amount and an amount at a specific time, t, can be plugged into the exponential function $A(t) = Pe^{rt}$ for A and P. Using properties of exponents and logarithms, one can then solve for the rate, r. This solution yields enough information to have the entire model, which can allow for an estimation of the quantity at any time, t, and the ability to solve various problems using that model.

Mathematical Models to Represent Real-World Situations

A mathematical model is a representation in mathematical terms of a real-world situation, and is widely used in science and engineering. Formulas are derived that model phenomena such as population growth and decay. In any model, simplifications must be made to create such formulas, and parameters within the model usually do not represent the physical world exactly. Once the model is formulated, its output can be compared to real-world scenarios to judge how valid the model is. If a model is deemed to be inaccurate, original assumptions and restrictions can be lifted that initially simplified the model.

Using Multiple Representations of Mathematical Concepts

There are many different areas of mathematics, and a single mathematical concept can have meaning in more than one area. Some of the main divisions of math include arithmetic, algebra, calculus, geometry, and statistics. A concept that spans across those divisions is *area*. Many different formulas in geometry involve calculating the area of different shapes. For example, area of a circle $A = \pi r^2$ is a quadratic function in r, the radius of the circle. In calculus, an area problem can involve calculating the area under a curve from two points on the x-axis, which is known as the definite integral. Also, the area between two curves is discussed. Finally, in statistics, the area under a density curve is defined to be probability.

Communicating Mathematical Ideas

Many different types of representations are useful in mathematics, and the most widely used are written symbols, pictures or diagrams, models, spoken words, and real-world experiences. Real-world experiences and spoken words are both representations that can be expressed by written symbols that impart mathematical meaning to the situation being discussed. Pictures or diagrams, including graphs and geometric figures, allow for visual representations of mathematical concepts. These external representations are widely used and have been developed for centuries. Similarly, written representations, such as symbolic methods like equations and functions, are also widely used and are used the most in math classes.

Using Visual Media

Students benefit from the use of visual media that represents mathematical information, and teachers should be able to go back and forth between each type. They should know which type of representation is useful in given a scenario. For example, a function can be represented by a diagram, a table, a graph, and a set of numbers simultaneously. Here is such an example:

Multiple Representations of a Function

Mapping

Table

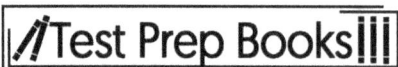

x	y
0	2
1	3
2	4
3	5
4	6

Graph

Ordered Pairs

{(0,2),(1,3),(2,4),(3,5),(4,6)}

Using Math Terminology

Using appropriate vocabulary that represents mathematical ideas is a critical skill in both being able to teach mathematics and use mathematical techniques to solve real-world situations. Each area in mathematics has its own set of definitions, and the translation of ideas onto paper requires a deep understanding of all the terminology. An important application of this idea is being able to translate word problems into equations that can be solved.

Algebra and Functions: Linear and Quadratic Equations and Inequalities

Rewriting Expressions

Algebraic expressions are made up of numbers, variables, and combinations of the two, using mathematical operations. Expressions can be rewritten based on their factors.

For example, the expression $6x + 4$ can be rewritten as $2(3x + 2)$ because 2 is a factor of both $6x$ and 4. More complex expressions can also be rewritten based on their factors. The expression $x^4 - 16$ can be rewritten as:

$$(x^2 - 4)(x^2 + 4)$$

This is a different type of factoring, where a difference of squares is factored into a sum and difference of the same two terms. With some expressions, the factoring process is simple and only leads to a different way to represent the expression. With others, factoring and rewriting the expression leads to more information about the given problem.

In the following quadratic equation, factoring the binomial leads to finding the zeros of the function:

$$x^2 - 5x + 6 = y$$

This equation factors into $(x - 3)(x - 2) = y$, where 2 and 3 are found to be the zeros of the function when y is set equal to zero. The zeros of any function are the x-values where the graph of the function on the coordinate plane crosses the x-axis.

Factoring an equation is a simple way to rewrite the equation and find the zeros, but factoring is not possible for every quadratic. Completing the square is one way to find zeros when factoring is not an option. The following equation cannot be factored:

$$x^2 + 10x - 9 = 0$$

The first step in this method is to move the constant to the right side of the equation, making it $x^2 + 10x = 9$.

Then, the coefficient of x is divided by 2 and squared. This number is then added to both sides of the equation, to make the equation still true. For this example, $\left(\frac{10}{2}\right)^2 = 25$ is added to both sides of the equation to obtain:

$$x^2 + 10x + 25 = 9 + 25$$

This expression simplifies to:

$$x^2 + 10x + 25 = 34$$

which can then be factored into:

$$(x + 5)^2 = 34$$

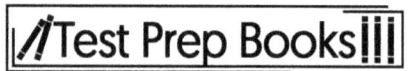

Solving for x then involves taking the square root of both sides and subtracting 5.

This leads to two zeros of the function:

$$x = \pm\sqrt{34} - 5$$

Depending on the type of answer the question seeks, a calculator may be used to find exact numbers.

Given a quadratic equation in standard form:

$$ax^2 + bx + c = 0$$

The sign of a tells whether the function has a minimum value or a maximum value. If $a > 0$, the graph opens up and has a minimum value. If $a < 0$, the graph opens down and has a maximum value. Depending on the way the quadratic equation is written, multiplication may need to occur before a max/min value is determined.

Exponential expressions can also be rewritten, just as quadratic equations. Properties of exponents must be understood. Multiplying two exponential expressions with the same base involves adding the exponents:

$$a^m a^n = a^{m+n}$$

Dividing two exponential expressions with the same base involves subtracting the exponents:

$$\frac{a^m}{a^n} = a^{m-n}$$

Raising an exponential expression to another exponent includes multiplying the exponents:

$$(a^m)^n = a^{mn}$$

The zero power always gives a value of 1: $a^0 = 1$. Raising either a product or a fraction to a power involves distributing that power:

$$(ab)^m = a^m b^m \text{ and } \left(\frac{a}{b}\right)^m = \frac{a^m}{b^m}$$

Finally, raising a number to a negative exponent is equivalent to the reciprocal including the positive exponent:

$$a^{-m} = \frac{1}{a^m}$$

Polynomial Identities

Difference of squares refers to a binomial composed of the difference of two squares. For example, $a^2 - b^2$ is a difference of squares. It can be written $(a)^2 - (b)^2$, and it can be factored into $(a - b)(a + b)$. Recognizing the difference of squares allows the expression to be rewritten easily because of the form it takes. For some expressions, factoring consists of more than one step. When factoring, it's important to always check to make sure that the result cannot be factored further. If it can, then the expression should be split further. If it cannot be, the factoring step is complete, and the expression is completely factored.

A sum and difference of cubes is another way to factor a polynomial expression. When the polynomial takes the form of addition or subtraction of two terms that can be written as a cube, a formula is given. The following graphic shows the factorization of a difference of cubes:

$$a^3 - b^3 = (a - b)(a^2 + ab + b^2)$$

same sign (first two arrows), opposite sign (bracket), always + (last arrow)

This form of factoring can be useful in finding the zeros of a function of degree 3. For example, when solving $x^3 - 27 = 0$, this rule needs to be used.

$x^3 - 27$ is first written as the difference two cubes, $(x)^3 - (3)^3$ and then factored into:

$$(x - 3)(x^2 + 3x + 9)$$

This expression may not be factored any further. Each factor is then set equal to zero. Therefore, one solution is found to be $x = 3$, and the other two solutions must be found using the quadratic formula. A sum of squares would have a similar process. The formula for factoring a sum of squares is:

$$a^3 + b^3 = (a + b)(a^2 - ab + b^2)$$

The opposite of factoring is multiplying. Multiplying a square of a binomial involves the following rules:

$$(a + b)^2 = a^2 + 2ab + b^2$$

and

$$(a - b)^2 = a^2 - 2ab + b^2$$

The binomial theorem for expansion can be used when the exponent on a binomial is larger than 2, and the multiplication would take a long time. The binomial theorem is given as:

$$(a + b)^n = \sum_{k=0}^{n} \binom{n}{k} a^{n-k} b^k$$

where

$$\binom{n}{k} = \frac{n!}{k!(n-k)!}$$

The **Remainder Theorem** can be helpful when evaluating polynomial functions $P(x)$ for a given value of x. A polynomial can be divided by $(x - a)$, if there is a remainder of 0.

This also means that $P(a) = 0$ and $(x - a)$ is a factor of $P(x)$.

In a similar sense, if P is evaluated at any other number b, $P(b)$ is equal to the remainder of dividing $P(x)$ by $(x - b)$.

Zeros of Polynomials

Finding the zeros of polynomial functions is the same process as finding the solutions of polynomial equations. These are the points at which the graph of the function crosses the x-axis. As stated previously, factors can be used to find the zeros of a polynomial function. The degree of the function shows the number of possible zeros. If the highest exponent on the independent variable is 4, then the degree is 4, and the number of possible zeros is 4. If there are complex solutions, the number of roots is less than the degree.

Given the function:

$$y = x^2 + 7x + 6$$

y can be set equal to zero, and the polynomial can be factored. The equation turns into:

$$0 = (x + 1)(x + 6)$$

where $x = -1$ and $x = -6$ are the zeros. Since this is a quadratic equation, the shape of the graph will be a parabola. Knowing that zeros represent the points where the parabola crosses the x-axis, the maximum or minimum point is the only other piece needed to sketch a rough graph of the function. By looking at the function in standard form, the coefficient of x is positive; therefore, the parabola opens up. Using the zeros and the minimum, the following rough sketch of the graph can be constructed:

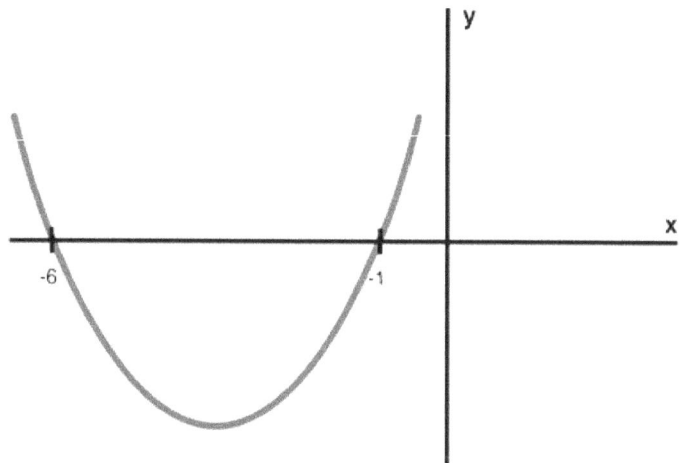

Operations with Polynomials

Addition and subtraction operations can be performed on polynomials with like terms. **Like terms refers to terms** that have the same variable and exponent. The two following polynomials can be added together by collecting like terms:

$$(x^2 + 3x - 4) + (4x^2 - 7x + 8)$$

The x^2 terms can be added as:

$$x^2 + 4x^2 = 5x^2$$

The x terms can be added as:

$$3x + -7x = -4x$$

and the constants can be added as:

$$-4 + 8 = 4$$

The following expression is the result of the addition:

$$5x^2 - 4x + 4$$

When subtracting polynomials, the same steps are followed, only subtracting like terms together.

Multiplication of polynomials can also be performed. Given the two polynomials, $(y^3 - 4)$ and $(x^2 + 8x - 7)$, each term in the first polynomial must be multiplied by each term in the second polynomial. The steps to multiply each term in the given example are as follows:

$$(y^3 * x^2) + (y^3 * 8x) + (y^3 * -7) + (-4 * x^2) + (-4 * 8x) + (-4 * -7)$$

Simplifying each multiplied part, yields:

$$x^2 y^3 + 8xy^3 - 7y^3 - 4x^2 - 32x + 28$$

None of the terms can be combined because there are no like terms in the final expression. Any polynomials can be multiplied by each other by following the same set of steps, then collecting like terms at the end.

Equations and Inequalities

The sum of a number and 5 is equal to -8 times the number. To find this unknown number, a simple equation can be written to represent the problem. Key words such as difference, equal, and times are used to form the following equation with one variable:

$$n + 5 = -8n$$

When solving for n, opposite operations are used. First, n is subtracted from $-8n$ across the equals sign, resulting in $5 = -9n$. Then, -9 is divided on both sides, leaving $n = -\frac{5}{9}$. This solution can be graphed on the number line with a dot as shown below:

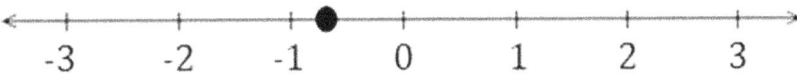

If the problem were changed to say, "The sum of a number and 5 is greater than -8 times the number," then an inequality would be used instead of an equation. Using key words again, *greater than* is represented by the symbol >. The inequality $n + 5 > -8n$ can be solved using the same techniques, resulting in $n < -\frac{5}{9}$. The only time solving an inequality differs from solving an equation is when a negative number is either multiplied times or divided by each side of the inequality. The sign must be switched in this case. For this example, the graph of the solution changes to the following graph because the solution represents all real numbers less than $-\frac{5}{9}$. Not included in this solution is $-\frac{5}{9}$ because it is a *less than* symbol, not *equal to*.

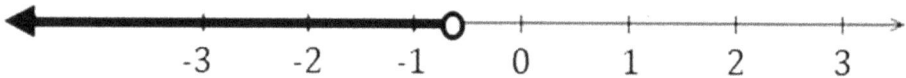

Equations and inequalities in two variables represent a relationship. Jim owns a car wash and charges $40 per car. The rent for the facility is $350 per month. An equation can be written to relate the number of cars Jim cleans to the money he makes per month. Let x represent the number of cars and y represent the profit Jim makes each month from the car wash. The equation

$$y = 40x - 350$$

can be used to show Jim's profit or loss. Since this equation has two variables, the coordinate plane can be used to show the relationship and predict profit or loss for Jim.

The following graph shows that Jim must wash at least nine cars to pay the rent, where $x = 9$. Anything nine cars and above yield a profit shown in the value on the y-axis.

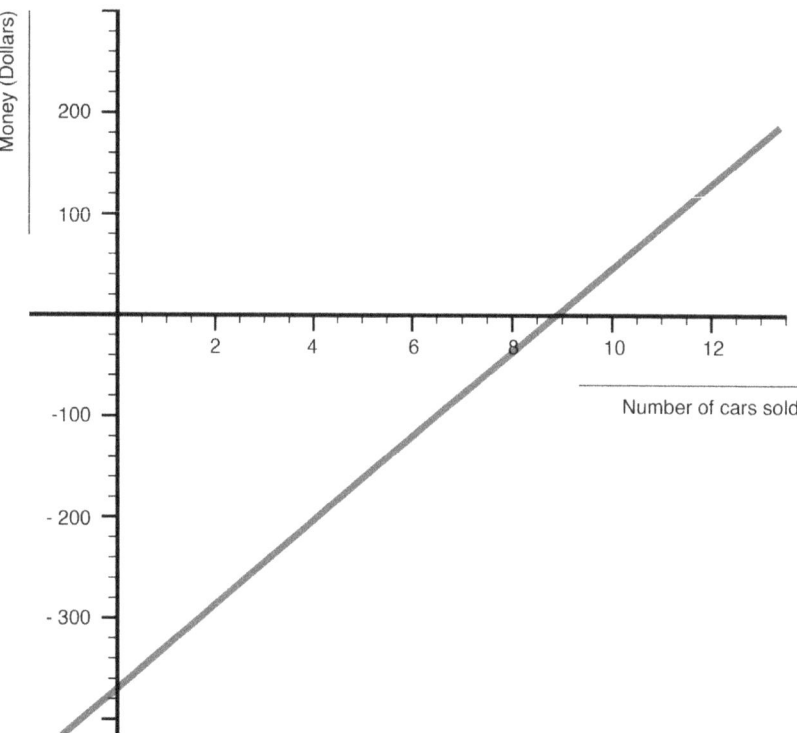

With a single equation in two variables, the solutions are limited only by the situation the equation represents. When two equations or inequalities are used, more constraints are added. For example, in a system of linear equations, there is often—although not always—only one answer. The point of intersection of two lines is the solution. For a system of inequalities, there are infinitely many answers.

The intersection of two solution sets gives the solution set of the system of inequalities. In the following graph, the darker shaded region is where two inequalities overlap. Any set of x and y found in that region satisfies both inequalities. The line with the positive slope is solid, meaning the values on that line are included in the solution. The line with the negative slope is dotted, so the coordinates on that line are not included.

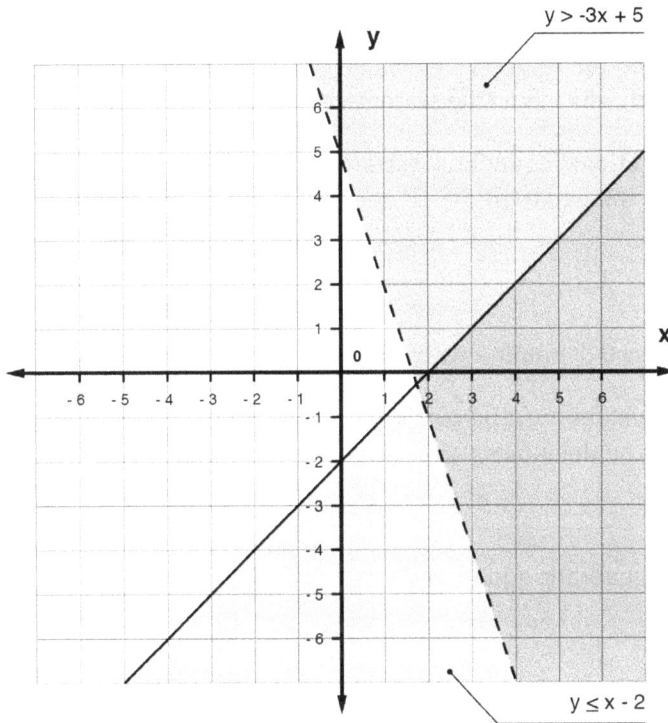

Formulas with two variables are equations used to represent a specific relationship. For example, the formula $d = rt$ represents the relationship between distance, rate, and time. If Bob travels at a rate of 35 miles per hour on his road trip from Westminster to Seneca, the formula $d = 35t$ can be used to represent his distance traveled in a specific length of time. Formulas can also be used to show different roles of the variables, transformed without any given numbers. Solving for r, the formula becomes $\frac{d}{t} = r$. The t is moved over by division so that *rate* is a function of distance and time.

Solving Equations

Solving equations with one variable is the process of isolating a variable on one side of the equation. For example:

$$3x - 7 = 20$$

The variable x needs to be isolated. Using opposite operations, the -7 is moved to the right side of the equation by adding seven to both sides:

$$3x - 7 + 7 = 20 + 7$$

This results in $3x = 27$.

Dividing by three on each side, $\frac{3x}{3} = \frac{27}{3}$, results in isolation of the variable. It is important to note that if an operation is performed on one side of the equals sign, it has to be performed on the other side to maintain equality. The solution is found to be $x = 9$.

This solution can be checked for accuracy by plugging $x=7$ in the original equation. After simplifying the equation, $20 = 20$ is found, which is a true statement.

When solving radical and rational equations, extraneous solutions must be accounted for when finding the answers. For example, the equation:

$$\frac{x}{x-5} = \frac{3x}{x+3}$$

has two values that create a 0 denominator: $x \neq 5, -3$.

When solving for x, these values must be considered because they cannot be solutions. In the given equation, solving for x can be done using cross-multiplication, yielding the equation:

$$x(x + 3) = 3x(x - 5)$$

Distributing results in the quadratic equation yields:

$$x^2 + 3x = 3x^2 - 15x$$

therefore, all terms must be moved to one side of the equal sign.

This results in $2x^2 - 18x = 0$, which in factored form is $2x(x - 9) = 0$.

Setting each factor equal to zero, the apparent solutions are $x = 0$ and $x = 9$. These two solutions are neither 5 nor -3, so they are viable solutions. Neither 0 nor 9 create a 0 denominator in the original equation.

A similar process exists when solving radical equations. One must check to make sure the solutions are defined in the original equations. Solving an equation containing a square root involves isolating the root and then squaring both sides of the equal sign. Solving a cube root equation involves isolating the radical and then cubing both sides. In either case, the variable can then be solved for because there are no longer radicals in the equation.

Methods for Solving Equations

Equations with one variable can be solved using the addition principle and multiplication principle. If $a = b$, then $a + c = b + c$, and $ac = bc$. Given the equation:

$$2x - 3 = 5x + 7$$

the first step is to combine the variable terms and the constant terms. Using the principles, expressions can be added and subtracted onto and off both sides of the equals sign, so the equation turns into

$$-10 = 3x$$

Dividing by 3 on both sides through the multiplication principle with $c = \frac{1}{3}$ results in the final answer of:

$$x = \frac{-10}{3}$$

Some equations have a higher degree and are not solved by simply using opposite operations. When an equation has a degree of 2, completing the square is an option. For example, the quadratic equation:

$$x^2 - 6x + 2 = 0$$

can be rewritten by completing the square. The goal of completing the square is to get the equation into the form:

$$(x - p)^2 = q$$

Using the example, the constant term 2 first needs to be moved over to the opposite side by subtracting. Then, the square can be completed by adding 9 to both sides, which is the square of half of the coefficient of the middle term $-6x$.

The current equation is:

$$x^2 - 6x + 9 = 7$$

The left side can be factored into a square of a binomial, resulting in:

$$(x - 3)^2 = 7$$

To solve for x, the square root of both sides should be taken, resulting in:

$(x - 3) = \pm\sqrt{7}$, and $x = 3 \pm \sqrt{7}$

Other ways of solving quadratic equations include graphing, factoring, and using the quadratic formula. The equation $y = x^2 - 4x + 3$ can be graphed on the coordinate plane, and the solutions can be observed where it crosses the x-axis. The graph will be a parabola that opens up with two solutions at 1 and 3.

The equation can also be factored to find the solutions. The original equation:

$$y = x^2 - 4x + 3$$

can be factored into:

$$y = (x - 1)(x - 3)$$

Setting this equal to zero, the x-values are found to be 1 and 3, just as on the graph. Solving by factoring and graphing are not always possible. The quadratic formula is a method of solving quadratic equations that always results in exact solutions.

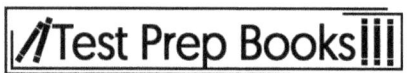

The formula is:

$$x = \frac{-b \pm \sqrt{b^2 - 4ac}}{2a}$$

where a, b, and c are the coefficients in the original equation in standard form $y = ax^2 + bx + c$. For this example:

$$x = \frac{4 \pm \sqrt{(-4)^2 - 4(1)(3)}}{2(1)}$$

$$\frac{4 \pm \sqrt{16 - 12}}{2} = \frac{4 \pm 2}{2} = 1, 3$$

The expression underneath the radical is called the **discriminant**. Without working out the entire formula, the value of the discriminant can reveal the nature of the solutions. If the value of the discriminant $b^2 - 4ac$ is positive, then there will be two real solutions. If the value is zero, there will be one real solution. If the value is negative, the two solutions will be imaginary or complex. If the solutions are complex, it means that the parabola never touches the x-axis. An example of a complex solution can be found by solving the following quadratic:

$$y = x^2 - 4x + 8$$

By using the quadratic formula, the solutions are found to be:

$$x = \frac{4 \pm \sqrt{(-4)^2 - 4(1)(8)}}{2(1)} = \frac{4 \pm \sqrt{16 - 32}}{2}$$

$$\frac{4 \pm \sqrt{-16}}{2} = 2 \pm 2i$$

The solutions both have a real part, 2, and an imaginary part, $2i$.

Systems of Equations

A **system of equations** is a group of equations that have the same variables or unknowns. These equations can be linear, but they are not always so. Finding a solution to a system of equations means finding the values of the variables that satisfy each equation. For a linear system of two equations and two variables, there could be a single solution, no solution, or infinitely many solutions.

A single solution occurs when there is one value for x and y that satisfies the system. This would be shown on the graph where the lines cross at exactly one point. When there is no solution, the lines are parallel and do not ever cross. With infinitely many solutions, the equations may look different, but they are the same line. One equation will be a multiple of the other, and on the graph, they lie on top of each other.

The process of elimination can be used to solve a system of equations. For example, the following equations make up a system:

$$x + 3y = 10 \text{ and } 2x - 5y = 9$$

Immediately adding these equations does not eliminate a variable, but it is possible to change the first equation by multiplying the whole equation by -2.

This changes the first equation to $-2x - 6y = -20$.

The equations can be then added to obtain $-11y = -11$.

Solving for y yields $y = 1$. To find the rest of the solution, 1 can be substituted in for y in either original equation to find the value of $x = 7$. The solution to the system is (7, 1) because it makes both equations true, and it is the point in which the lines intersect. If the system is *dependent*—having infinitely many solutions—then both variables will cancel out when the elimination method is used, resulting in an equation that is true for many values of x and y. Since the system is dependent, both equations can be simplified to the same equation or line.

A system can also be solved using **substitution**. This involves solving one equation for a variable and then plugging that solved equation into the other equation in the system. For example:

$$x - y = -2$$

and

$$3x + 2y = 9$$

can be solved using substitution. The first equation can be solved for x, where $x = -2 + y$. Then it can be plugged into the other equation:

$$3(-2 + y) + 2y = 9$$

Solving for y yields $-6 + 3y + 2y = 9$, where $y = 3$. If $y = 3$, then $x = 1$.

This solution can be checked by plugging in these values for the variables in each equation to see if it makes a true statement.

Finally, a solution to a system of equations can be found graphically. The solution to a linear system is the point or points where the lines cross. The values of x and y represent the coordinates (x, y) where the lines intersect. Using the same system of equations as above, they can be solved for y to put them in slope-intercept form, $y = mx + b$.

These equations become $y = x + 2$ and:

$$y = -\frac{3}{2}x + 4.5$$

The slope is the coefficient of x, and the y-intercept is the constant value. This system with the solution is shown below:

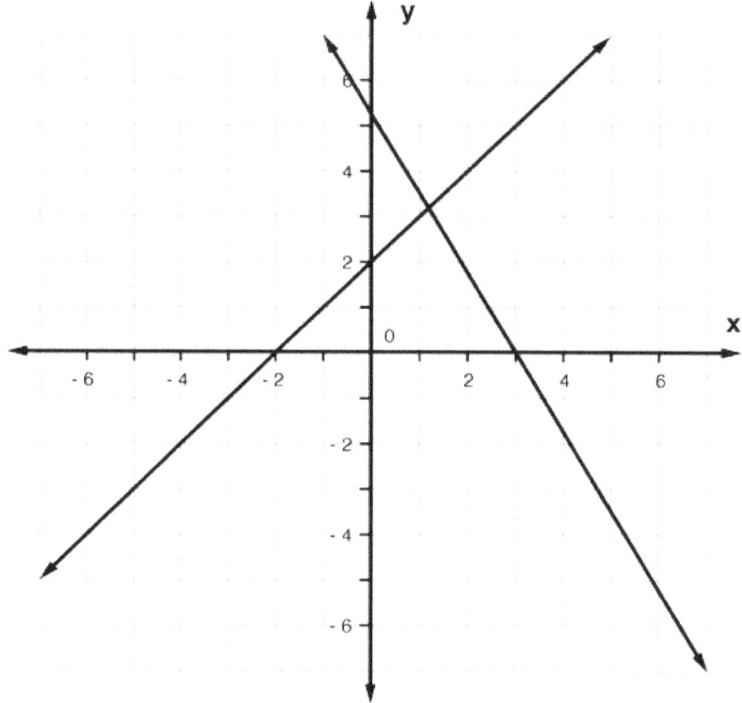

A system of equations may also be made up of a linear and a quadratic equation. These systems may have one solution, two solutions, or no solutions. The graph of these systems involves one straight line and one parabola. Algebraically, these systems can be solved by solving the linear equation for one variable and plugging that answer in to the quadratic equation. If possible, the equation can then be solved to find part of the answer. The graphing method is commonly used for these types of systems. On a graph, these two lines can be found to intersect at one point, at two points across the parabola, or at no points.

Matrices can also be used to solve systems of linear equations. Specifically, for systems, the coefficients of the linear equations in standard form are the entries in the matrix. Using the same system of linear equations as above, $x - y = -2$ and $3x + 2y = 9$, the matrix to represent the system is:

$$[1\ -1\ 3\ 2\,][x\ y\,] = [-2\ 9\,]$$

To solve this system using matrices, the inverse matrix must be found. For a general 2x2 matrix, $[a\ b\ c\ d\,]$, the inverse matrix is found by the expression:

$$\frac{1}{ad - bc}[d\ -b\ -c\ a\,]$$

The inverse matrix for the system given is:

$$\frac{1}{2 - -3}[2\ 1\ -3\ 1\,] = \frac{1}{5}[2\ 1\ -3\ 1\,]$$

The next step in solving is to multiply this identity matrix by the system matrix.

Quantitative Reasoning Section

This is given by the following equation:

$$\frac{1}{5}[2\ 1\ -3\ 1][1\ -1\ 3\ 2][x\ y] = [-2\ 9][2\ 1\ -3\ 1]\frac{1}{5}$$

This simplifies to:

$$\frac{1}{5}[5\ 0\ 0\ 5][x\ y] = \frac{1}{5}[5\ 15]$$

Solving for the solution matrix, the answer is:

$$[1\ 0\ 0\ 1][x\ y] = [1\ 3]$$

Since the first matrix is the identity matrix, the solution is $x = 1$ and $y = 3$.

Finding solutions to systems of equations is essentially finding what values of the variables make both equations true. It is finding the input value that yields the same output value in both equations. For functions $g(x)$ and $f(x)$, the equation $g(x) = f(x)$ means the output values are being set equal to each other.

Solving for the value of x means finding the x-coordinate that gives the same output in both functions.

For example, $f(x) = x + 2$ and $g(x) = -3x + 10$ is a system of equations.

Setting $f(x) = g(x)$ yields the equation $x + 2 = -3x + 10$.

Solving for x, gives the x-coordinate $x = 2$ where the two lines cross. This value can also be found by using a table or a graph. On a table, both equations can be given the same inputs, and the outputs can be recorded to find the point(s) where the lines cross. Any method of solving finds the same solution, but some methods are more appropriate for some systems of equations than others.

Systems of Linear Inequalities

Systems of **linear inequalities** are like systems of equations, but the solutions are different. Since inequalities have infinitely many solutions, their systems also have infinitely many solutions. Finding the solutions of inequalities involves graphs. A system of two equations and two inequalities is linear; thus, the lines can be graphed using slope-intercept form. If the inequality has an equal sign, the line is solid. If the inequality only has a greater than or less than symbol, the line on the graph is dotted. Dashed lines indicate that points lying on the line are not included in the solution. After the lines are graphed, a region is shaded on one side of the line. This side is found by determining if a point—known as a **test point**—lying on one side of the line produces a true inequality. If it does, that side of the graph is shaded. If the point produces a false inequality, the line is shaded on the opposite side from the point. The graph of a system of inequalities involves shading the intersection of the two shaded regions.

Simple Events, Probabilities of Compound Events, and Conditional Probabilities

Simple and Compound Events
A **simple event** consists of only one outcome. The most popular simple event is flipping a coin, which results in either heads or tails. A **compound event** results in more than one outcome and consists of more than one simple event. An example of a compound event is flipping a coin while tossing a die. The

result is either heads or tails on the coin and a number from one to six on the die. The probability of a simple event is calculated by dividing the number of possible outcomes by the total number of outcomes. Therefore, the probability of obtaining heads on a coin is $\frac{1}{2}$, and the probability of rolling a 6 on a die is $\frac{1}{6}$. The probability of compound events is calculated using the basic idea of the probability of simple events. If the two events are independent, the probability of one outcome is equal to the product of the probabilities of each simple event. For example, the probability of obtaining heads on a coin and rolling a 6 is equal to:

$$\frac{1}{2} \times \frac{1}{6} = \frac{1}{12}$$

The probability of either A or B occurring is equal to the sum of the probabilities minus the probability that both A and B will occur. Therefore, the probability of obtaining either heads on a coin or rolling a 6 on a die is:

$$\frac{1}{2} + \frac{1}{6} - \frac{1}{12} = \frac{7}{12}$$

The two events aren't mutually exclusive because they can happen at the same time. If two events are mutually exclusive, and the probability of both events occurring at the same time is zero, the probability of event A or B occurring equals the sum of both probabilities. An example of calculating the probability of two mutually exclusive events is determining the probability of pulling a king or a queen from a deck of cards. The two events cannot occur at the same time.

Geometry

Points, Lines, Planes, and Angles

A point is a place, not a thing, and therefore has no dimensions or size. A set of points that lies on the same line is called collinear. A set of points that lies on the same plane is called coplanar.

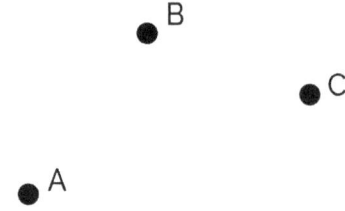

The image above displays point A, point B, and point C.

A line is as series of points that extends in both directions without ending. It consists of an infinite number of points and is drawn with arrows on both ends to indicate it extends infinitely. Lines can be named by two points on the line or with a single, cursive, lower case letter. The lines below are named: line *AB* or line *BA* or $\overleftrightarrow{AB}$ or $\overleftrightarrow{BA}$; and line *m*.

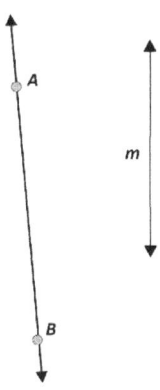

Two lines are considered parallel to each other if, while extending infinitely, they will never intersect (or meet). Parallel lines point in the same direction and are always the same distance apart. Two lines are considered perpendicular if they intersect to form right angles. Right angles are 90°. Typically, a small box is drawn at the intersection point to indicate the right angle.

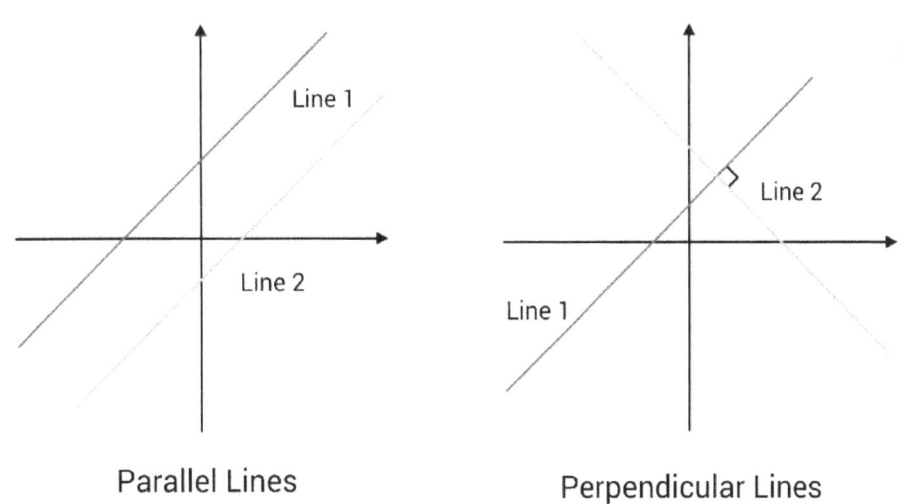

Parallel Lines   Perpendicular Lines

Line 1 is parallel to line 2 in the left image and is written as line 1 || line 2. Line 1 is perpendicular to line 2 in the right image and is written as line 1 ⊥ line 2.

A ray has a specific starting point and extends in one direction without ending. The endpoint of a ray is its starting point. Rays are named using the endpoint first, and any other point on the ray. The following ray can be named ray AB and written $\overrightarrow{AB}$.

A line segment has specific starting and ending points. A line segment consists of two endpoints and all the points in between. Line segments are named by the two endpoints. The example below is named segment GH or segment HG, written $\overline{GH}$ or $\overline{HG}$.

Solving Problems in the Coordinate Plane

The location of a point on a coordinate grid is identified by writing it as an ordered pair. An ordered pair is a set of numbers indicating the x-and y-coordinates of the point. Ordered pairs are written in the form (x, y) where x and y are values which indicate their respective coordinates. For example, the point (3, -2) has an x-coordinate of 3 and a y-coordinate of -2.

Plotting a point on the coordinate plane with a given coordinate means starting from the origin $(0, 0)$. To determine the value of the x-coordinate, move right (positive number) or left (negative number) along the x-axis. Next, move up (positive number) or down (negative number) to the value of the y-coordinate. Finally, plot and label the point. For example, plotting the point $(1, -2)$ requires starting from the origin and moving right along the x-axis to positive one, then moving down until straight across from negative 2 on the y-axis. The point is plotted and labeled. This point, along with three other points, are plotted and labeled on the graph below:

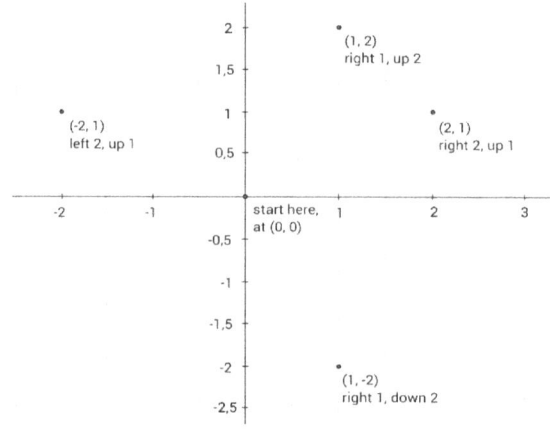

To write the coordinates of a point on the coordinate grid, a line should be traced directly above or below the point until reaching the x-axis (noting the value on the x-axis). Then, returning to the point, a line should be traced directly to the right or left of the point until reaching the y-axis (noting the value on the y-axis). The ordered pair (x, y) should be written with the values determined for the x- and y-coordinates.

Polygons can be drawn in the coordinate plane given the coordinates of their vertices. These coordinates can be used to determine the perimeter and area of the figure. Suppose triangle RQP has vertices located at the points: $R(-2, 0)$, $Q(2, 2)$, and $P(2, 0)$. By plotting the points for the three vertices, the triangle can be constructed as follows:

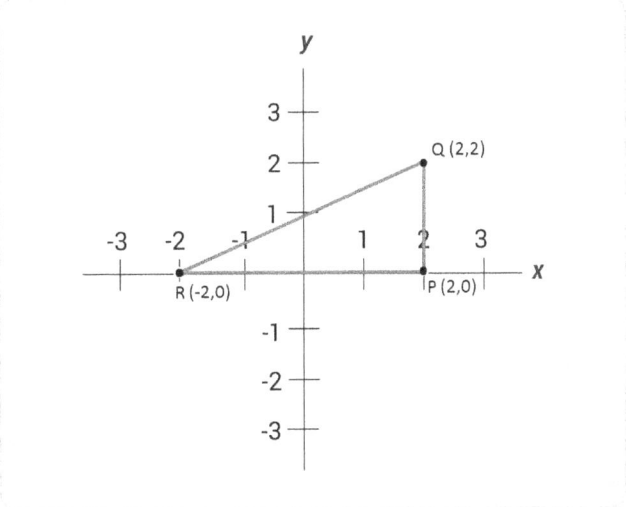

Because points R and P have the same y-coordinates (they are directly across from each other), the distance between them is determined by subtracting their x-coordinates (or simply counting units from one point to the other): $2 - (-2) = 4$. Therefore, the length of side RP is 4 units. Because points Q and P have the same x-coordinate (they are directly above and below each other), the distance between them is determined by subtracting their y-coordinates (or counting units between them): $2 - 0 = 2$. Therefore, the length of side PQ is 2 units. Knowing the length of side RP, which is the base of the triangle, and the length of side PQ, which is the height of the triangle, the area of the figure can be determined by using the formula:

$$A = \frac{1}{2}bh$$

To determine the perimeter of the triangle, the lengths of all three sides are needed. Points R and Q are neither directly across nor directly above and below each other. Therefore, the distance formula must be used to find the length of side RQ. The distance formula is as follows:

$$d = \sqrt{(x_2 - x_1)^2 + (y_2 - y_1)^2}$$

$$d = \sqrt{(2 - (-2))^2 + (2 - 0)^2}$$

$$d = \sqrt{(4)^2 + (2)^2}$$

$$d = \sqrt{16 + 4} \rightarrow d = \sqrt{20}$$

The perimeter is determined by adding the lengths of the three sides of the triangle.

Two- and Three-Dimensional Shapes

A polygon is a closed geometric figure in a plane (flat surface) consisting of at least 3 sides formed by line segments. These are often defined as two-dimensional shapes. Common two-dimensional shapes include circles, triangles, squares, rectangles, pentagons, and hexagons. Note that a circle is a two-dimensional shape without sides.

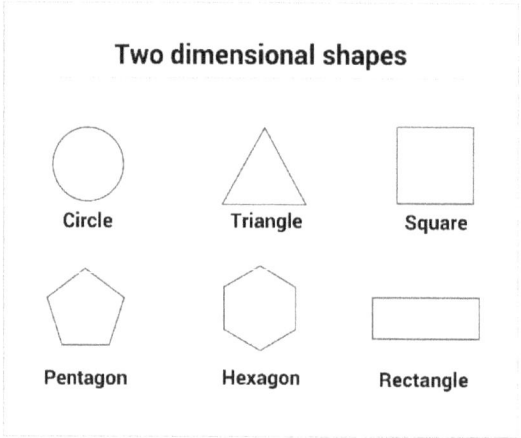

Quantitative Reasoning Section

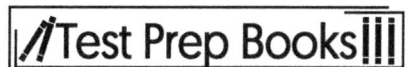

A solid figure, or simple solid, is a figure that encloses a part of space. Some solids consist of flat surfaces only while others include curved surfaces. Solid figures are often defined as three-dimensional shapes. Common three-dimensional shapes include spheres, prisms, cubes, pyramids, cylinders, and cones.

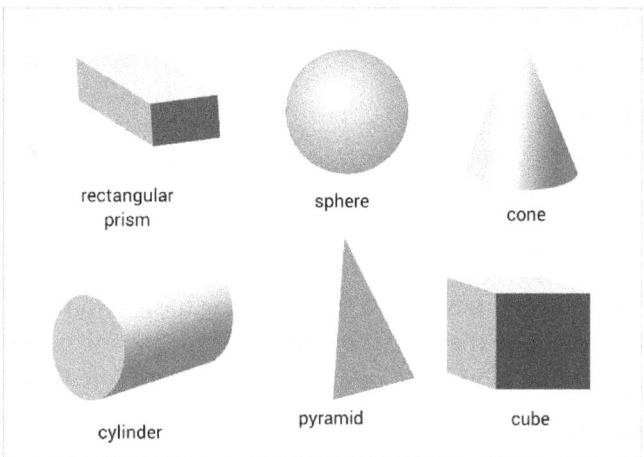

Composing two- or three-dimensional shapes involves putting together two or more shapes to create a new larger figure. For example, a semi-circle (half circle), rectangle, and two triangles can be used to compose the figure of the sailboat shown below.

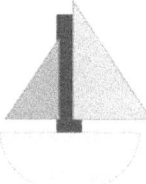

Similarly, solid figures can be placed together to compose an endless number of three-dimensional objects.

Decomposing two- and three-dimensional figures involves breaking the shapes apart into smaller, simpler shapes. Consider the following two-dimensional representations of a house:

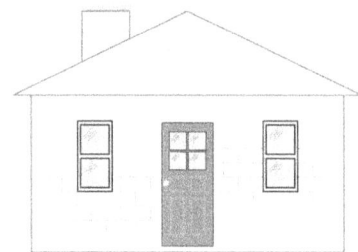

This complex figure can be decomposed into the following basic two-dimensional shapes: large rectangle (body of house); large triangle (roof); small rectangle and small triangle (chimney). Decomposing figures is often done more than one way. To illustrate, the figure of the house could also be decomposed into: two large triangles (body); two medium triangles (roof); two smaller triangles of unequal size (chimney).

Polygons and Solids

A polygon is a closed two-dimensional figure consisting of three or more sides. Polygons can be either convex or concave. A polygon that has interior angles all measuring less than 180° is convex. A concave polygon has one or more interior angles measuring greater than 180°. Examples are shown below:

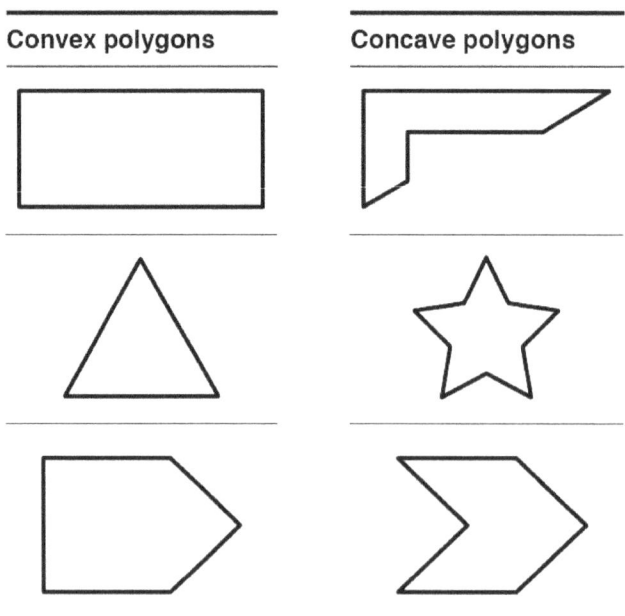

Polygons can be classified by the number of sides (also equal to the number of angles) they have. The following are the names of polygons with a given number of sides or angles:

# of Sides	Name of Polygon
3	Triangle
4	Quadrilateral
5	Pentagon
6	Hexagon
7	Septagon (or heptagon)
8	Octagon
9	Nonagon
10	Decagon

Equiangular polygons are polygons in which the measure of every interior angle is the same. The sides of equilateral polygons are always the same length. If a polygon is both equiangular and equilateral, the polygon is defined as a regular polygon. Examples are shown below:

 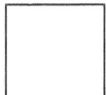 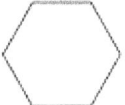

Triangles can be further classified by their sides and angles. A triangle with its largest angle measuring 90° is a right triangle. A triangle with the largest angle less than 90° is an acute triangle. A triangle with the largest angle greater than 90° is an obtuse triangle.

  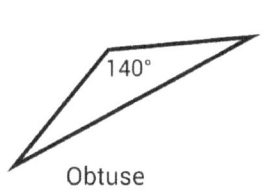

Acute
3 acute angles

Right
1 right angle

Obtuse
1 obtuse angle

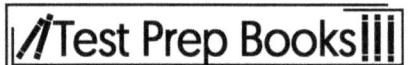

A triangle consisting of two equal sides and two equal angles is an isosceles triangle. A triangle with three equal sides and three equal angles is an equilateral triangle. A triangle with no equal sides or angles is a scalene triangle.

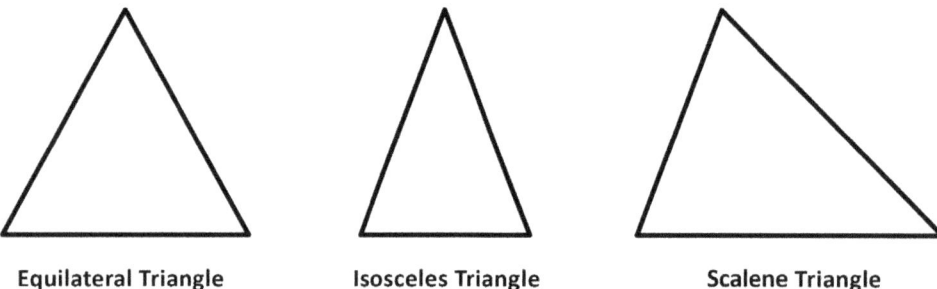

Equilateral Triangle   Isosceles Triangle   Scalene Triangle

Quadrilaterals can be further classified according to their sides and angles. A quadrilateral with exactly one pair of parallel sides is called a trapezoid. A quadrilateral that shows both pairs of opposite sides parallel is a parallelogram. Parallelograms include rhombuses, rectangles, and squares. A rhombus has four equal sides. A rectangle has four equal angles (90° each). A square has four 90° angles and four equal sides. Therefore, a square is both a rhombus and a rectangle.

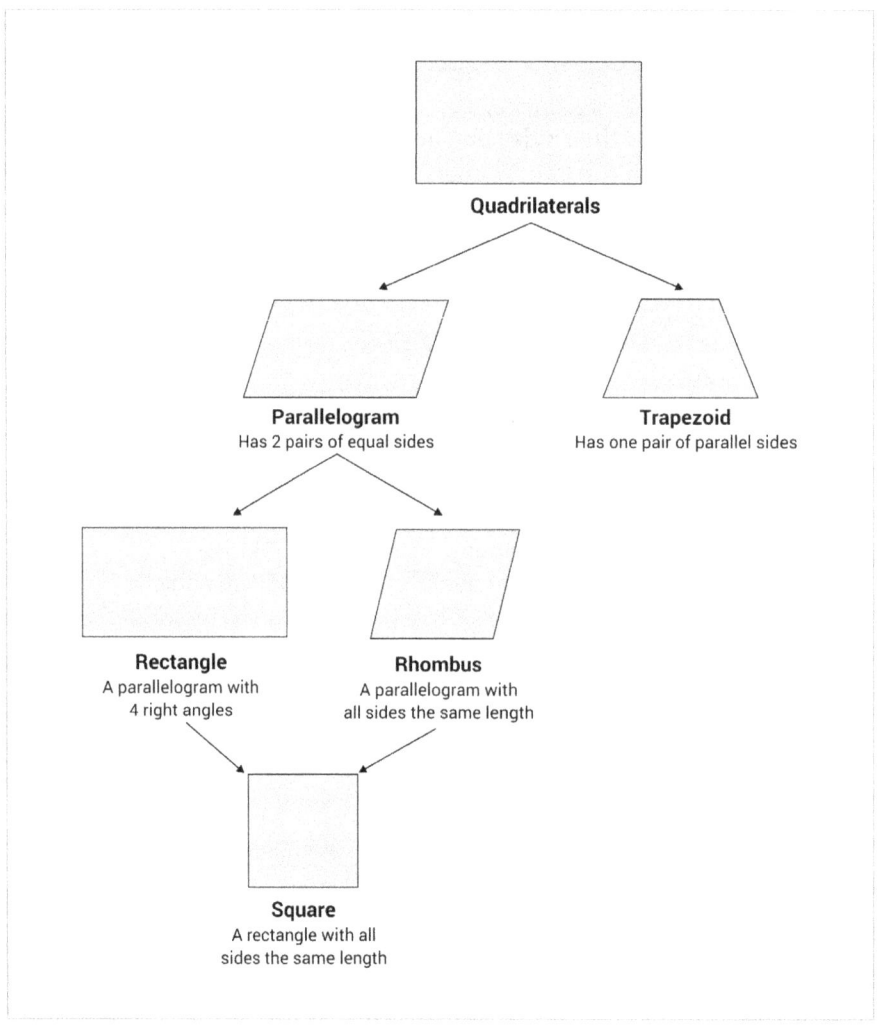

A solid is a three-dimensional figure that encloses a part of space. Solids consisting of all flat surfaces that are polygons are called polyhedrons. The two-dimensional surfaces that make up a polyhedron are called faces. Types of polyhedrons include prisms and pyramids. A prism consists of two parallel faces that are congruent (or the same shape and same size), and lateral faces going around (which are parallelograms).

A prism is further classified by the shape of its base, as shown below:

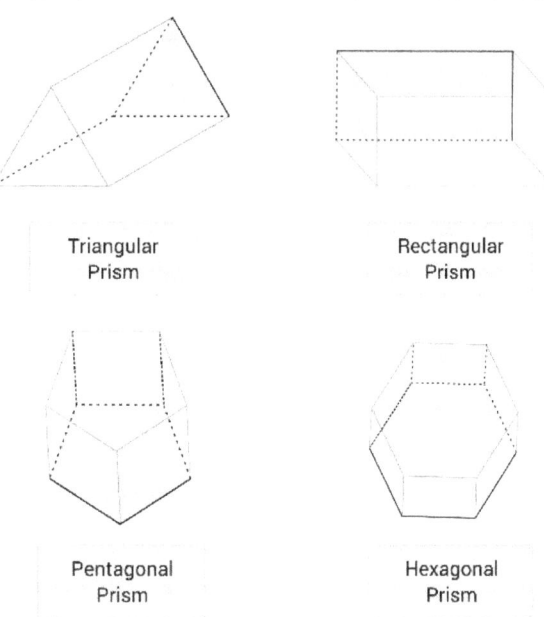

A pyramid consists of lateral faces (triangles) that meet at a common point called the vertex and one other face that is a polygon, called the base. A pyramid can be further classified by the shape of its base, as shown below:

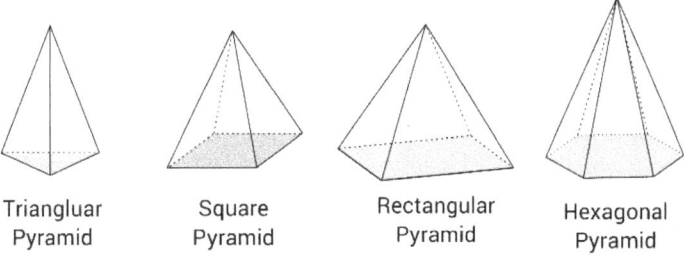

A tetrahedron is another name for a triangular pyramid. All the faces of a tetrahedron are triangles.

Solids that are not polyhedrons include spheres, cylinders, and cones. A sphere is the set of all points a given distance from a given center point. A sphere is commonly thought of as a three-dimensional circle. A cylinder consists of two parallel, congruent (same size) circles and a lateral curved surface. A cone consists of a circle as its base and a lateral curved surface that narrows to a point called the vertex.

Similar polygons are the same shape but different sizes. More specifically, their corresponding angle measures are congruent (or equal) and the length of their sides is proportional. For example, all sides of one polygon may be double the length of the sides of another. Likewise, similar solids are the same shape but different sizes. Any corresponding faces or bases of similar solids are the same polygons that are proportional by a consistent value.

Properties of certain polygons allow that the perimeter may be obtained by using formulas. A rectangle consists of two sides called the length (*l*), which have equal measures, and two sides called the width (*w*), which have equal measures. Therefore, the perimeter (*P*) of a rectangle can be expressed as *P* = *l* + *l* + *w* + *w*. This can be simplified to produce the following formula to find the perimeter of a rectangle:

$$P = 2l + 2w \text{ or } P = 2(l + w)$$

A regular polygon is one in which all sides have equal length and all interior angles have equal measures, such as a square and an equilateral triangle. To find the perimeter of a regular polygon, the length of one side is multiplied by the number of sides. For example, to find the perimeter of an equilateral triangle with a side of length of 4 feet, 4 feet is multiplied by 3 (number of sides of a triangle). The perimeter of a regular octagon (8 sides) with a side of length of $\frac{1}{2}$cm is $\frac{1}{2} cm \times 8 = 4 cm$.

Classification of Angles

An angle consists of two rays that have a common endpoint. This common endpoint is called the vertex of the angle. The two rays can be called sides of the angle. The angle below has a vertex at point *B* and the sides consist of ray *BA* and ray *BC*. An angle can be named in three ways:

1. Using the vertex and a point from each side, with the vertex letter in the middle.
2. Using only the vertex. This can only be used if it is the only angle with that vertex.
3. Using a number that is written inside the angle.

The angle below can be written ∠*ABC* (read angle *ABC*), ∠*CBA*, ∠*B*, or ∠1:

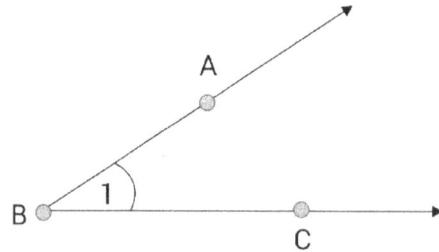

An angle divides a plane, or flat surface, into three parts: the angle itself, the interior (inside) of the angle, and the exterior (outside) of the angle. The figure below shows point M on the interior of the angle and point N on the exterior of the angle:

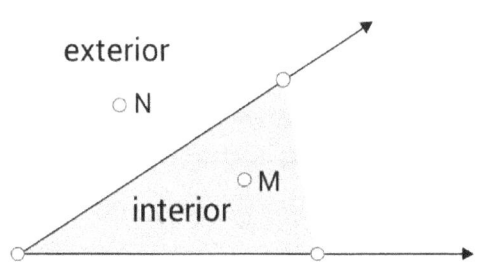

Angles can be measured in units called degrees, with the symbol °. The degree measure of an angle is between 0° and 180° and can be obtained by using a protractor. A straight angle (or simply a line) measures exactly 180°. A right angle's sides meet at the vertex to create a square corner. A right-angle measures exactly 90° and is typically indicated by a box drawn in the interior of the angle. An acute angle has an interior that is narrower than a right angle. The measure of an acute angle is any value less than 90° and greater than 0°. For example, 89.9°, 47°, 12°, and 1°. An obtuse angle has an interior that is wider than a right angle. The measure of an obtuse angle is any value greater than 90° but less than 180°. For example, 90.1°, 110°, 150°, and 179.9°.

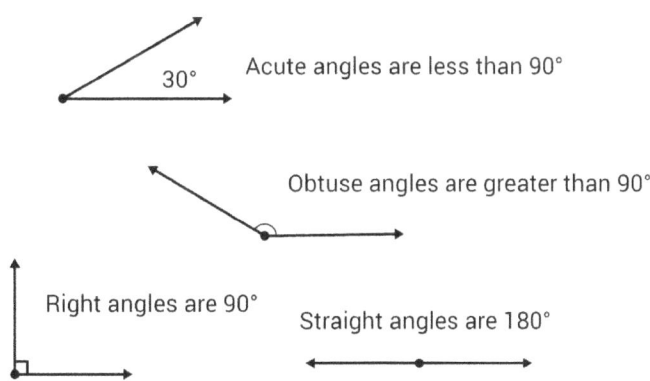

Effects of Changes to Dimensions on Area and Volume

Similar polygons are figures that are the same shape but different sizes. Likewise, similar solids are different sizes but are the same shape. In both cases, corresponding angles in the same positions for both figures are congruent (equal), and corresponding sides are proportional in length. For example, the triangles below are similar. The following pairs of corresponding angles are congruent: ∠A and ∠D; ∠B and ∠E; ∠C and ∠F. The corresponding sides are proportional:

$$\frac{AB}{DE} = \frac{6}{3} = 2$$

$$\frac{BC}{EF} = \frac{9}{4.5} = 2$$

$$\frac{CA}{FD} = \frac{10}{5} = 2$$

In other words, triangle ABC is the same shape but twice as large as triangle DEF.

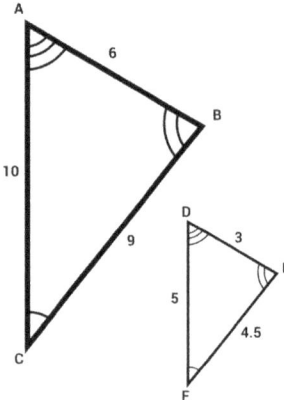

An example of similar triangular pyramids is shown below:

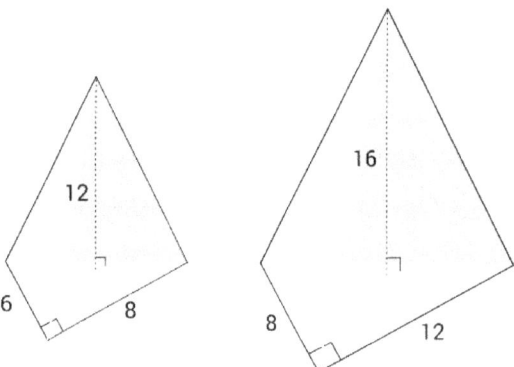

Given the nature of two- and three-dimensional measurements, changing dimensions by a given scale (multiplier) does not change the area of volume by the same scale. Consider a rectangle with a length of 5 centimeters and a width of 4 centimeters. The area of the rectangle is $20cm^2$. Doubling the dimensions of the rectangle (multiplying by a scale factor of 2) to 10 centimeters and 8 centimeters *does not* double the area to $40cm^2$. Area is a two-dimensional measurement (measured in square units).

Therefore, the dimensions are multiplied by a scale that is squared (raised to the second power) to determine the scale of the corresponding areas.

For the previous example, the length and width are multiplied by 2. Therefore, the area is multiplied by 2^2, or 4. The area of a 5cm × 4cm rectangle is $20cm^2$. The area of a 10cm × 8cm rectangle is $80cm^2$.

Volume is a three-dimensional measurement, which is measured in cubic units. Therefore, the scale between dimensions of similar solids is cubed (raised to the third power) to determine the scale between their volumes. Consider similar right rectangular prisms: one with a length of 8 inches, a width of 24 inches, and a height of 16 inches; the second with a length of 4 inches, a width of 12 inches, and a height of 8 inches.

The first prism, multiplied by a scalar of $\frac{1}{2}$, produces the measurement of the second prism. The volume of the first prism, multiplied by $(\frac{1}{2})^3$, which equals $\frac{1}{8}$, produces the volume of the second prism.

The volume of the first prism is 8in × 24in × 16in which equals $3,072 in^3$. The volume of the second prism is 4in × 12in × 8in which equals:

$$384 in^3 \ (3,072 in^3 \times \frac{1}{8} = 384 in^3)$$

The rules for squaring the scalar for area and cubing the scalar for volume only hold true for similar figures. In other words, if only one dimension is changed (changing the width of a rectangle but not the length) or dimensions are changed at different rates (the length of a prism is doubled and its height is tripled) the figures are not similar (same shape). Therefore, the rules above do not apply.

Congruence and Similarity in Terms of Transformations

Rigid Motion

A **rigid motion** is a transformation that preserves distance and length. Every line segment in the resulting image is congruent to the corresponding line segment in the pre-image. Congruence between two figures means a series of transformations (or a rigid motion) can be defined that maps one of the figures onto the other. Basically, two figures are congruent if they have the same shape and size.

Dilation

A shape is dilated, or a **dilation** occurs, when each side of the original image is multiplied by a given scale factor. If the scale factor is less than 1 and greater than 0, the dilation contracts the shape, and the resulting shape is smaller. If the scale factor equals 1, the resulting shape is the same size, and the dilation is a rigid motion. Finally, if the scale factor is greater than 1, the resulting shape is larger and the dilation expands the shape. The **center of dilation** is the point where the distance from it to any point on the new shape equals the scale factor times the distance from the center to the corresponding point in the pre-image. Dilation isn't an isometric transformation because distance isn't preserved. However, angle measure, parallel lines, and points on a line all remain unchanged.

The following figure is an example of translation, rotation, dilation, and reflection:

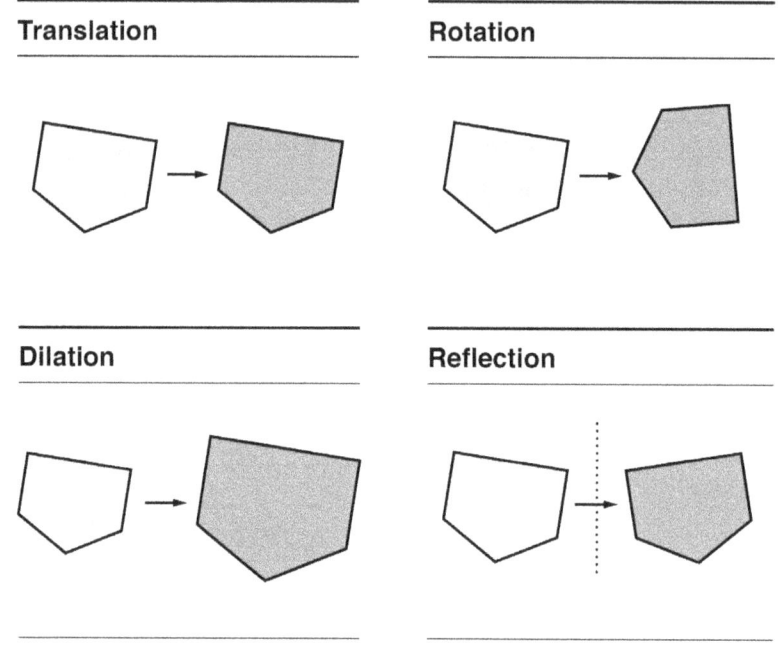

Determining Congruence

Two figures are congruent if there is a rigid motion that can map one figure onto the other. Therefore, all pairs of sides and angles within the image and pre-image must be congruent. For example, in triangles, each pair of the three sides and three angles must be congruent. Similarly, in two four-sided figures, each pair of the four sides and four angles must be congruent.

Similarity

Two figures are **similar** if there is a combination of translations, reflections, rotations, and dilations, which maps one figure onto the other. The difference between congruence and similarity is that dilation can be used in similarity. Therefore, side lengths between each shape can differ. However, angle measure must be preserved within this definition. If two polygons differ in size so that the lengths of corresponding line segments differ by the same factor, but corresponding angles have the same measurement, they are similar.

Triangle Congruence

There are five theorems to show that triangles are congruent when it's unknown whether each pair of angles and sides are congruent. Each theorem is a shortcut that involves different combinations of sides and angles that must be true for the two triangles to be congruent. For example, **side-side-side (SSS)** states that if all sides are equal, the triangles are congruent.

Side-angle-side (SAS) states that if two pairs of sides are equal and the included angles are congruent, then the triangles are congruent. Similarly, **angle-side-angle (ASA)** states that if two pairs of angles are congruent and the included side lengths are equal, the triangles are similar. **Angle-angle-side (AAS)** states that two triangles are congruent if they have two pairs of congruent angles and a pair of corresponding equal side lengths that aren't included. Finally, **hypotenuse-leg (HL)** states that if two right triangles have equal hypotenuses and an equal pair of shorter sides, then the triangles are congruent. An important item to note is that angle-angle-angle (**AAA**) is not enough information to have congruence. It's important to understand why these rules work by using rigid motions to show congruence between the triangles with the given properties. For example, three reflections are needed to show why **SAS** follows from the definition of congruence.

Similarity for Two Triangles

If two angles of one triangle are congruent with two angles of a second triangle, the triangles are similar. This is because, within any triangle, the sum of the angle measurements is 180 degrees. Therefore, if two are congruent, the third angle must also be congruent because their measurements are equal. Three congruent pairs of angles mean that the triangles are similar.

Proving Congruence and Similarity

The criteria needed to prove triangles are congruent involves both angle and side congruence. Both pairs of related angles and sides need to be of the same measurement to use congruence in a proof. The criteria to prove similarity in triangles involves proportionality of side lengths. Angles must be congruent in similar triangles; however, corresponding side lengths only need to be a constant multiple of each other. Once similarity is established, it can be used in proofs as well. Relationships in geometric figures other than triangles can be proven using triangle congruence and similarity. If a similar or congruent triangle can be found within another type of geometric figure, their criteria can be used to prove a relationship about a given formula. For instance, a rectangle can be broken up into two congruent triangles.

Relationships Between Angles

Supplementary angles add up to 180 degrees. **Vertical angles** are two nonadjacent angles formed by two intersecting lines. **Corresponding angles** are two angles in the same position whenever a straight line (known as a **transversal**) crosses two others. If the two lines are parallel, the corresponding angles are equal. In the following diagram, angles 1 and 3 are corresponding angles but aren't equal to each other:

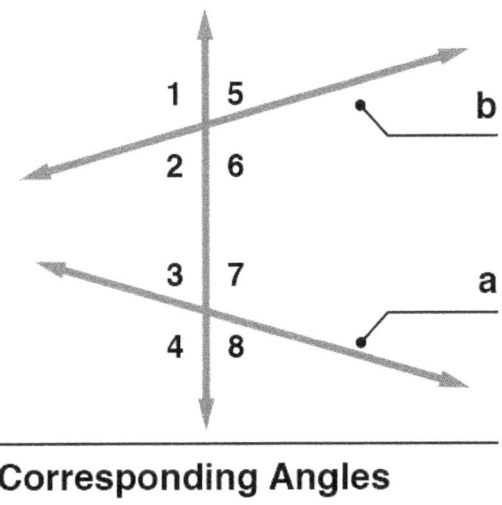

Corresponding Angles

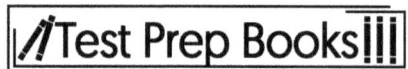

Alternate interior angles are also a pair of angles formed when two lines are crossed by a transversal. They are opposite angles that exist inside of the two lines. In the corresponding angles diagram above, angles 2 and 7 are alternate interior angles, as well as angles 6 and 3. **Alternate exterior angles** are opposite angles formed by a transversal but, in contrast to interior angles, exterior angles exist outside the two original lines. Therefore, angles 1 and 8 are alternate exterior angles and so are angles 5 and 4. Finally, **consecutive interior angles** are pairs of angles formed by a transversal. These angles are located on the same side of the transversal and inside the two original lines. Therefore, angles 2 and 3 are a pair of consecutive interior angles, and so are angles 6 and 7. These definitions are instrumental in solving many problems that involve determining relationships between angles.

Medians, Midpoints, and Altitudes

A **median** of a triangle is a line segment that connects a vertex to the midpoint on the other side of the triangle. A triangle has three medians, and their point of intersection is known as the **centroid**. An **altitude** is a line drawn from a vertex perpendicular to the opposite side. A triangle has three altitudes, and their point of intersection is known as the **orthocenter**. An altitude can actually exist outside, inside, or on the triangle depending on the placement of the vertex. Many problems involve these definitions. For example, given one endpoint of a line segment and the midpoint, the other endpoint can be determined by using the midpoint formula. In addition, area problems heavily depend on these definitions. For example, it can be proven that the median of a triangle divides it into two regions of equal areas. The actual formula for the area of a triangle depends on its altitude.

Special Triangles

An **isosceles triangle** contains at least two equal sides. Therefore, it must also contain two equal angles and, subsequently, contain two medians of the same length. An isosceles triangle can also be labelled as an **equilateral triangle** (which contains three equal sides and three equal angles) when it meets these conditions. In an equilateral triangle, the measure of each angle is always 60 degrees. Also within an equilateral triangle, the medians are of the same length. A **scalene triangle** can never be an equilateral or an isosceles triangle because it contains no equal sides and no equal angles. Also, medians in a scalene triangle can't have the same length. However, a **right triangle**, which is a triangle containing a 90-degree angle, can be a scalene triangle. There are two types of special right triangles. The **30-60-90 right triangle** has angle measurements of 30 degrees, 60 degrees, and 90 degrees. Because of the nature of this triangle, and through the use of the Pythagorean theorem, the side lengths have a special relationship. If x is the length opposite the 30-degree angle, the length opposite the 60-degree angle is $\sqrt{3}x$, and the hypotenuse has length $2x$. The *45-45-90 right triangle* is also special as it contains two angle measurements of 45 degrees. It can be proven that, if x is the length of the two equal sides, the hypotenuse is $x\sqrt{2}$. The properties of all of these special triangles are extremely useful in determining both side lengths and angle measurements in problems where some of these quantities are given and some are not.

Special Quadrilaterals

A special quadrilateral is one in which both pairs of opposite sides are parallel. This type of quadrilateral is known as a **parallelogram**. A parallelogram has six important properties:

- Opposite sides are congruent.
- Opposite angles are congruent.
- Within a parallelogram, consecutive angles are supplementary, so their measurements total 180 degrees.
- If one angle is a right angle, all of them have to be right angles.

- The diagonals of the angles bisect each other.
- These diagonals form two congruent triangles.

A parallelogram with four congruent sides is a **rhombus**. A quadrilateral containing only one set of parallel sides is known as a **trapezoid**. The parallel sides are known as bases, and the other two sides are known as legs. If the legs are congruent, the trapezoid can be labelled an **isosceles trapezoid**. An important property of a trapezoid is that their diagonals are congruent. Also, the median of a trapezoid is parallel to the bases, and its length is equal to half of the sum of the base lengths.

Quadrilateral Relationships

Rectangles, squares, and rhombuses are **polygons** with four sides. By definition, all rectangles are parallelograms, but only some rectangles are squares. However, some parallelograms are rectangles. Also, it's true that all squares are rectangles, and some rhombuses are squares. There are no rectangles, squares, or rhombuses that are trapezoids though, because they have more than one set of parallel sides.

Diagonals and Angles

Diagonals are lines (excluding sides) that connect two vertices within a polygon. **Mutually bisecting diagonals** intersect at their midpoints. Parallelograms, rectangles, squares, and rhombuses have mutually bisecting diagonals. However, trapezoids don't have such lines. **Perpendicular diagonals** occur when they form four right triangles at their point of intersection. Squares and rhombuses have perpendicular diagonals, but trapezoids, rectangles, and parallelograms do not. Finally, **perpendicular bisecting** diagonals (also known as **perpendicular bisectors**) form four right triangles at their point of intersection, but this intersection is also the midpoint of the two lines. Both rhombuses and squares have perpendicular bisecting angles, but trapezoids, rectangles, and parallelograms do not. Knowing these definitions can help tremendously in problems that involve both angles and diagonals.

Polygons with More Than Four Sides

A **pentagon** is a five-sided figure. A six-sided shape is a **hexagon**. A seven-sided figure is classified as a **heptagon**, and an eight-sided figure is called an **octagon**. An important characteristic is whether a polygon is regular or irregular. If it's **regular**, the side lengths and angle measurements are all equal. An **irregular** polygon has unequal side lengths and angle measurements. Mathematical problems involving polygons with more than four sides usually involve side length and angle measurements. The sum of all internal angles in a polygon equals $180(n - 2)$ degrees, where n is the number of sides. Therefore, the total of all internal angles in a pentagon is 540 degrees because there are five sides so $180(5 - 2) = 540$ degrees. Unfortunately, area formulas don't exist for polygons with more than four sides. However, their shapes can be split up into triangles, and the formula for area of a triangle can be applied and totaled to obtain the area for the entire figure.

Congruency

Two figures are congruent if they have the same shape and same size. The two figures could have been rotated, reflected, or translated. Two figures are similar if they have been rotated, reflected, translated, and resized. Angle measure is preserved in similar figures. Both angle and side length are preserved in congruent figures.

Basic Trigonometric Ratios in Right Triangles

Trigonometric Functions

Within similar triangles, corresponding sides are proportional, and angles are congruent. In addition, within similar triangles, the ratio of the side lengths is the same. This property is true even if side lengths are different. Within right triangles, trigonometric ratios can be defined for the acute angle within the triangle. The functions are defined through ratios in a right triangle. Sine of acute angle, A, is opposite over hypotenuse, cosine is adjacent over hypotenuse, and tangent is opposite over adjacent. Note that expanding or shrinking the triangle won't change the ratios. However, changing the angle measurements will alter the calculations.

Complementary Angles

Angles that add up to 90 degrees are *complementary*. Within a right triangle, two complementary angles exist because the third angle is always 90 degrees. In this scenario, the *sine* of one of the complementary angles is equal to the *cosine* of the other angle. The opposite is also true. This relationship exists because sine and cosine will be calculated as the ratios of the same side lengths.

Pythagorean Theorem

The *Pythagorean theorem* is an important relationship between the three sides of a right triangle. It states that the square of the side opposite the right triangle, known as the *hypotenuse* (denoted as c^2), is equal to the sum of the squares of the other two sides ($a^2 + b^2$). Thus, $a^2 + b^2 = c^2$.

Both the trigonometric functions and the Pythagorean theorem can be used in problems that involve finding either a missing side or a missing angle of a right triangle. To do so, one must look to see what sides and angles are given and select the correct relationship that will help find the missing value. These relationships can also be used to solve application problems involving right triangles. Often, it's helpful to draw a figure to represent the problem to see what's missing.

Solving Line Problems

Two lines are parallel if they have the same slope and a different intercept. Two lines are perpendicular if the product of their slope equals -1. Parallel lines never intersect unless they are the same line, and perpendicular lines intersect at a right angle. If two lines aren't parallel, they must intersect at one point. Determining equations of lines based on properties of parallel and perpendicular lines appears in word problems. To find an equation of a line, both the slope and a point the line goes through are necessary. Therefore, if an equation of a line is needed that's parallel to a given line and runs through a specified point, the slope of the given line and the point are plugged into the point-slope form of an equation of a line. Secondly, if an equation of a line is needed that's perpendicular to a given line running through a specified point, the negative reciprocal of the slope of the given line and the point are plugged into the point-slope form. Also, if the point of intersection of two lines is known, that point will be used to solve the set of equations. Therefore, to solve a system of equations, the point of intersection must be found. If a set of two equations with two unknown variables has no solution, the lines are parallel.

Solving Problems with Parallel and Perpendicular Lines

Two lines can be parallel, perpendicular, or neither. If two lines are parallel, they have the same slope. This is proven using the idea of similar triangles. Consider the following diagram with two parallel lines, L1 and L2:

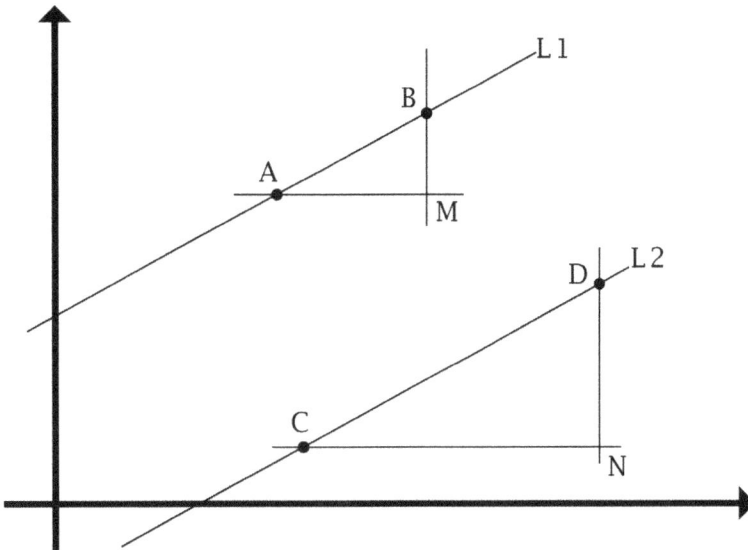

A and B are points on L1, and C and D are points on L2. Right triangles are formed with vertex M and N where lines BM and DN are parallel to the y-axis and AM and CN are parallel to the x-axis. Because all three sets of lines are parallel, the triangles are similar. Therefore, $\frac{BM}{DN} = \frac{MA}{NC}$. This shows that the rise/run is equal for lines L1 and L2. Hence, their slopes are equal.

Secondly, if two lines are perpendicular, the product of their slopes equals -1. This means that their slopes are negative reciprocals of each other. Consider two perpendicular lines, l and n:

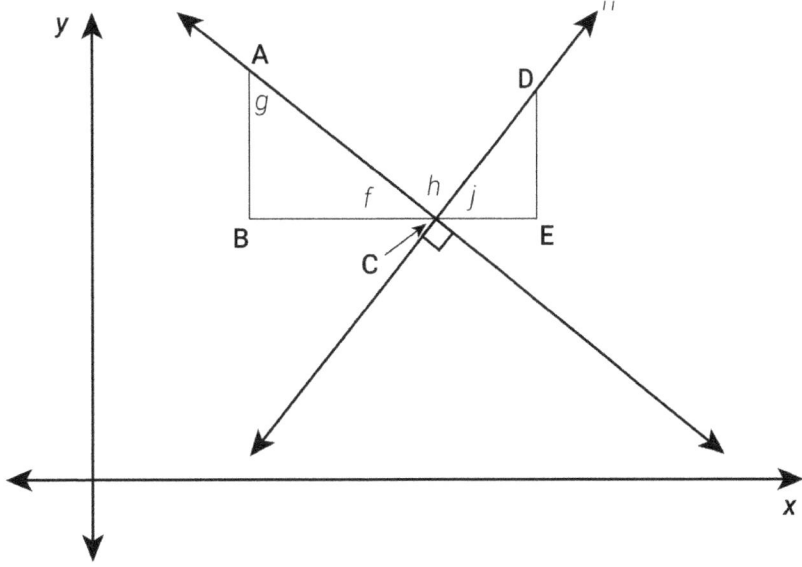

Right triangles ABC and CDE are formed so that lines BC and CE are parallel to the x-axis, and AB and DE are parallel to the y-axis. Because line BE is a straight line, angles:

$$f + h + i = 180 \text{ degrees}$$

However, angle h is a right angle, so $f + j = 90 \text{ degrees}$.

By construction, $f + g = 90$, which means that $g = j$.

Therefore, because angles $B = E$ and $g = j$, the triangles are similar and $\frac{AB}{BC} = \frac{CE}{DE}$.

Because slope is equal to rise/run, the slope of line l is $-\frac{AB}{BC}$ and the slope of line n is $\frac{DE}{CE}$. Multiplying the slopes together gives:

$$-\frac{AB}{BC} \cdot \frac{DE}{CE} = -\frac{CE}{DE} \cdot \frac{DE}{CE} = -1$$

This proves that the product of the slopes of two perpendicular lines equals -1. Both parallel and perpendicular lines can be integral in many geometric proofs, so knowing and understanding their properties is crucial for problem-solving.

Perimeter and Area

Perimeter is the measurement of a distance around something. Think of perimeter as the length of the boundary, like a fence. In contrast, area is the space occupied by a defined enclosure, like a field enclosed by a fence.

The perimeter of a polygon is the distance around the outside of the two-dimensional figure. Perimeter is a one-dimensional measurement and is therefore expressed in linear units such as centimeters (*cm*), feet (*ft.*), and miles (*mi*). The perimeter (*P*) of the figure below is calculated by:

$$P = 9m + 5m + 4m + 6m + 8m \rightarrow P = 32\ m$$

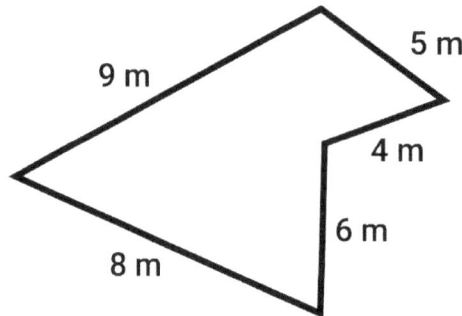

The perimeter of a square is measured by adding together all of the sides. Since a square has four equal sides, its perimeter can be calculated by multiplying the length of one side by 4. Thus, the formula is $P = 4 \times s$, where s equals one side. The area of a square is calculated by squaring the length of one side, which is expressed as the formula $A = s^2$.

Quantitative Reasoning Section

Like a square, a rectangle's perimeter is measured by adding together all of the sides. But as the sides are unequal, the formula is different. A rectangle has equal values for its lengths (long sides) and equal values for its widths (short sides), so the perimeter formula for a rectangle is:

$$P = l + l + w + w = 2l + 2w$$

where l equals length and w equals width. The area is found by multiplying the length by the width, so the formula is $A = l \times w$.

A triangle's perimeter is measured by adding together the three sides, so the formula is $P = a + b + c$, where $a, b,$ and c are the values of the three sides. The area is calculated by multiplying the length of the base times the height times ½, so the formula is:

$$A = \frac{1}{2} \times b \times h = \frac{bh}{2}$$

The base is the bottom of the triangle, and the height is the distance from the base to the peak. If a problem asks to calculate the area of a triangle, it will provide the base and height.

A circle's perimeter—also known as its circumference—is measured by multiplying the diameter (the straight line measured from one end to the direct opposite end of the circle) by π, so the formula is $\pi \times d$. This is sometimes expressed by the formula:

$$C = 2 \times \pi \times r$$

where r is the radius of the circle. These formulas are equivalent, as the radius equals half of the diameter. The area of a circle is calculated through the formula $A = \pi \times r^2$.

The test will indicate either to leave the answer with π attached or to calculate to the nearest decimal place, which means multiplying by 3.14 for π.

The perimeter of a parallelogram is measured by adding the lengths and widths together. Thus, the formula is the same as for a rectangle:

$$P = l + l + w + w = 2l + 2w$$

However, the area formula differs from the rectangle. For a parallelogram, the area is calculated by multiplying the length by the height: $A = h \times l$

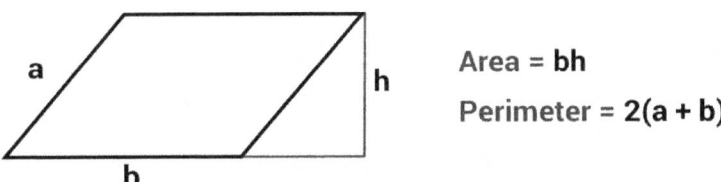

The perimeter of a trapezoid is calculated by adding the two unequal bases and two equal sides, so the formula is

$$P = a + b_1 + c + b_2$$

Although unlikely to be a test question, the formula for the area of a trapezoid is $A = \frac{b_1 + b_2}{2} \times h$, where h equals height, and b_1 and b_2 equal the bases.

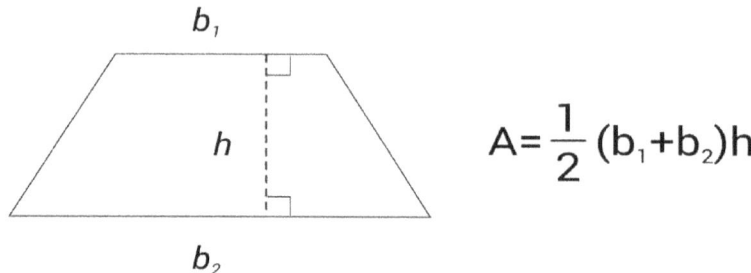

Irregular Shapes

The perimeter of an irregular polygon is found by adding the lengths of all of the sides. In cases where all of the sides are given, this will be very straightforward, as it will simply involve finding the sum of the provided lengths. Other times, a side length may be missing and must be determined before the perimeter can be calculated. Consider the example below:

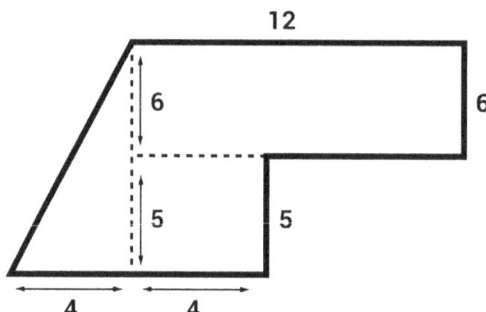

All of the side lengths are provided except for the angled side on the left. Test takers should notice that this is the hypotenuse of a right triangle. The other two sides of the triangle are provided (the base is 4 and the height is 6 + 5 = 11). The Pythagorean Theorem can be used to find the length of the hypotenuse, remembering that $a^2 + b^2 = c^2$.

Substituting the side values provided yields $(4)^2 + (11)^2 = c^2$.

Therefore, $c = \sqrt{16 + 121} = 11.7$

Finally, the perimeter can be found by adding this new side length with the other provided lengths to get the total length around the figure: 4+4+5+8+6+12+11.7=50.7.

Although units are not provided in this figure, remember that reporting units with a measurement is important.

The area of an irregular polygon is found by decomposing, or breaking apart, the figure into smaller shapes. When the area of the smaller shapes is determined, these areas are added together to produce the total area of the area of the original figure. Consider the same example provided before:

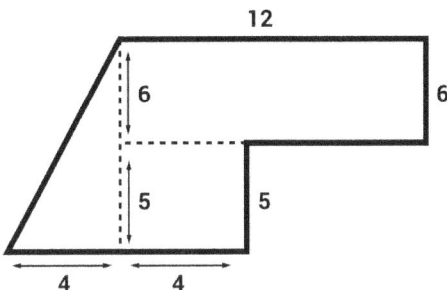

The irregular polygon is decomposed into two rectangles and a triangle. The area of the large rectangles

$$(A = l \times w \rightarrow A = 12 \times 6)$$

is 72 square units. The area of the small rectangle is 20 square units ($A = 4 \times 5$).

The area of the triangle ($A = \frac{1}{2} \times b \times h \rightarrow A = \frac{1}{2} \times 4 \times 11$) is 22 square units.

The sum of the areas of these figures produces the total area of the original polygon:

$$A = 72 + 20 + 22 \rightarrow A = 114 \text{ square units}$$

Surface Area of Three-Dimensional Figures

The area of a two-dimensional figure refers to the number of square units needed to cover the interior region of the figure. This concept is similar to wallpaper covering the flat surface of a wall. For example, if a rectangle has an area of 21 square centimeters (written $21cm^2$), it will take 21 squares, each with sides one centimeter in length, to cover the interior region of the rectangle. Note that area is measured in square units such as: square feet or ft^2; square yards or yd^2; square miles or mi^2.

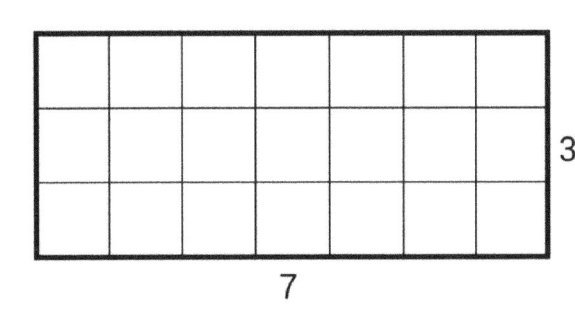

The surface area of a three-dimensional figure refers to the number of square units needed to cover the entire surface of the figure. This concept is similar to using wrapping paper to completely cover the outside of a box. For example, if a triangular pyramid has a surface area of 17 square inches (written $17in^2$), it will take 17 squares, each with sides one inch in length, to cover the entire surface of the pyramid. Surface area is also measured in square units.

Many three-dimensional figures (solid figures) can be represented by nets consisting of rectangles and triangles. The surface area of such solids can be determined by adding the areas of each of its faces and bases. Finding the surface area using this method requires calculating the areas of rectangles and triangles. To find the area (A) of a rectangle, the length (l) is multiplied by the width:

$$(w) \rightarrow A = l \times w$$

The area of a rectangle with a length of 8cm and a width of 4cm is calculated:

$$A = (8cm) \times (4cm) \rightarrow A = 32cm^2$$

To calculate the area (A) of a triangle, the product of $\frac{1}{2}$, the base (b), and the height (h) is found → $A = \frac{1}{2} \times b \times h$. The height of a triangle is measured from the base to the vertex opposite of it forming a right angle with the base. The area of a triangle with a base of 11cm and a height of 6cm is calculated:

$$A = \frac{1}{2} \times (11cm) \times (6cm) \rightarrow A = 33cm^2$$

Consider the following triangular prism, which is represented by a net consisting of two triangles and three rectangles:

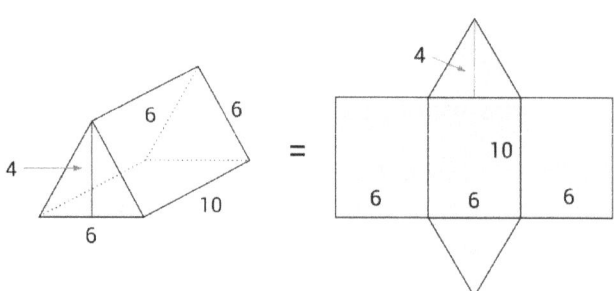

The surface area of the prism can be determined by adding the areas of each of its faces and bases. The surface area (SA) = area of triangle + area of triangle + area of rectangle + area of rectangle + area of rectangle.

$$SA = \left(\frac{1}{2} \times b \times h\right) + \left(\frac{1}{2} \times b \times h\right) + (l \times w) + (l \times w) + (l \times w)$$

$$SA = \left(\frac{1}{2} \times 6 \times 4\right) + \left(\frac{1}{2} \times 6 \times 4\right) + (6 \times 10) + (6 \times 10) + (6 \times 10)$$

$$SA = (12) + (12) + (60) + (60) + (60)$$

$$SA = 204 \text{ square units}$$

Circles

Circle Angles

The distance from the middle of a circle to any other point on the circle is known as the **radius**. A **chord** of a circle is a straight line formed when its endpoints are allowed to be any two points on the circle. Many angles exist within a circle. A **central angle** is formed by using two radii as its rays and the center of the circle as its vertex. An inscribed angle is formed by using two chords as its rays, and its vertex is a point on the circle itself.

Finally, a **circumscribed angle** has a vertex that is a point outside the circle and rays that intersect with the circle. Some relationships exist between these types of angles, and, in order to define these relationships, arc measure must be understood. An **arc** of a circle is a portion of the circumference. Finding the **arc measure** is the same as finding the degree measure of the central angle that intersects the circle to form the arc. The measure of an inscribed angle is half the measure of its intercepted arc. It's also true that the measure of a circumscribed angle is equal to 180 degrees minus the measure of the central angle that forms the arc in the angle.

Quadrilateral Angles

If a quadrilateral is inscribed in a circle, the sum of its opposite angles is 180 degrees. Consider the quadrilateral ABCD centered at the point O:

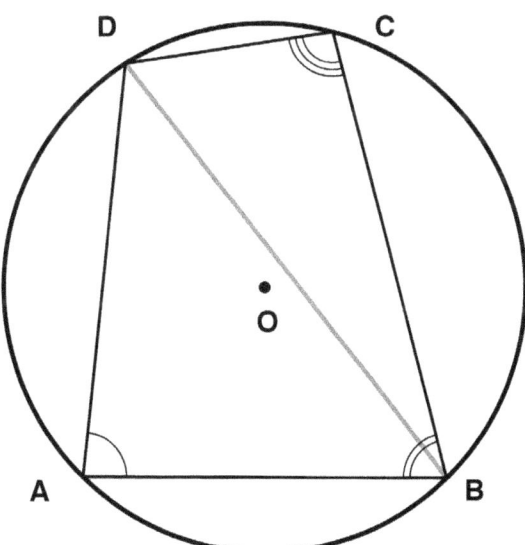

Each of the four line segments within the quadrilateral is a chord of the circle. Consider the diagonal DB. Angle DAB is an inscribed angle leaning on the arc DCB. Therefore, angle DAB is half the measure of the arc DCB. Conversely, angle DCB is an inscribed angle leaning on the arc DAB. Therefore, angle DCB is half the measure of the arc DAB. The sum of arcs DCB and DAB is 360 degrees because they make up the entire circle. Therefore, the sum of angles DAB and DCB equals half of 360 degrees, which is 180 degrees.

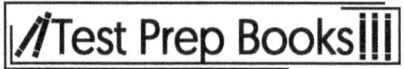

Quantitative Reasoning Section

Functions

A **function** is defined as a relationship between inputs and outputs where there is only one output value for a given input. As an example, the following function is in function notation:

$$f(x) = 3x - 4$$

The $f(x)$ represents the output value for an input of x. If $x = 2$, the equation becomes:

$$f(2) = 3(2) - 4 = 6 - 4 = 2$$

The input of 2 yields an output of 2, forming the ordered pair $(2, 2)$. The following set of ordered pairs corresponds to the given function: $(2, 2), (0, -4), (-2, -10)$. The set of all possible inputs of a function is its **domain**, and all possible outputs is called the **range**. By definition, each member of the domain is paired with only one member of the range.

Functions can also be defined **recursively**. In this form, they are not defined **explicitly** in terms of variables. Instead, they are defined using previously evaluated function outputs, starting with either $f(0)$ or $f(1)$. An example of a recursively defined function is:

$$f(1) = 2, f(n) = 2f(n-1) + 2n, n > 1$$

The domain of this function is the set of all integers.

Domain and Range

The domain and range of a function can be found visually by its plot on the coordinate plane. In the function $f(x) = x^2 - 3$, for example, the domain is all real numbers because the parabola can stretch infinitely far left and right with no restrictions. This means that any input value from the real number system will yield an output in the real number system. For the range, the inequality $y \geq -3$ would be used to describe the possible output values because the parabola has a minimum at $y = -3$. This means there will not be any real output values less than -3 because -3 is the lowest value the function reaches on the y-axis.

These same answers for domain and range can be found by observing a table. The table below shows that from input values $x = -1$ to $x = 1$, the output results in a minimum of -3. On each side of $x = 0$, the numbers increase, showing that the range is all real numbers greater than or equal to -3.

x (domain/input)	y (range/output)
-2	1
-1	-2
0	-3
-1	-2
2	1

Function Behavior

Different types of functions behave in different ways. A function is defined to be increasing over a subset of its domain if for all $x_1 \geq x_2$ in that interval, $f(x_1) \geq f(x_2)$. Also, a function is decreasing over an interval if for all $x_1 \geq x_2$ in that interval, $f(x_1) \leq f(x_2)$. A point in which a function changes from increasing to decreasing can also be labeled as the **maximum value** of a function if it is the largest point the graph reaches on the y-axis. A point in which a function changes from decreasing to increasing can be labeled as the **minimum value** of a function if it is the smallest point the graph reaches on the y-axis. Maximum and minimum values are also known as **extreme values**. The graph of a **continuous function** does not have any breaks or jumps in the graph. This description is not true of all functions. A **radical function**, for example, $f(x) = \sqrt{x}$, has a restriction for the domain and range because there are no real negative inputs or outputs for this function. The domain can be stated as $x \geq 0$, and the range is $y \geq 0$.

A **piecewise-defined** function also has a different appearance on the graph. In the following function, there are three equations defined over different intervals. It is a function because there is only one y-value for each x-value, passing the **Vertical Line Test**. The domain is all real numbers less than or equal to 6. The range is all real numbers greater than zero.

Example
The graphic below is an example of a piecewise function. It shows that the function x^2 is used when x is less than 2, 6 is used if x equals 2, and that the function $10 - x$ is used if x is greater than 2 but less than or equal to 6.

$$f(x) = \begin{cases} x^2 & \text{if } x < 2 \\ 6 & \text{if } x = 2 \\ 10 - x & \text{if } x > 2 \text{ and } x \leq 6 \end{cases}$$

The graph below shows how to graph this function.

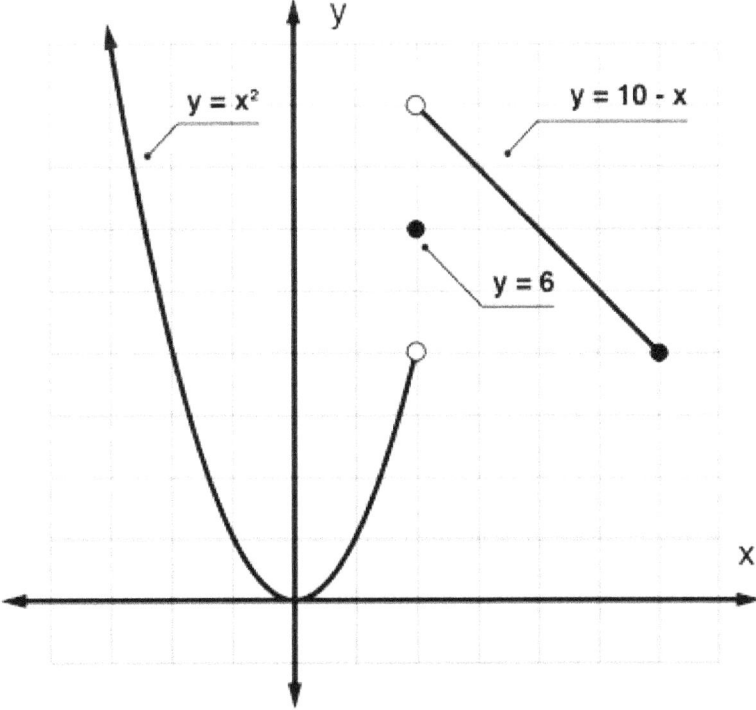

Logarithmic and exponential functions also have different behavior than other functions. These two types of functions are inverses of each other. The **inverse** of a function can be found by switching the place of x and y, and solving for y. When this is done for the exponential equation, $y = 2^x$, the function $y = \log_2 x$ is found. The general form of a **logarithmic function** is $y = \log_b x$, which says b raised to the y power equals x.

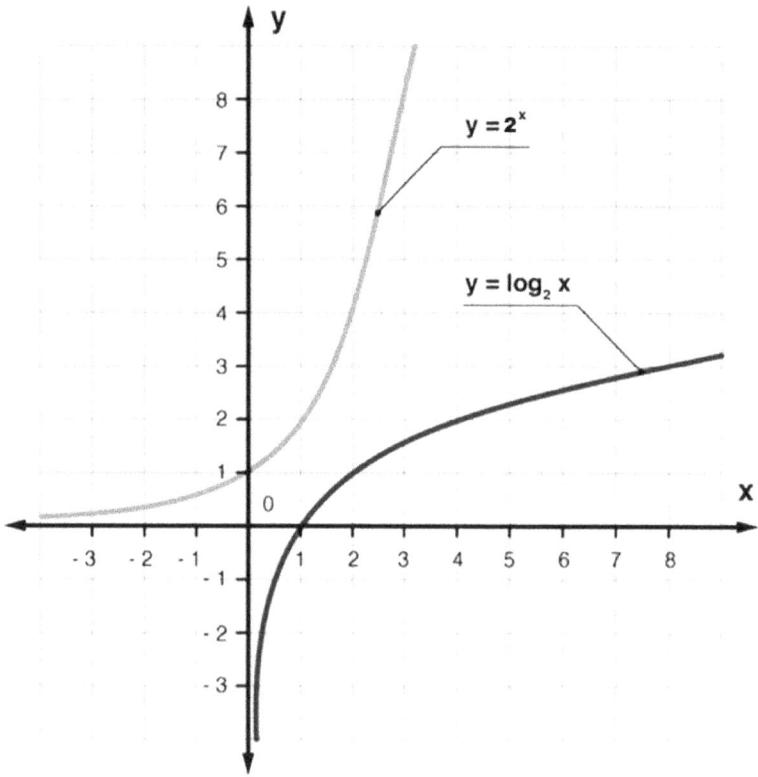

The thick black line on the graph above represents the logarithmic function $y = \log_2 x$. This curve passes through the point $(1, 0)$, just as all log functions do, because any value $b^0 = 1$. The graph of this logarithmic function starts very close to zero, but does not touch the y-axis. The output value will never be zero by the definition of logarithms. The thinner gray line seen above represents the exponential function $y = 2^x$. The behavior of this function is opposite the logarithmic function because the graph of an inverse function is the graph of the original function flipped over the line $y = x$. The curve passes through the point $(0, 1)$ because any number raised to the zero power is one. This curve also gets very close to the x-axis but never touches it because an exponential expression never has an output of zero. The x-axis on this graph is called a horizontal asymptote. An **asymptote** is a line that represents a boundary for a function. It shows a value that the function will get close to, but never reach.

Functions can also be described as being even, odd, or neither. If $f(-x) = f(x)$, the function is **even**. For example, the function $f(x) = x^2 - 2$ is even. Plugging in $x = 2$ yields an output of $y = 2$. After changing the input to $x = -2$, the output is still $y = 2$. The output is the same for opposite inputs. Another way to observe an even function is by the symmetry of the graph. If the graph is symmetrical about the axis, then the function is even. If the graph is symmetric about the origin, then the function is **odd**. Algebraically, if $f(-x) = -f(x)$, the function is odd.

Also, a function can be described as **periodic** if it repeats itself in regular intervals. Common periodic functions are trigonometric functions. For example, $y = \sin x$ is a periodic function with period 2π because it repeats itself every 2π units along the x-axis.

Building a Function

Functions can be built out of the context of a situation. For example, the relationship between the money paid for a gym membership and the months that someone has been a member can be described through a function. If the one-time membership fee is $40 and the monthly fee is $30, then the function can be written $f(x) = 30x + 40$. The x-value represents the number of months the person has been part of the gym, while the output is the total money paid for the membership. The table below shows this relationship. It is a representation of the function because the initial cost is $40 and the cost increases each month by $30.

x (months)	y (money paid to gym)
0	40
1	70
2	100
3	130

Functions can also be built from existing functions. For example, a given function $f(x)$ can be transformed by adding a constant, multiplying by a constant, or changing the input value by a constant. The new function $g(x) = f(x) + k$ represents a vertical shift of the original function. In $f(x) = 3x - 2$, a vertical shift 4 units up would be:

$$g(x) = 3x - 2 + 4 = 3x + 2$$

Multiplying the function by a constant k represents a vertical stretch, based on whether the constant is greater than or less than 1. The function

$$g(x) = kf(x) = 4(3x - 2) = 12x - 8$$

represents a stretch. Changing the input x by a constant forms the function:

$$g(x) = f(x + k) = 3(x + 4) - 2 = 3x + 12 - 2 = 3x + 10$$

and this represents a horizontal shift to the left 4 units. If $(x - 4)$ was plugged into the function, it would represent a vertical shift.

A **composition function** can also be formed by plugging one function into another. In function notation, this is written:

$$(f \circ g)(x) = f(g(x))$$

For two functions $f(x) = x^2$ and $g(x) = x - 3$, the composition function becomes:

$$f(g(x)) = (x - 3)^2 = x^2 - 6x + 9$$

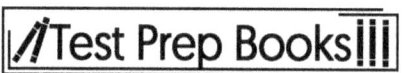

The composition of functions can also be used to verify if two functions are inverses of each other. Given the two functions $f(x) = 2x + 5$ and $g(x) = \frac{x-5}{2}$, the composition function can be found $(f \circ g)(x)$. Solving this equation yields:

$$f(g(x)) = 2\left(\frac{x-5}{2}\right) + 5 = x - 5 + 5 = x$$

It also is true that $g(f(x)) = x$. Since the composition of these two functions gives a simplified answer of x, this verifies that $f(x)$ and $g(x)$ are inverse functions. The domain of $f(g(x))$ is the set of all x-values in the domain of $g(x)$ such that $g(x)$ is in the domain of $f(x)$. Basically, both $f(g(x))$ and $g(x)$ have to be defined.

To build an inverse of a function, $f(x)$ needs to be replaced with y, and the x and y values need to be switched. Then, the equation can be solved for y. For example, given the equation $y = e^{2x}$, the inverse can be found by rewriting the equation $x = e^{2y}$. The natural logarithm of both sides is taken down, and the exponent is brought down to form the equation:

$$\ln(x) = \ln(e)\, 2y$$

$\ln(e)=1$, which yields the equation $\ln(x) = 2y$. Dividing both sides by 2 yields the inverse equation

$$\frac{\ln(x)}{2} = y = f^{-1}(x)$$

The domain of an inverse function is the range of the original function, and the range of an inverse function is the domain of the original function. Therefore, an ordered pair (x, y) on either a graph or a table corresponding to $f(x)$ means that the ordered pair (y, x) exists on the graph of $f^{-1}(x)$. Basically, if $f(x) = y$, then $f^{-1}(y) = x$. For a function to have an inverse, it must be one-to-one. That means it must pass the **Horizontal Line Test,** and if any horizontal line passes through the graph of the function twice, a function is not one-to-one. The domain of a function that is not one-to-one can be restricted to an interval in which the function is one-to-one, to be able to define an inverse function.

Functions can also be formed from combinations of existing functions.

Given $f(x)$ and $g(x)$, the following can be built:

$$f + g$$

$$f - g$$

$$fg$$

$$\frac{f}{g}$$

The domains of $f + g$, $f - g$, and fg are the intersection of the domains of f and g. The domain of $\frac{f}{g}$ is the same set, excluding those values that make $g(x) = 0$.

For example, if:

$$f(x) = 2x + 3$$

$$g(x) = x + 1$$

then

$$\frac{f}{g} = \frac{2x + 3}{x + 1}$$

Its domain is all real numbers except -1.

Common Functions

Three common functions used to model different relationships between quantities are linear, quadratic, and exponential functions. **Linear functions** are the simplest of the three, and the independent variable x has an exponent of 1. Written in the most common form, $y = mx + b$, the coefficient of x indicates how fast the function grows at a constant rate, and the b-value denotes the starting point. A **quadratic function** has an exponent of 2 on the independent variable x. Standard form for this type of function is $y = ax^2 + bx + c$, and the graph is a parabola. These type functions grow at a changing rate. **An exponential function** has an independent variable in the exponent $y = ab^x$. The graph of these types of functions is described as **growth** or **decay**, based on whether the **base**, b, is greater than or less than 1. These functions are different from quadratic functions because the base stays constant. A common base is base e.

The following three functions model a linear, quadratic, and exponential function respectively: $y = 2x$, $y = x^2$, and $y = 2^x$. Their graphs are shown below. The first graph, modeling the linear function, shows that the growth is constant over each interval. With a horizontal change of 1, the vertical change is 2. It models constant positive growth. The second graph shows the quadratic function, which is a curve that is symmetric across the y-axis. The growth is not constant, but the change is mirrored over the axis. The last graph models the exponential function, where the horizontal change of 1 yields a vertical change that increases more and more with each iteration of horizontal change. The exponential graph gets very close to the x-axis, but never touches it, meaning there is an asymptote there. The y-value can never be zero because the base of 2 can never be raised to an input value that yields an output of zero.

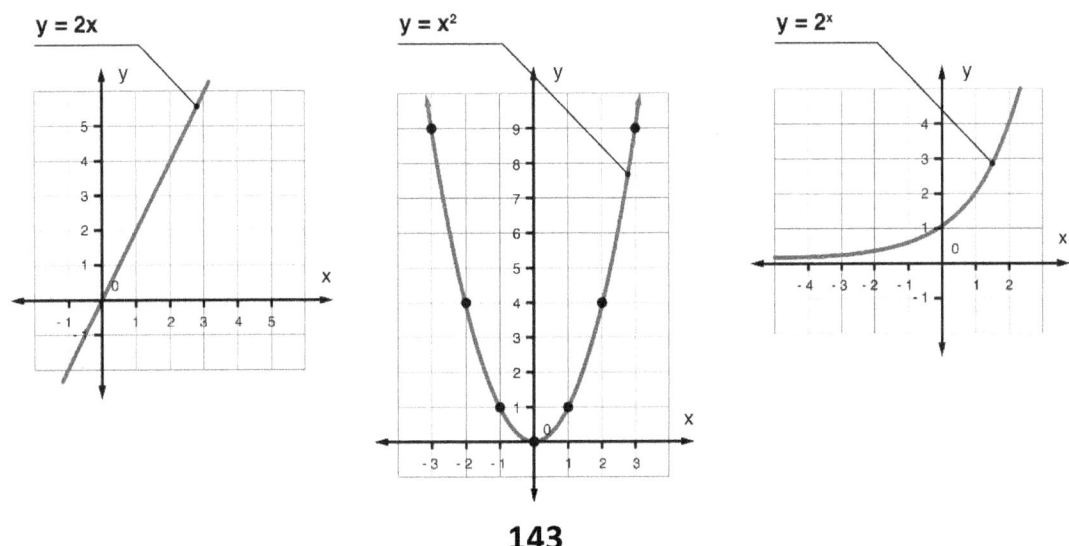

The three tables below show specific values for three types of functions. The third column in each table shows the change in the y-values for each interval. The first table shows a constant change of 2 for each equal interval, which matches the slope in the equation $y = 2x$. The second table shows an increasing change, but it also has a pattern. The increase is changing by 2 more each time, so the change is quadratic. The third table shows the change as factors of the base, 2. It shows a continuing pattern of factors of the base.

$y = 2x$		
x	y	Δy
1	2	
2	4	2
3	6	2
4	8	2
5	10	2

$y = x^2$		
x	y	Δy
1	1	
2	4	3
3	9	5
4	16	7
5	25	9

$y = 2^x$		
x	y	Δy
1	2	
2	4	2
3	8	4
4	16	8
5	32	16

Given a table of values, the type of function can be determined by observing the change in y over equal intervals. For example, the tables below model two functions. The changes in interval for the x-values is 1 for both tables. For the first table, the y-values increase by 5 for each interval. Since the change is constant, the situation can be described as a linear function. The equation would be:

$$y = 5x + 3$$

For the second table, the change for y is 20, 100, and 500, respectively. The increases are multiples of 5, meaning the situation can be modeled by an exponential function. The equation below models this situation:

$$y = 5^x + 3$$

$y = 5x + 3$	
x	y
1	8
2	13
3	18
4	23

$y = 5^x + 3$	
x	y
1	8
2	28
3	128
4	628

Quadratic equations can be used to model real-world area problems. For example, a farmer may have a rectangular field that he needs to sow with seed. The field has length $x + 8$ and width $2x$. The formula for area should be used: $A = lw$. Therefore:

$$A = (x + 8) \times 2x = 2x^2 + 16x$$

The possible values for the length and width can be shown in a table, with input x and output A. If the equation was graphed, the possible area values can be seen on the y-axis for given x-values.

Exponential growth and decay can be found in real-world situations. For example, if a piece of notebook paper is folded 25 times, the thickness of the paper can be found. To model this situation, a table can be used. The initial point is one-fold, which yields a thickness of 2 papers. For the second fold, the thickness is 4. Since the thickness doubles each time, the table below shows the thickness for the next few folds. Notice the thickness changes by the same factor each time. Since this change for a constant interval of folds is a factor of 2, the function is exponential. The equation for this is $y = 2^x$. For twenty-five folds, the thickness would be 33,554,432 papers.

x (folds)	y (paper thickness)
0	1
1	2
2	4
3	8
4	16
5	32

One exponential formula that is commonly used is the **interest formula**: $A = Pe^{rt}$. In this formula, interest is compounded continuously. A is the value of the investment after the time, t, in years. P is the initial amount of the investment, r is the interest rate, and e is the constant equal to approximately 2.718. Given an initial amount of $200 and a time of 3 years, if interest is compounded continuously at a rate of 6%, the total investment value can be found by plugging each value into the formula. The invested value at the end is $239.44. In more complex problems, the final investment may be given, and the rate may be the unknown. In this case, the formula becomes $239.44 = 200e^{r3}$. Solving for r requires isolating the exponential expression on one side by dividing by 200, yielding the equation $1.20 = e^{r3}$. Taking the natural log of both sides results in $\ln(1.2) = r3$. Using a calculator to evaluate the logarithmic expression, $r = 0.06 = 6\%$.

When working with logarithms and exponential expressions, it is important to remember the relationship between the two. In general, the logarithmic form is $y = log_b x$ for an exponential form $b^y = x$. Logarithms and exponential functions are inverses of each other.

Trigonometric Functions

Trigonometric functions are also used to describe behavior in mathematics. **Trigonometry** is the relationship between the angles and sides of a triangle. **Trigonometric functions** include sine, cosine, tangent, secant, cosecant, and cotangent. The functions are defined through ratios in a right triangle. **SOHCAHTOA** is a common acronym used to remember these ratios, which are defined by the relationships of the sides and angles relative to the right angle. **Sine** is opposite over hypotenuse, **cosine** is adjacent over hypotenuse, and **tangent** is opposite over adjacent. These ratios are the reciprocals of secant, cosecant, and cotangent, respectively. Angles can be measured in degrees or radians. Here is a diagram of SOHCAHTOA:

SOH $\sin\theta = \dfrac{\text{opposite}}{\text{hypotenuse}}$

CAH $\cos\theta = \dfrac{\text{adjacent}}{\text{hypotenuse}}$

TOA $\tan\theta = \dfrac{\text{opposite}}{\text{adjacent}}$

A **radian** is equal to the angle that subtends the arc with the same length as the radius of the circle. It is another unit for measuring angles, in addition to degrees. The **unit circle** is used to describe different radian measurements and the trigonometric ratios for special angles. The circle has a center at the origin, $(0, 0)$, and a radius of 1, which can be seen below. The points where the circle crosses an axis are labeled.

The Unit Circle

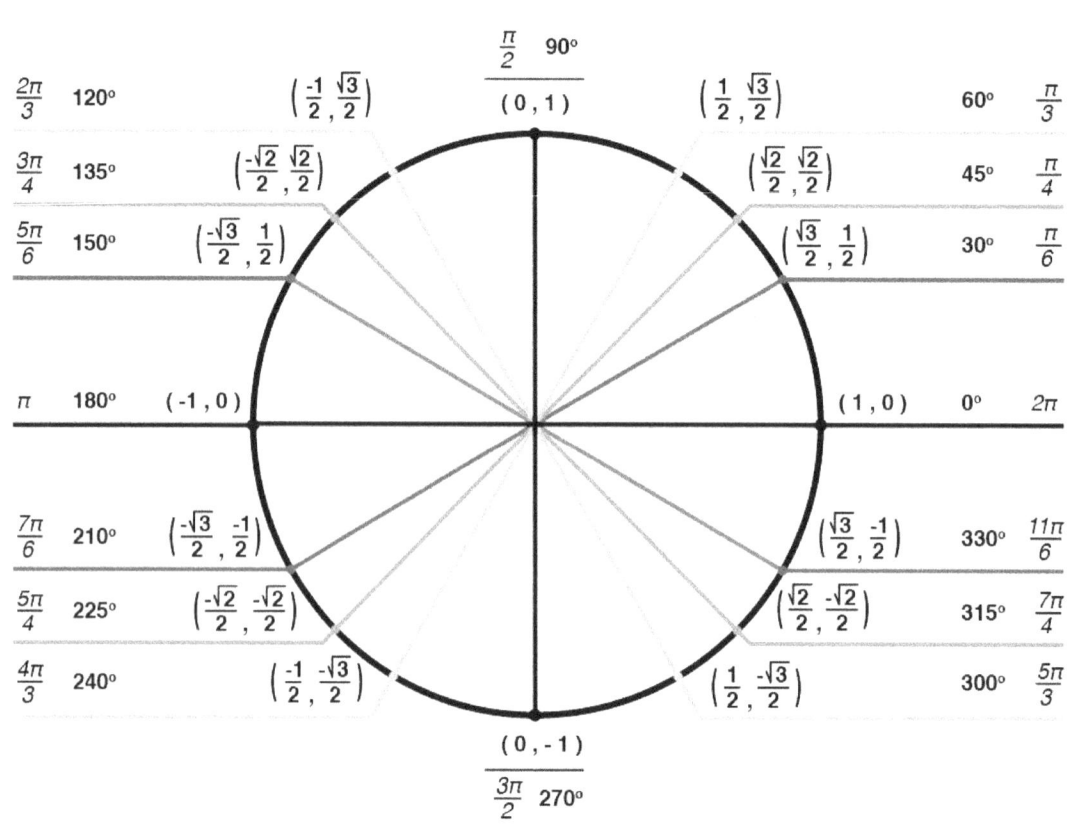

Quantitative Reasoning Section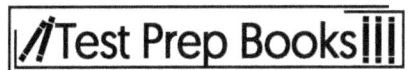

The circle begins on the right-hand side of the x-axis at 0 radians. Since the circumference of a circle is $2\pi r$ and the radius $r = 1$, the circumference is 2π. Zero and 2π are labeled as radian measurements at the point $(1, 0)$ on the graph. The radian measures around the rest of the circle are labeled also in relation to π; π is at the point $(-1, 0)$, also known as 180 degrees. Since these two measurements are equal, $\pi = 180$ degrees written as a ratio can be used to convert degrees to radians or vice versa. For example, to convert 30 degrees to radians, 30 degrees $\times \frac{\pi}{180 \text{ degrees}}$ can be used to obtain $\frac{1}{6}\pi$ or $\frac{\pi}{6}$. This radian measure is a point the unit circle

The coordinates labeled on the unit circle are found based on two common right triangles. The ratios formed in the coordinates can be found using these triangles. Each of these triangles can be inserted into the circle to correspond 30, 45, and 60 degrees or $\frac{\pi}{6}, \frac{\pi}{4}$, and $\frac{\pi}{3}$ radians.

By letting the hypotenuse length of these triangles equal 1, these triangles can be placed inside the unit circle. These coordinates can be used to find the trigonometric ratio for any of the radian measurements on the circle.

Given any (x, y) on the unit circle, $\sin(\theta) = y$, $\cos(\theta) = x$, and $\tan(\theta) = \frac{y}{x}$. The value θ is the angle that spans the arc around the unit circle. For example, finding $\sin\left(\frac{\pi}{4}\right)$ means finding the y-value corresponding to the angle $\theta = \frac{\pi}{4}$. The answer is $\frac{\sqrt{2}}{2}$. Finding $\cos\left(\frac{\pi}{3}\right)$ means finding the x-value corresponding to the angle $\theta = \frac{\pi}{3}$. The answer is $\frac{1}{2}$ or 0.5. Both angles lie in the first quadrant of the unit circle. Trigonometric ratios can also be calculated for radian measures past $\frac{\pi}{2}$, or 90 degrees. Since the same special angles can be moved around the circle, the results only differ with a change in sign. This can be seen at two points labeled in the second and third quadrant.

Trigonometric functions are periodic. Both sine and cosine have period 2π. For each input angle value, the output value follows around the unit circle. Once it reaches the starting point, it continues around and around the circle. It is true that:

$$\sin(0) = \sin(2\pi) = \sin(4\pi), \text{ etc.}$$

and

$$\cos(0) = \cos(2\pi) = \cos(4\pi)$$

Tangent has period π, and its output values repeat themselves every half of the unit circle. The domain of sine and cosine are all real numbers, and the domain of tangent is all real numbers, except the points where cosine equals zero. It is also true that

$$\sin(-x) = -\sin x$$

$$\cos(-x) = \cos(x)$$

$$\tan(-x) = -\tan(x)$$

Thus, sine and tangent are odd functions, while cosine is an even function. Sine and tangent are symmetric with respect the origin, and cosine is symmetric with respect to the y-axis.

The graph of trigonometric functions can be used to model different situations. General forms are:

$$y = a \sin b(x - h) + k$$

and

$$y = a \cos b (x - h) + k$$

The variable a represents the **amplitude**, which shows the maximum and minimum value of the function. The b is used to find the **period** by using the ratio $\frac{2\pi}{b}$, h is the **horizontal shift**, and k is the **vertical shift**.

The equation $y = \sin(x)$ is shown on the following graph with the thick black line. The stretched graph of $y = 2 \sin(x)$ is shown in solid black, and the shrunken graph $y = \frac{1}{2}\sin(x)$ is shown with the dotted line.

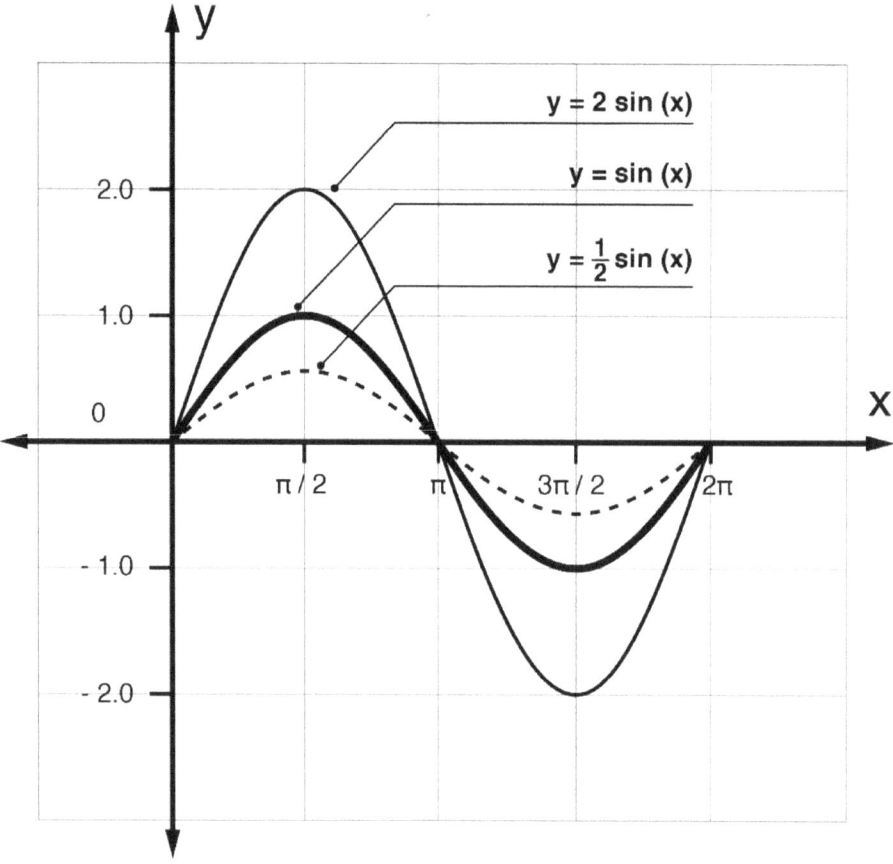

Trigonometric functions are used to find unknown ratios for a given angle measure. The inverse of these trig functions is used to find the unknown angle, given a ratio. For example, the expression $\arcsin\left(\frac{1}{2}\right)$ means finding the value of x for $\sin(x) = \frac{1}{2}$. Since $\sin(\theta) = \frac{y}{1}$ on the unit circle, the angle whose y-value is $\frac{1}{2}$ is $\frac{\pi}{6}$. The inverse of any of the trigonometric functions can be used to find a missing angle

Quantitative Reasoning Section

measurement. Values not found on the unit circle can be found using the trigonometric functions on the calculator, making sure its mode is set to degrees or radians.

In order for the inverse to exist, the function must be one-to-one over its domain. There cannot be two input values connected to the same output. For example, the following graphs show the functions $y = \cos(x)$ and $y = \arccos(x)$. In order to have an inverse, the domain of cosine is restricted from 0 to π.

Therefore, the range of its inverse function is $[0, \pi]$.

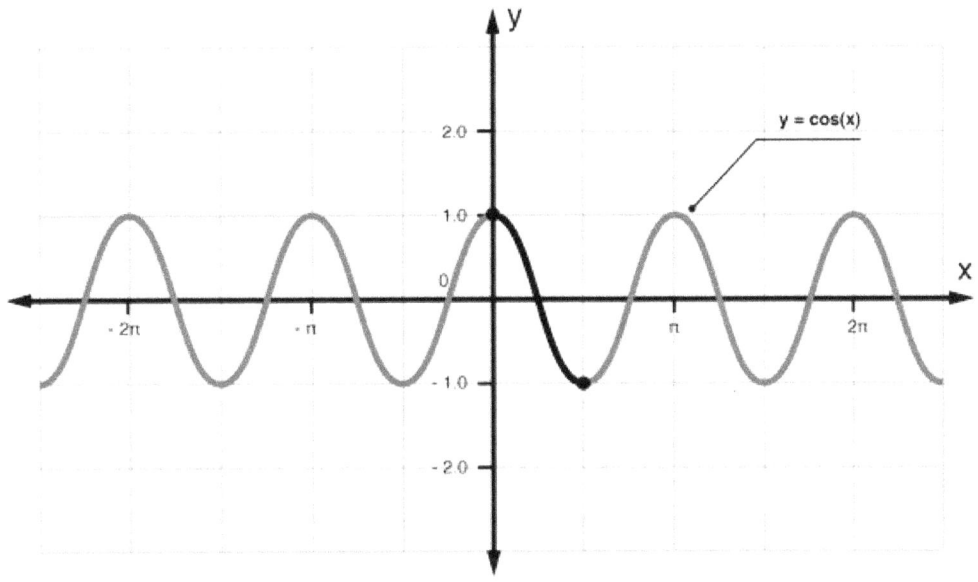

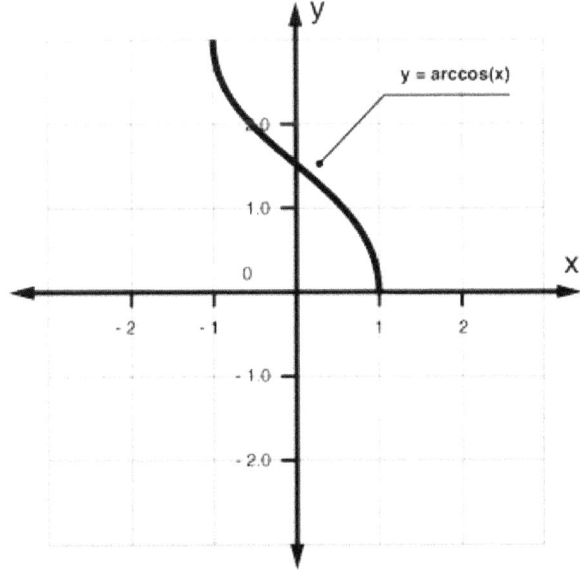

Inverses of trigonometric functions can be used to solve real-world problems. For example, there are many situations where the lengths of a perceived triangle can be found, but the angles are unknown. Consider a problem where the height of a flag (25 feet) and the distance on the ground to the flag is given (42 feet). The unknown, x, is the angle. To find this angle, the equation $\tan x = \frac{42}{25}$ is used. To solve for x, the inverse function can be used to turn the equation into $\tan^{-1} \frac{42}{25} = x$. Using the calculator, in degree mode, the answer is found to be $x = 59.2$ degrees

Trigonometric Identities

From the unit circle, the trigonometric ratios were found for the special right triangle with a hypotenuse of 1.

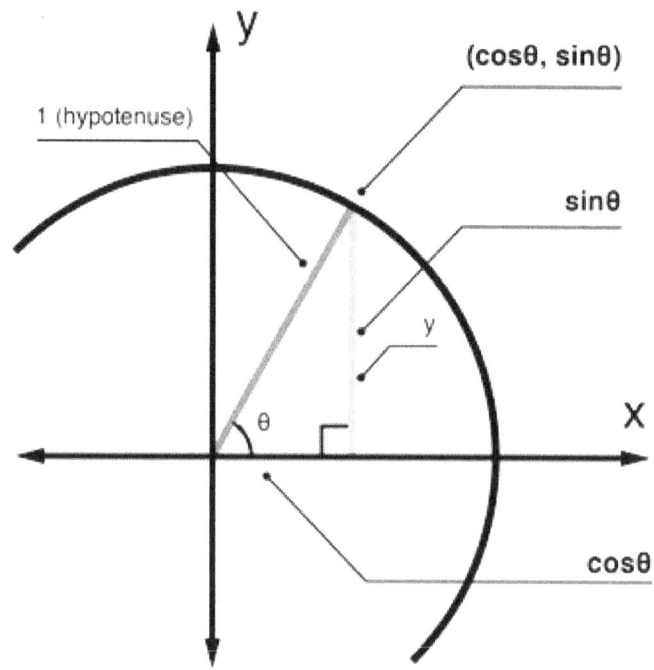

From this triangle, the following **Pythagorean identities** are formed:

$$\sin^2 \theta + \cos^2 \theta = 1$$

$$\tan^2 \theta + 1 = \sec^2 \theta$$

$$1 + \cot^2 \theta = \csc^2 \theta$$

The second two identities are formed by manipulating the first identity. Since identities are statements that are true for any value of the variable, then they may be used to manipulate equations. For example, a problem may ask for simplification of the expression:

$$\cos^2 x + \cos^2 x \tan^2 x$$

Using the fact that:

$$\tan(x) = \frac{\sin x}{\cos x}$$

$\frac{\sin^2 x}{\cos^2 x}$ can then be substituted in for $\tan^2 x$, making the expression:

$$\cos^2 x + \cos^2 x \frac{\sin^2 x}{\cos^2 x}$$

Then the two $\cos^2 x$ terms on top and bottom cancel each other out, simplifying the expression to:

$$\cos^2 x + \sin^2 x$$

By the first Pythagorean identity stated above, the expression can be turned into:

$$\cos^2 x + \sin^2 x = 1$$

Another set of trigonometric identities are the **double-angle formulas**:

$$\sin 2\alpha = 2 \sin \alpha \cos \alpha$$

$$\cos 2\alpha = \begin{cases} \cos^2 \alpha - \sin^2 \alpha \\ 2\cos^2 \alpha - 1 \\ 1 - 2\sin^2 \alpha \end{cases}$$

Using these formulas, the following identity can be proved:

$$\sin 2x = \frac{2 \tan x}{1 + \tan^2 x}$$

By using one of the Pythagorean identities, the denominator can be rewritten as:

$$1 + \tan^2 x = \sec^2 x$$

By knowing the reciprocals of the trigonometric identities, the secant term can be rewritten to form the equation:

$$\sin 2x = \frac{2 \tan x}{1} * \cos^2 x$$

Replacing $\tan(x)$, the equation becomes:

$$\sin 2x = \frac{2 \sin x}{\cos x} * \cos^2 x$$

The $\cos x$ can cancel out. The new equation is:

$$\sin 2x = 2 \sin x * \cos x$$

This final equation is one of the double-angle formulas.

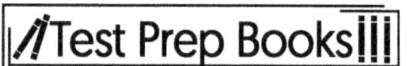

Other trigonometric identities such as half-angle formulas, sum and difference formulas, and difference of angles formulas can be used to prove and rewrite trigonometric equations. Depending on the given equation or expression, the correct identities need to be chosen to write equivalent statements.

The graph of sine is equal to the graph of cosine, shifted $\frac{\pi}{2}$ units. Therefore, the function $y = \sin x$ is equal to:

$$y = \cos(\frac{\pi}{2} - x)$$

Within functions, adding a constant to the independent variable shifts the graph either left or right. By shifting the cosine graph, the curve lies on top of the sine function. By transforming the function, the two equations give the same output for any given input.

Functions of Two Variables

The graph of a function of one variable can be represented in the xy-plane and is known as a **curve**. When a function has two variables, the function is graphed in three-dimensional space, and the graph is known as a **surface**. The graph is the set of all ordered triples (x, y, z) that satisfy the function. Within three-dimensional space, there is a third axis known as the **z-axis.**

Solving Trigonometric Functions

Solving trigonometric functions can be done with a knowledge of the unit circle and the trigonometric identities. It requires the use of opposite operations combined with trigonometric ratios for special triangles. For example, the problem may require solving the equation $2\cos^2 x - \sqrt{3} \cos x = 0$ for the values of x between 0 and 180 degrees. The first step is to factor out the $\cos x$ term, resulting in:

$$\cos x (2 \cos x - \sqrt{3}) = 0$$

By the factoring method of solving, each factor can be set equal to zero:

$$\cos x = 0$$

$$(2 \cos x - \sqrt{3}) = 0$$

The second equation can be solved to yield the following equation:

$$\cos x = \frac{\sqrt{3}}{2}$$

Now that the value of x is found, the trigonometric ratios can be used to find the solutions of $x = 30$ and 90 degrees.

Solving trigonometric functions requires the use of algebra to isolate the variable and a knowledge of trigonometric ratios to find the value of the variable. The unit circle can be used to find answers for special triangles. Beyond those triangles, a calculator can be used to solve for variables within the trigonometric functions.

Solving Logarithmic and Exponential Functions

To solve an equation involving exponential expressions, the goal is to isolate the exponential expression. Once this process is completed, the logarithm—with the base equaling the base of the exponent of both sides—needs to be taken to get an expression for the variable. If the base is e, the natural log of both sides needs to be taken.

To solve an equation with logarithms, the given equation needs to be written in exponential form, using the fact that $\log_b y = x$ means $b^x = y$, and then solved for the given variable. Lastly, properties of logarithms can be used to simplify more than one logarithmic expression into one.

Practice Quiz

1. One person can fold 5 loads of laundry in 30 minutes. If a second person helps to fold the laundry, it can be done in 20 minutes. How long would it take the second person to fold 5 laundry loads by themselves?
    a. 60 minutes
    b. 30 minutes
    c. 20 minutes
    d. 80 minutes

2. The line $y = -5$ is shown on the (x, y)- coordinate plane and is reflected across the x-axis. Which of the following is true about this new line?
    a. It is vertical.
    b. It is parallel to $x = 5$.
    c. It is perpendicular to $x = 5$.
    d. It has an undefined slope.

3. The area of a rectangle is 150 square meters, and its perimeter is equal to 70 meters. What is the width of the rectangle?
    a. 10 meters
    b. 30 meters
    c. 70 meters
    d. 12 meters

4. How many integers between 1 and 40 meet both of the conditions below?
    I. The integer is prime.
    II. The integer is odd.
    a. 14
    b. 12
    c. 10
    d. 11

5. In Jim's school, there are a total of 650 boys and girls. There are 3 girls for every 2 boys. How many students are girls?
    a. 260
    b. 130
    c. 65
    d. 390

See answers on the next page.

Answer Explanations

1. A: The first person's rate of time for folding 5 loads of laundry is $\frac{1}{30}$, and the second person's rate is $\frac{1}{x}$, where x is the unknown time. Therefore, $\frac{1}{30}(20) + \frac{1}{x}(20) = 1$. This simplifies to $\frac{2}{3} + \frac{20}{x} = 1$. Multiply both sides by $3x$ to obtain $2x + 60 = 3x$. Solving for x results in $x = 60$. The second person takes 60 minutes to fold 5 loads of laundry.

2. C: The line $y = -5$ is horizontal. Even if it is reflected across the x-axis, it remains a horizontal line. Therefore, it has a slope of 0, and any vertical line is perpendicular to it. The line $x = 5$ is vertical, so it is perpendicular to it.

3. B: Area is equal to length times width. Therefore, $150 = L \times W$. Perimeter is equal to $2L + 2W$. Therefore, $70 = 2L + 2W$. We can solve the area equation for L as $L = \frac{150}{W}$. Plug this into the perimeter equation to obtain $70 = 2\left(\frac{150}{W}\right) + 2W$. Multiply both sides by W to obtain $70W = 300 + 2W^2$, which can be rewritten as $2W^2 - 70W + 300 = 0$. Dividing by 2 results in $W^2 - 35W + 150 = (W - 30)(W - 5) = 0$. This equation has two solutions: 5 and 30. The option given is a width of 30 meters.

4. D: The integers between 1 and 40 that are both odd and prime are 3, 5, 7, 11, 13, 17, 19, 23, 29, 31, and 37. Therefore, there are 11 of them.

5. D: Three girls for every two boys can be expressed as a ratio: 3 : 2. This can be visualized as splitting the school into 5 groups: 3 girl groups and 2 boy groups. The number of students that are in each group can be found by dividing the total number of students by 5:

$$\frac{650 \text{ students}}{5 \text{ groups}} = \frac{130 \text{ students}}{\text{group}}$$

To find the total number of girls, multiply the number of students per group (130) by the number of girl groups in the school (3). This equals 390, Choice D.

Practice Test #1

Verbal Reasoning

Passage: Literature

This passage is adapted from a translation of Homer's The Hymn to Demeter, *created in the late sixth or early seventh century BC.*

[1] I begin to sing of rich-haired Demeter, awful goddess—of her and her trim-ankled daughter whom Aidoneus rapt away, given to him by all-seeing Zeus the loud-thunderer.

[2] Apart from Demeter, lady of the golden sword and glorious fruits, she was playing with the deep-bosomed daughters of Oceanus and gathering flowers over a soft meadow, roses and crocuses and beautiful violets, irises also and hyacinths and the narcissus, which Earth made to grow at the will of Zeus and to please the Host of Many, to be a snare for the bloom-like girl—a marvelous, radiant flower. It was a thing of awe whether for deathless gods or mortal men to see: from its root grew a hundred blooms, and it smelled most sweetly, so that all wide heaven above and the whole earth and the sea's salt swell laughed for joy. And the girl was amazed and reached out with both hands to take the lovely toy; but the wide-pathed earth yawned there in the plain of Nysa, and the lord, Host of Many, with his immortal horses sprang out upon her—the Son of Cronos, He who has many names.

[3] He caught her up reluctant on his golden car and bare her away lamenting. Then she cried out shrilly with her voice, calling upon her father, the Son of Cronos, who is most high and excellent. But no one, either of the deathless gods or of mortal men, heard her voice, nor yet the olive-trees bearing rich fruit: only tender-hearted Hecate, bright-coiffed, the daughter of Persaeus, heard the girl from her cave, and the lord Helios, Hyperion's bright son, as she cried to her father, the Son of Cronos. But he was sitting aloof, apart from the gods, in his temple where many pray, and receiving sweet offerings from mortal men. So he, that Son of Cronos, of many names, who is Ruler of Many and Host of Many, was bearing her away by leave of Zeus on his immortal chariot—his own brother's child and all unwilling.

[4] And so long as she, the goddess, yet beheld earth and starry heaven and the strong-flowing sea where fishes shoal, and the rays of the sun, and still hoped to see her dear mother and the tribes of the eternal gods, so long hope calmed her great heart for all her trouble....and the heights of the mountains and the depths of the sea rang with her immortal voice: and her queenly mother heard her.

[5] Bitter pain seized her heart, and she rent the covering upon her divine hair with her dear hands: her dark cloak she cast down from both her shoulders and sped, like a wild-bird, over the firm land and yielding sea, seeking her child. But no one would tell her the truth, neither god nor mortal men; and of the birds of omen none came with true news for her. Then for nine days queenly Deo wandered over the earth with flaming torches in her hands, so grieved that she never tasted ambrosia and the sweet draught of

nectar, nor sprinkled her body with water. But when the tenth enlightening dawn had come, Hecate, with a torch in her hands, met her, and spoke to her and told her news:

[6] 'Queenly Demeter, bringer of seasons and giver of good gifts, what god of heaven or what mortal man has rapt away Persephone and pierced with sorrow your dear heart? For I heard her voice, yet saw not with my eyes who it was. But I tell you truly and shortly all I know.'

[7] So, then, said Hecate. And the daughter of rich-haired Rhea answered her not, but sped swiftly with her, holding flaming torches in her hands. So they came to Helios, who is watchman of both gods and men, and stood in front of his horses: and the bright goddess enquired of him: 'Helios, do you at least regard me, goddess as I am, if ever by word or deed of mine I have cheered your heart and spirit. Through the fruitless air I heard the thrilling cry of my daughter whom I bare, sweet scion of my body and lovely in form, as of one seized violently; though with my eyes I saw nothing. But you—for with your beams you look down from the bright upper air Over all the earth and sea—tell me truly of my dear child, if you have seen her anywhere, what god or mortal man has violently seized her against her will and mine, and so made off.'

[8] So said she. And the Son of Hyperion answered her: 'Queen Demeter, daughter of rich-haired Rhea, I will tell you the truth; for I greatly reverence and pity you in your grief for your trim-ankled daughter. None other of the deathless gods is to blame, but only cloud-gathering Zeus who gave her to Hades, her father's brother, to be called his buxom wife. And Hades seized her and took her loudly crying in his chariot down to his realm of mist and gloom. Yet, goddess, cease your loud lament and keep not vain anger unrelentingly: Aidoneus, the Ruler of Many, is no unfitting husband among the deathless gods for your child, being your own brother and born of the same stock: also, for honor, he has that third share which he received when division was made at the first, and is appointed lord of those among whom he dwells.'

1. The passage makes clear that Helios views Hades as
    a. A merciless kidnapper
    b. A fine husband for Persephone
    c. A good brother to Demeter
    d. Unfitting among the deathless gods

2. This passage is primarily
    a. A lament
    b. A warning
    c. A narrative
    d. Descriptive

3. What is the purpose of referring to Demeter as "awful goddess" in Paragraph 1, Sentence 1?
    a. To establish her as a figure inspiring reverence
    b. To establish her as fearsome and frightening
    c. To condemn her as an overprotective parent
    d. To indicate that she is the true villain of this story

4. Which of these sentences in the passage provides the best support for the idea that Hades was not a lone actor in his kidnapping of Persephone?
   a. Paragraph 2, Sentence 3 ("And the girl...many names.")
   b. Paragraph 4, Sentence 1 ("And so long...heard her.")
   c. Paragraph 8, Sentence 5 ("Yet, goddess...dwells.")
   d. Paragraph 3, Sentence 5 ("So he...unwilling.")

5. Based on the passage, Demeter will most likely
   a. Be met with great opposition in her attempt to get her daughter back
   b. Have Hades punished by Zeus for what he has done
   c. Eventually give up on her search
   d. Convince Helios that he is wrong to call Hades a fitting husband for Persephone

6. What purpose does the description of Persephone's unwillingness in Paragraph 3 serve?
   a. It undermines the idea that Persephone went with Hades willingly, as Helios later claims.
   b. It gives the reader perspective on the facts of the situation so that Demeter's grief and worry can be given proper weight as the passage continues.
   c. It prevents the reader from mistaking the passage for a story about Demeter's search for her daughter.
   d. It gives the reader a reason to side with Helios later.

7. The word *bare* in Paragraph 7, Sentence 4 most closely means
   a. Naked
   b. Revealed
   c. Saw
   d. Gave birth to

8. Which paragraph contains the best evidence to support the idea that the rest of the deathless gods will not be as sympathetic to Demeter's plight as Hecate has been?
   a. Paragraph 3
   b. Paragraph 4
   c. Paragraph 8
   d. Paragraph 6

9. Hyperion : Helios ::
   a. Demeter : Rhea
   b. Demeter : Persephone
   c. Hecate : Demeter
   d. Hyperion : Demeter

10. Persephone : willing ::
    a. Hecate : unhelpful
    b. Helios : wise
    c. Hades : rash
    d. Cronos : fatherly

Passage: Science

This passage is adapted from Charles Darwin's On the Origin of Species, *published in 1859.*

[1] Whether natural selection has really thus acted in nature, in modifying and adapting the various forms of life to their several conditions and stations, must be judged of by the general tenor and balance of evidence given in the following chapters. But we already see how it entails extinction; and how largely extinction has acted in the world's history, geology plainly declares. Natural selection, also, leads to divergence of character; for more living beings can be supported on the same area the more they diverge in structure, habits, and constitution, of which we see proof by looking at the inhabitants of any small spot or at naturalized productions. Therefore during the modification of the descendants of any one species, and during the incessant struggle of all species to increase in numbers, the more diversified these descendants become, the better will be their chance of succeeding in the battle of life. Thus the small differences distinguishing varieties of the same species, will steadily tend to increase till they come to equal the greater differences between species of the same genus, or even of distinct genera.

[2] The affinities of all the beings of the same class have sometimes been represented by a great tree. I believe this simile largely speaks the truth. The green and budding twigs may represent existing species; and those produced during each former year may represent the long succession of extinct species. At each period of growth all the growing twigs have tried to branch out on all sides, and to overtop and kill the surrounding twigs and branches, in the same manner as species and groups of species have tried to overmaster other species in the great battle for life. The limbs divided into great branches, and these into lesser and lesser branches, were themselves once, when the tree was small, budding twigs; and this connection of the former and present buds by ramifying branches may well represent the classification of all extinct and living species in groups subordinate to groups. Of the many twigs which flourished when the tree was a mere bush, only two or three, now grown into great branches, yet survive and bear all the other branches; so with the species which lived during long-past geological periods, very few now have living and modified descendants. From the first growth of the tree, many a limb and branch has decayed and dropped off; and these lost branches of various sizes may represent those whole orders, families, and genera which have now no living representatives, and which are known to us only from having been found in a fossil state. As we here and there see a thin straggling branch springing from a fork low down in a tree, and which by some chance has been favored and is still alive on its summit, so we occasionally see an animal like the Ornithorhynchus or Lepidosiren, which in some small degree connects by its affinities two large branches of life, and which has apparently been saved from fatal competition by having inhabited a protected station. As buds give rise by growth to fresh buds, and these, if vigorous, branch out and overtop on all sides many a feebler branch, so by generation I believe it has been with the great Tree of Life, which fills with its dead and broken branches the crust of the earth, and covers the surface with its ever branching and beautiful ramifications.

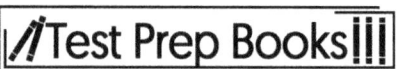

Diagram visual of the "Tree of Life" idea proposed by Charles Darwin:

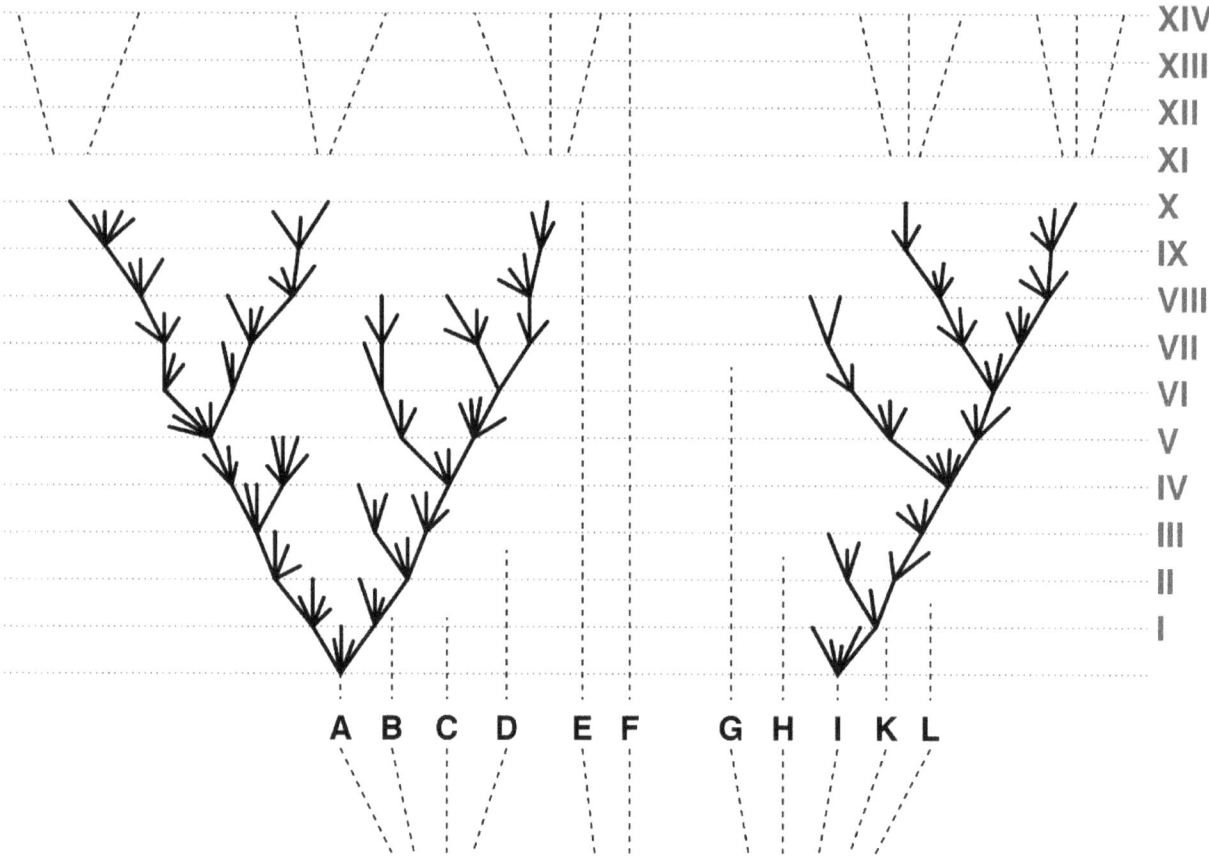

11. What is the main focus of this passage?
    a. The process of natural selection and its effects
    b. The evolutionary struggles of various animals
    c. The complex root systems of trees
    d. The communication signals between different species

12. What does the author argue that natural selection means for living beings?
    a. Habitat destruction
    b. Diversity of descendants
    c. Geological disaster
    d. Fatal genetic modifications

13. What does the passage suggest connects the classification of species with the Tree of Life?
    a. Struggle for survival
    b. Threat of extinction
    c. Divergence of character
    d. Ability for mutation

14. Why does the author mention Ornithorhynchus and Lepidosiren?
    a. To demonstrate the connection between different branches
    b. To give examples of species that have gone extinct
    c. To show the effect of the "decaying branch"
    d. To highlight adaptation based on geographical location

15. Based on the passage, what inference can be made about the impact of divergence on the possibility for survival of a species?
    a. Divergence has no impact on the chance of survival.
    b. Divergence decreases the chance of survival.
    c. Divergence increases the chance of survival.
    d. Divergence eventually leads to ultimate extinction.

16. In Paragraph 1, Sentence 4, the word *incessant* most nearly means
    a. Unusual
    b. Expeditious
    c. Sporadic
    d. Ceaseless

17. How does the purpose of the second paragraph differ from that of the first?
    a. The first paragraph introduces the struggle for survival, while the second paragraph explains the importance of dominant traits.
    b. The first paragraph focuses on natural selection, while the second paragraph focuses on the Tree of Life as a metaphor for the evolutionary process.
    c. The first paragraph focuses on the theory of evolution, while the second paragraph lays out the threat of extinction.
    d. The first paragraph focuses on natural selection, while the second paragraph focuses on specific examples of species affected by natural selection.

18. What does the author mean by "ramifying branches" in Paragraph 2, Sentence 4?
    a. The phrase refers to the branches increasing in complexity and representing various species.
    b. The phrase refers to dying branches that represent extinct species.
    c. The phrase refers to the branches with budding twigs that represent new evolutionary traits.
    d. The phrase refers to the variation in branch size, which represents the strength of a species.

19. Natural selection : divergence in character ::
    a. Analog : digital
    b. Bank : loans
    c. Trees : deforestation
    d. Studying : good grades

20. Twig : branch ::
    a. Deed : house
    b. Foal : steed
    c. Week : month
    d. Water : hydration

Passage: Philosophy/Religion

This passage is adapted from René Descartes' Discourse on the Method of Rightly Conducting One's Reason and of Seeking Truth in the Sciences, *published in 1637.*

[1] Good sense is, of all things among men, the most equally distributed; for every one thinks himself so abundantly provided with it, that those even who are the most difficult to satisfy in everything else, do not usually desire a larger measure of this quality than they already possess. And in this it is not likely that all are mistaken the conviction is rather to be held as testifying that the power of judging aright and of distinguishing truth from error, which is properly what is called good sense or reason, is by nature equal in all men; and that the diversity of our opinions, consequently, does not arise from some being endowed with a larger share of reason than others, but solely from this, that we conduct our thoughts along different ways, and do not fix our attention on the same objects. For to be possessed of a vigorous mind is not enough; the prime requisite is rightly to apply it. The greatest minds, as they are capable of the highest excellences, are open likewise to the greatest aberrations; and those who travel very slowly may yet make far greater progress, provided they keep always to the straight road, than those who, while they run, forsake it.

[2] For myself, I have never fancied my mind to be in any respect more perfect than those of the generality; on the contrary, I have often wished that I were equal to some others in promptitude of thought, or in clearness and distinctness of imagination, or in fullness and readiness of memory. And besides these, I know of no other qualities that contribute to the perfection of the mind; for as to the reason or sense, inasmuch as it is that alone which constitutes us men, and distinguishes us from the brutes, I am disposed to believe that it is to be found complete in each individual; and on this point to adopt the common opinion of philosophers, who say that the difference of greater and less holds only among the accidents, and not among the forms or natures of individuals of the same species.

[3] I will not hesitate, however, to avow my belief that it has been my singular good fortune to have very early in life fallen in with certain tracks which have conducted me to considerations and maxims, of which I have formed a method that gives me the means, as I think, of gradually augmenting my knowledge, and of raising it by little and little to the highest point which the mediocrity of my talents and the brief duration of my life will permit me to reach. For I have already reaped from it such fruits that, although I have been accustomed to think lowly enough of myself, and although when I look with the eye of a philosopher at the varied courses and pursuits of mankind at large, I find scarcely one which does not appear in vain and useless, I nevertheless derive the highest satisfaction from the progress I conceive myself to have already made in the search after truth, and cannot help entertaining such expectations of the future as to believe that if, among the occupations of men as men, there is any one really excellent and important, it is that which I have chosen.

[4] After all, it is possible I may be mistaken; and it is but a little copper and glass, perhaps, that I take for gold and diamonds. I know how very liable we are to delusion in what relates to ourselves, and also how much the judgments of our friends are to be suspected when given in our favor. But I shall endeavor in this discourse to describe the

paths I have followed, and to delineate my life as in a picture, in order that each one may also be able to judge of them for himself, and that in the general opinion entertained of them, as gathered from current report, I myself may have a new help towards instruction to be added to those I have been in the habit of employing.

21. What is the main purpose of this passage?
   a. The author is reflecting on the equality of human reason and shares some considerations regarding his own journey.
   b. The author is asserting that good sense is not afforded to all humans and states that he is on a path towards improving his reasoning abilities.
   c. The author is attempting to persuade readers to question their abilities to use good sense and emphasizes that he is an authority on the subject.
   d. The author claims that humanity does not need philosophers as every human is capable of making their own fair judgements about life.

22. In which line of the passage does the author acknowledge that he may be incorrect in his beliefs?
   a. Paragraph 1, Sentence 4 ("The greatest minds... forsake it.")
   b. Paragraph 2, Sentence 1 ("For myself... readiness of memory.")
   c. Paragraph 3, Sentence 2 ("For I have... which I have chosen.")
   d. Paragraph 4, Sentence 1 ("After all... gold and diamonds.")

23. Which of the following is an inference that can be made from the text?
   a. The author often makes mistakes and is cautious with his beliefs because of that.
   b. Those who act unreasonably do not lack reason, only the desire to use it.
   c. Those gifted with sense have an obligation to lead others, namely through philosophy.
   d. The author believes he is better than those who do not pursue the truth as he has.

24. Which line from the text provides the best evidence for why the author believes this subject is important to discuss?
   a. Paragraph 1, Sentence 3 ("For to be possessed...rightly to apply it.")
   b. Paragraph 2, Sentence 2 ("And besides these... the same species.")
   c. Paragraph 3, Sentence 1 ("I will not hesitate... life will permit me to reach.")
   d. Paragraph 4, Sentence 2 ("But I shall... habit of employing.")

25. What common theme do Paragraph 2 and Paragraph 3 share?
   a. They both discuss the pros and cons of having natural good sense.
   b. They both question the popular opinions of philosophers of the time.
   c. They both encourage the reader to utilize the good sense they have been given and to gain more knowledge.
   d. They both focus on the author's thoughts and experiences regarding his own good sense and pursuit of the truth.

26. What does the author believe regarding differing opinions among humans?
   a. Opinions come from variations in thinking processes.
   b. Opinions are irrelevant when facts are presented.
   c. Opinions are a form of self-expression and should be celebrated.
   d. Opinions are shaped by our childhood experiences.

27. What inference can be made from Paragraph 3?
    a. The author believes he has an endless capacity for knowledge.
    b. The author looks down upon people who do not attempt to educate themselves in all that life has to offer.
    c. The author values the conviction to strengthen one's mind as opposed to relying on our inherent abilities that are received at birth.
    d. The author is content with all he has learned and does not wish to make any further pursuits.

28. What type of evidence is the following sentence?

    "The greatest minds, as they are capable of the highest excellences, are open likewise to the greatest aberrations; and those who travel very slowly may yet make far greater progress, provided they keep always to the straight road, than those who, while they run, forsake it."

    a. Empirical
    b. Anecdotal
    c. Illustrative
    d. Circumstantial

29. Humans : good sense ::
    a. Economy : communism
    b. Science : chemistry
    c. Birds : feathers
    d. President : citizens

30. Glass : diamonds ::
    a. Plastic : platinum
    b. Cotton : fleece
    c. Pebble : boulder
    d. Tiger : bear

Passage: Historical/Founding Documents

Passage A

This passage is adapted from Aristotle's Politics (A Treatise on Government), *created in the fourth century BC.*

> [1] But whether any person is such by nature, and whether it is advantageous and just for any one to be a slave or no, or whether all slavery is contrary to nature, shall be considered hereafter; not that it is difficult to determine it upon general principles, or to understand it from matters of fact; for that some should govern, and others be governed, is not only necessary but useful, and from the hour of their birth some are marked out for those purposes, and others for the other, and there are many species of both sorts. And the better those are who are governed the better also is the government, as for instance of man, rather than the brute creation: for the more excellent the materials are with which the work is finished, the more excellent certainly is the work; and wherever there is a governor and a governed, there certainly is some work produced; for whatsoever is composed of many parts, which jointly become one, whether conjunct or separate, evidently show the marks of governing and governed;

and this is true of every living thing in all nature; nay, even in some things which partake not of life, as in music; but this probably would be a disquisition too foreign to our present purpose. Every living thing in the first place is composed of soul and body, of these the one is by nature the governor, the other the governed; now if we would know what is natural, we ought to search for it in those subjects in which nature appears most perfect, and not in those which are corrupted; we should therefore examine into a man who is most perfectly formed both in soul and body, in whom this is evident, for in the depraved and vicious the body seems to rule rather than the soul, on account of their being corrupt and contrary to nature.

Passage B
This passage is adapted from James Madison's "Federalist No. 10," published in 1787, from The Federalist Papers *by Alexander Hamilton, John Jay, and James Madison.*

[1] Liberty is to faction what air is to fire, an aliment without which it instantly expires. But it could not be less folly to abolish liberty, which is essential to political life, because it nourishes faction, than it would be to wish the annihilation of air, which is essential to animal life, because it imparts to fire its destructive agency.

[2] As long as the reason of man continues fallible, and he is at liberty to exercise it, different opinions will be formed. As long as the connection subsists between his reason and his self-love, his opinions and his passions will have a reciprocal influence on each other; and the former will be objects to which the latter will attach themselves. The diversity in the faculties of men, from which the rights of property originate, is not less an insuperable obstacle to a uniformity of interests. The protection of these faculties is the first object of government. From the protection of different and unequal faculties of acquiring property, the possession of different degrees and kinds of property immediately results; and from the influence of these on the sentiments and views of the respective proprietors, ensues a division of the society into different interests and parties.

[3] The latent causes of faction are thus sown in the nature of man; and we see them everywhere brought into different degrees of activity, according to the different circumstances of civil society. A zeal for different opinions concerning religion, concerning government, and many other points, as well of speculation as of practice; an attachment to different leaders ambitiously contending for pre-eminence and power; or to persons of other descriptions whose fortunes have been interesting to the human passions, have, in turn, divided mankind into parties, inflamed them with mutual animosity, and rendered them much more disposed to vex and oppress each other than to co-operate for their common good. The regulation of these various and interfering interests forms the principal task of modern legislation, and involves the spirit of party and faction in the necessary and ordinary operations of the government.

31. Exploration of what theme is shared between these two passages?
    a. The nature of governance
    b. Foreign invasion
    c. Corruption
    d. Political factions

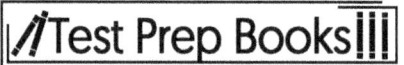

32. How do the authors address the concept of liberty and politics?
    a. Passage A focuses on how some individuals are inherently meant for slavery, while Passage B argues that liberty should be suppressed to avoid factions in society.
    b. Passage A claims that humans should be tested on their leadership capabilities before entering politics, while Passage B states that factions ruin the possibility of liberty within a society.
    c. Passage A focuses on the roles of individuals to fulfill their liberty, while Passage B emphasizes that liberty leads to the creation of factions.
    d. Passage A states that liberty is contained within the soul of mankind, while Passage B argues that liberty comes from the ego of mankind.

33. What does Aristotle suggest about corruption and human nature?
    a. Corruption is inevitable, and there is no real way to prevent it.
    b. Corruption is temporary and changes as democracy runs its course.
    c. Corruption can only be overcome through societal upheaval and political protest.
    d. Corruption is a result of societal structures and can be prevented by picking good leaders.

34. How does Madison support his argument about factions within society?
    a. By explaining how factionalism comes from diversity in opinions and interests
    b. By giving examples of societies that have experienced factionalism
    c. By providing an emotional appeal to the importance of human passion
    d. By comparing different forms of government and how they address factions

35. What does Aristotle believe regarding the soul and body?
    a. Those who are perfectly formed in soul and body are best suited to govern.
    b. The soul and body are irrelevant to human governance.
    c. The soul and body cannot be tainted with corruption in those who govern.
    d. The body is often taken over by passion and depravity whereas the mind is not.

36. Which quote from the Aristotle passage best describes his thoughts on natural order in society?
    a. "...for whatsoever is composed of many parts, which jointly become one, whether conjunct or separate, evidently show the marks of governing and governed..."
    b. "...we ought to search for it in those subjects in which nature appears most perfect..."
    c. "...for that some should govern, and others be governed, is not only necessary but useful, and from the hour of their birth some are marked out for those purposes, and others for the other..."
    d. "...for in the depraved and vicious the body seems to rule rather than the soul, on account of their being corrupt and contrary to nature."

37. In what way do these two passages differ from one another?
    a. Passage A focuses on slavery, while Passage B focuses on liberty in democracy.
    b. Passage A focuses on individual roles, while Passage B focuses on how people are grouped together into factions.
    c. Passage A focuses on the corruption of government, while Passage B focuses on human nature.
    d. Passage A focuses on the inevitable failures within a political system, while Passage B focuses on the danger of civil unrest.

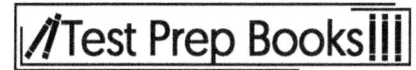

38. In Passage B, Paragraph 2, Sentence 3, the word *insuperable* most nearly means
    a. Achievable
    b. Unexpected
    c. Difficult
    d. Unconquerable

39. Diverse opinions : factions ::
    a. Labor : taxation
    b. Legislation : laws
    c. Spark : fire
    d. Diplomat : peacekeeper

40. Government : corruption ::
    a. Crops : disease
    b. School : principal
    c. Life : afterlife
    d. Exercise : health

Grammar and Writing

Passage One: Philosophy/Religion

This passage is adapted from G. K. Chesterton's Eugenics and Other Evils, *published in 1922.*

It is not really difficult to sum up the essence of Eugenics: though some of the Eugenists seem to be rather vague about it. The movement consists of [41] two parts; a moral basis, which is common to all, and a scheme of social application which varies a good deal. For the moral basis, it is obvious that man's ethical responsibility varies with his knowledge of consequences. If I were in charge of a baby (like Dr. Johnson in that tower of vision), and if the baby was ill through having eaten the soap, I might possibly send for a doctor. I might be calling him away from much more serious cases, from the bedsides of babies whose diet had been far more deadly; but I should be justified. I could not be expected to know enough about his other patients to be obliged (or even entitled) [42] to sacrificed to them the baby for whom I was primarily and directly responsible. Now the Eugenic moral basis is this; that the baby for whom we are primarily and directly responsible is the babe unborn. [43] That is, that we know (or may come to know) enough of certain inevitable tendencies in biology to consider the fruit of some contemplated union in that direct and clear light of conscience which we can now only fix on the other partner in that union. The one duty can conceivably be as definite as or more definite than the other. The baby that does not exist can be considered even before the wife who does. Now it is essential to grasp that this is a comparatively new note in morality. [44] Of course sane people always thought the aim of marriage was the procreation of children to the glory of God or according to the plan of Nature; but whether they counted such children as God's reward for service or Nature's premium on sanity, they always left the reward to God or the premium to Nature, as a less definable thing. The only person (and this is the point) towards [45] whom one could have precise duties was the partner in the process. Directly considering the partner's claims was the nearest one could get to indirectly considering the claims of posterity. [46] If the women

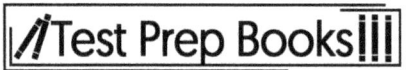

of the harem sang praises of the hero as the Moslem mounted his horse, it was because this was the due of a man; if the Christian knight helped his wife off her horse, it was because this was the due of a woman. Definite and detailed dues of this kind they did not predicate of the babe unborn; regarding him in that agnostic and opportunist light in which Mr. Browdie regarded the hypothetical child of Miss Squeers. Thinking these sex relations healthy, they naturally hoped they would produce [47] strong investments; but that was all. The Moslem woman doubtless expected Allah to send beautiful sons to an obedient wife; but she would not have allowed any direct vision of such sons to alter the obedience itself. She would not [48] have said "I will now be a disobedient wife; as the learned leech informs me that great prophets are often the children of disobedient wives." The knight doubtless hoped that the saints would help him to strong children, if he did all the duties of his station, one of which might be helping his wife off her horse; but he would not have refrained from doing this because he had read in a book that a course of falling off horses often resulted in the birth of a genius. Both Moslem and Christian would have thought such speculations not only [49] imminent but utterly unpractical. I quite agree with [50] them; but that is not the point here.

41. two parts; a moral basis,
    a. NO CHANGE
    b. two parts: a moral basis,
    c. two parts—a moral basis,
    d. two parts… a moral basis,

42. to sacrificed
    a. NO CHANGE
    b. to be sacrificial
    c. sacrificing
    d. to sacrifice

43. Which of the following choices represents the clearest and most concise way to convey all the information in the sentence?

    That is, that we know (or may come to know) enough of certain inevitable tendencies in biology to consider the fruit of some contemplated union in that direct and clear light of conscience which we can now only fix on the other partner in that union.

    a. NO CHANGE
    b. We know (or may come to know) enough of certain inevitable tendencies in biology to consider the fruit of relationships, primarily by focusing on both partners within the union.
    c. We know (or may come to know) enough of certain inevitable tendencies in biology to consider potential outcomes of relationships; however, we primarily focus on one partner within the union.
    d. We understand the inevitable outcomes of contemplated unions, especially for one partner within the union.

Practice Test #1

44. Which of the following choices represents the clearest and most concise way to convey all the information in the sentence?

> Of course sane people always thought the aim of marriage was the procreation of children to the glory of God or according to the plan of Nature; but whether they counted such children as God's reward for service or Nature's premium on sanity, they always left the reward to God or the premium to Nature, as a less definable thing.

a. NO CHANGE
b. Sane people always believed that procreation was to the glory of God, while others believed it was Nature's plan; these opinions were well-defined and represented humanity's differences.
c. Some people believed that the procreation of children was for the glory of God, while those who were misled believed that it was simply a part of the plan of Nature. Their beliefs were a less definable thing.
d. Sane people always believed the aim of marriage was having children to the glory of God or according to Nature's plan; however, the reward to God or premium to nature was less definable.

45. whom
a. NO CHANGE
b. whose
c. which
d. them

46. What is the purpose of having two independent clauses in this sentence?

> If the women of the harem sang praises of the hero as the Moslem mounted his horse, it was because this was the due of a man; if the Christian knight helped his wife off her horse, it was because this was the due of a woman.

a. To provide an argument for why women are more likely to be concerned about posterity than men
b. To explain that the women of the harem sang praises of the hero due to the Christian knight helping his wife
c. To compare the motivation behind the actions of the harem women and the Christian knight
d. To show that the women within the harem are not as morally concerned as the Christian knight

47. Which of the examples fits best in the paragraph?

> Thinking these sex relations healthy, they naturally hoped they would produce [7] strong investments; but that was all.

a. NO CHANGE
b. male heirs
c. healthy children
d. efficient laborers

169

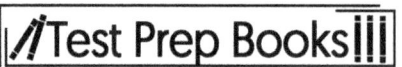

48. have said "I will
    a. NO CHANGE
    b. have said, "I will
    c. have said… "I will
    d. have said, 'I will

49. imminent
    a. NO CHANGE
    b. idealistic
    c. illustrious
    d. impious

50. them; but
    a. NO CHANGE
    b. them but
    c. them, but
    d. them. But

Passage Two: Historical

Edgar Allan Poe was a revolutionary author [51] that is considered a major figure in world literature. He is best known for his unique macabre writing style in the short story genre, as well as his invention of the detective genre. He was an American writing pioneer and left a lasting mark on literature from the 19th century and beyond. Born on [52] January 19 1809, in Boston, Massachusetts, Poe had a life fraught with tragedy and personal struggle. However, a grand literary talent emerged [53] despite the unfortunate events of his childhood.

Poe's father abandoned the family early on. His mother, a well-known actress, succumbed to tuberculosis when Poe was only two years old. He was then taken in by John Allan, a wealthy tobacco merchant, but their relationship was strained. Poe received a strong education because of Allan. However, the two often fought terribly, and this made for a [54] taciturn upbringing. Poe's childhood left a lasting impact on his later work, which often explored themes of loss, death, and the macabre.

In 1827, Poe published his first collection of poetry, *Tamerlane and Other Poems*. It unfortunately went largely unnoticed. After the failure, Poe enlisted in the United States Army under the pseudonym Edgar A. Perry, but this journey was short-lived. He sought admission to West Point but was dismissed. Luckily, he had already set his sights on a literary career.

The turning point in Poe's literary career came in 1833 with the publication of his short story "MS. Found in a Bottle," which won a literary contest and earned him recognition in the writing world. This was the beginning of Poe's mastery of the short story format, where he would go on to write some of his most famous works.

Poe's legacy lies in his contributions to the short story and his mastery of Gothic themes. "The Fall of the House of Usher," "The Tell-Tale Heart," and "The Black Cat" [55] is just a few of his most celebrated works. These stories showcase Poe's ability to make the reader feel an intense sense of dread. He often picks apart the darkest recesses of the human psyche. He is also credited with the creation of the detective fiction genre, which was initially seen in the form of the [56] character, C. Auguste Dupin, who predates Sherlock Holmes and other iconic fictional detectives.

"The Raven," arguably Poe's most famous poem, was published in 1845 and brought him recognition beyond just the literary world. Its melancholic tone and repetitive use of the word *nevermore* contributed to its impressive popularity.

His new fame and success aside, Poe's personal life continued to be marred by tragedy. In 1847, his wife, Virginia, succumbed to tuberculosis. [57] This unfortunate turn of events plunged Poe into a profound depression. Poe's final years [58] included: financial woes, alcoholism, and severely erratic behavior. Undoubtedly, these were caused or made worse by his mental health struggles.

Poe's death on October 7, 1849, remains a mystery that the public can only speculate on. He was found delirious on the streets of Baltimore and died mere days later in a hospital. There are numerous theories regarding the cause of death, including suggestions of alcohol poisoning or even rabies. None of Poe's medical records survive, including his death certificate. Thus, the true cause of Poe's death will remain uncertain, an appropriately haunting ending for a troubled soul.

Poe's impact on American literature only grew after his death. His exploration of the macabre influenced subsequent generations of writers, such as H. P. Lovecraft. [59] Poe's morbid writing and fascination with the [60] darkest parts of the human mind have made him a cultural icon. His works have been turned into movies and TV shows for a more modern audience.

51. that
    a. NO CHANGE
    b. whom
    c. who
    d. he

52. January 19 1809, in Boston, Massachusetts,
    a. NO CHANGE
    b. January 19, 1809, in Boston Massachusetts,
    c. January 19, 1809 in Boston, Massachusetts
    d. January 19, 1809, in Boston, Massachusetts,

53. Which of the examples fits best in the paragraph?

    However, a grand literary talent emerged despite the unfortunate events of his childhood.

    a. NO CHANGE
    b. despite the lack of popularity for macabre writing.
    c. despite constant interruption by his fans and contemporaries.
    d. despite the harsh criticism from his peers.

54. taciturn
    a. NO CHANGE
    b. tedious
    c. turbulent
    d. tenuous

55. is just
    a. NO CHANGE
    b. be just
    c. are just
    d. were just

56. character, C. Auguste Dupin, who
    a. NO CHANGE
    b. character C. Auguste Dupin who
    c. character C. Auguste Dupin. Who
    d. character C. Auguste Dupin, who

57. What is the tone of the sentence?

    <u>This unfortunate turn of events plunged Poe into a profound depression.</u>

    a. Accusatory
    b. Cynical
    c. Somber
    d. Caustic

58. included:
    a. NO CHANGE
    b. included
    c. included,
    d. included…

59. What is the tone of this sentence?

    Poe's morbid writing and fascination with the darkest parts of the human mind have made him a cultural icon.

    a. Hopeful
    b. Critical
    c. Abhorring
    d. Laudatory

60. Which of the examples fits best in the paragraph?

Poe's morbid writing and fascination with the darkest parts of the human mind have made him a cultural icon.

a. NO CHANGE
b. indomitable spirit of humanity
c. miracles of scientific discovery
d. psychological effects of chronic illness

Passage Three: Science

This passage is adapted from Albert Einstein's Relativity: The Special and the General Theory, *first published in 1916.*

The surface of a marble table is spread out in front of me. I can get from any one point on this table to any other point by passing continuously from one point to a "neighboring" one, and repeating this process a (large) number of times, or, in other words, by going from point to point without executing "jumps." I am sure the reader will appreciate with sufficient clearness what I mean here by "neighboring" and by "jumps" (if he is not too [61] patriotic). We express this property of the surface by describing the latter as a continuum.

Let us now imagine that a large number of little rods of equal length have been made, [62] its lengths being small compared with the dimensions of the marble slab. When I say they are of equal length, I mean that one can be laid on any other without the ends overlapping. We next lay four of these little rods on the marble slab so that they constitute a quadrilateral figure (a square), the diagonals of which are equally long. To ensure the equality of the diagonals, we make use of a little testing-rod. To this square we add similar ones, each of which has one rod in common with the first. We proceed in like manner with each of these square until finally the whole marble slab is laid out with squares. The arrangement is such, that each side of a [63] square belong to two squares and each corner to four squares.

[64] It is a veritable wonder that we can carry out this business without getting into the greatest difficulties. We only need to think of the following. If at any moment three squares meet at a corner, then two sides of the fourth square are already laid, and, as a consequence, the arrangement of the remaining [65] three sides of the square is already completely determined. But I am now no longer able to adjust the quadrilateral so that its diagonals may be equal. If they are equal of their own accord, then this is an especial favor of the marble slab and of the little [66] rods; about which I can only be thankfully surprised. We must experience many such surprises if the [67] construction is to be successful.

If everything has really gone smoothly, then I say that the points of the marble slab constitute a Euclidean continuum with respect to the little rod, which has been used as a "distance" (line-interval). By choosing one corner of a square as "origin" I can characterize every other corner of a square with reference to this origin by means of two numbers. I only need state how many rods I must pass over when, starting from the

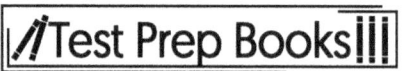

Practice Test #1

origin, I proceed towards the "right" and then "upwards," in order to arrive at the corner of the square under consideration. These two numbers are then the "Cartesian co-ordinates" of this corner with reference to the "Cartesian co-ordinate system" which is determined by the arrangement of little rods.

By making use of the following modification of this abstract experiment, we recognize that there must also be cases in which the experiment would be unsuccessful. We shall suppose that the rods "expand" by an amount proportional to the increase of temperature. We heat the central part of the marble slab, but not the periphery, in which case [68] two of my little rods can still be brought into coincidence at every position on the table. [69] But our construction of squares must necessarily come into disorder during the heating, because the little rods on the central region of the table expand, whereas those on the outer part do not.

With reference to our little rods—defined as unit lengths—the marble slab is no longer a Euclidean continuum, and we are also no longer in the position of defining Cartesian co-ordinates directly with their aid, since the above construction can no longer be carried out. But since there are other things which are not influenced in a similar manner to the little rods (or perhaps not at all) by the temperature of the table, it is possible quite naturally to maintain the point of view that the marble slab is a "Euclidean continuum." This can be done in a satisfactory [70] manner, by making a more subtle stipulation about the measurement or the comparison of lengths.

61. patriotic
    a. NO CHANGE
    b. penitent
    c. pedantic
    d. perfidious

62. its lengths
    a. NO CHANGE
    b. the lengths
    c. their lengths
    d. its length

63. square belong to
    a. NO CHANGE
    b. squares belong to
    c. squares belongs to
    d. square belongs to

64. What is the tone of this sentence?

    It is a veritable wonder that we can carry out this business without getting into the greatest difficulties.

    a. Sarcastic
    b. Cautionary
    c. Disappointed
    d. Appreciative

65. Which of the examples fits best in the sentence?

    If at any moment three squares meet at a corner, then two sides of the fourth square are already laid, and, as a consequence, the arrangement of the remaining three sides of the square is already completely determined.

    a. NO CHANGE
    b. two sides
    c. four sides
    d. one side

66. rods; about
    a. NO CHANGE
    b. rods about
    c. rods: about
    d. rods, about

67. What is the word *construction* in this sentence referring to?

    We must experience many such surprises if the construction is to be successful.

    a. The quadrilateral figure
    b. The marble slab
    c. The rods
    d. Both B and C

68. two of my little rods
    a. NO CHANGE
    b. two of their little rods
    c. two of our little rods
    d. two of his little rods

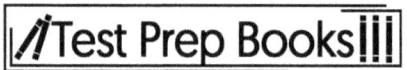

69. Which of the following choices represents the clearest and most concise way to convey all the information in the sentence?

> But our construction of squares must necessarily come into disorder during the heating, because the little rods on the central region of the table expand, whereas those on the outer part do not.

   a. NO CHANGE
   b. Our construction of squares comes into disorder during heating, because the central region rods expand, while those on the outer part do not.
   c. The construction of squares is disordered during the heating of the marble slab, as the rods in the central region of the table expand, and the rods on the outer part expand as well.
   d. Our construction of squares comes into order during the heating, because the central region rods expand, and the outer rods do not.

70. manner, by
   a. NO CHANGE
   b. manner: by
   c. manner by,
   d. manner by

Passage Four: Modern/Influential Thinker

This passage is adapted from Jimmy Carter's "A Crisis of Confidence" speech, given July 15, 1979.

> These ten days confirmed my belief in the decency and the strength and the wisdom of the American people, but it also bore out some of my long-standing concerns about our nation's underlying problems.
>
> [71] <u>I know, of course, being president</u>, that government actions and legislation can be very important. That's why I've worked hard to put my campaign promises into law—and I have to admit, with just mixed success. But after listening to the American people I have been reminded again that all the legislation in the world can't fix what's wrong with America. So, I want to speak to you first tonight about a subject even more serious than energy or inflation. I want to talk to you right now about a fundamental threat to American democracy.
>
> I do not mean our political and civil liberties. [72] <u>It</u> will endure. [73] <u>And I do not refer to the outward strength of America, a nation that is at peace tonight everywhere in the world, with unmatched economic power and military might.</u>
>
> The threat is nearly invisible in ordinary ways. It is a crisis of confidence. It is a crisis that strikes at the very heart and soul and spirit of our national will. We can see this crisis in the growing doubt about the meaning of our own lives and in the loss of a unity of purpose for our nation.
>
> The erosion of our confidence in the future is threatening to destroy the social and the political fabric of America.
>
> The confidence that we have always had as a people is not simply some romantic dream or a proverb in a dusty book that we read just on the Fourth of July.

It is the idea which founded our nation and has guided our development as a people. Confidence in the future has supported everything else—public institutions and private enterprise, our own families, and the very Constitution of the United States. Confidence has defined our course and has served as a link between [74] nations. We've always believed in something called progress. We've always had a faith that the days of our children would be better than our own.

Our people are losing that faith, not only in government itself but in the ability as citizens to serve as the ultimate rulers and shapers of our democracy. As a people we know our past and we are proud of it. Our progress has been part of the living history of America, even the world. [75] We always believed that we were part of a great movement of humanity itself called democracy, involved in the search for freedom, and that belief has always strengthened us in our purpose. But just as we are losing our confidence in the future, we are also beginning to close the door on our past.

In a nation that was proud of hard work, strong families, close-knit communities, and our faith in God, too many of us now tend to worship self-indulgence and consumption. Human identity is no longer defined by what one does, but by what one owns. But we've discovered that owning things and consuming things does not satisfy [76] my longing for meaning. We've learned that piling up material goods cannot fill the emptiness of lives which have [77] no confidence or purpose.

The symptoms of this crisis of the American spirit are all around us. For the first time in the history of our [78] country a majority of our people believe that the next five years will be worse than the past five years. Two-thirds of our people do not even vote. The productivity of American workers is actually dropping, and the willingness of Americans to save for the future has fallen below that of all other people in the Western world.

As you know, there is a growing disrespect for government and for churches and for schools, the news media, and other institutions. This is not a message of happiness or [79] relevance, but it is the truth and it is a warning.

These changes did not happen overnight. They've come upon us gradually over the last [80] generation; years that were filled with shocks and tragedy.

71. I know, of course, being president
    a. NO CHANGE
    b. I know, of course. Being president
    c. I know, of course; being president
    d. I know of course being president

72. It
    a. NO CHANGE
    b. They
    c. I
    d. We

73. Which of the following choices represents the clearest and most concise way to convey all the information in the sentence?

   And I do not refer to the outward strength of America, a nation that is at peace tonight everywhere in the world, with unmatched economic power and military might.

   a. NO CHANGE
   b. I am not referring to America's strength, since despite not being at peace tonight, we have unmatched economic power and military might.
   c. I am speaking of the strength of America, a nation that is at peace tonight, with economic power and military might.
   d. I am not referring to the strength of America, a nation that is at peace tonight, with unmatched economic and military power.

74. Which of the examples fits best in the paragraph?

   Confidence has defined our course and has served as a link between nations.

   a. NO CHANGE
   b. cultures
   c. generations
   d. species

75. Which of the following choices represents the clearest and most concise way to convey all the information in the sentence?

   We always believed that we were part of a great movement of humanity itself called democracy, involved in the search for freedom, and that belief has always strengthened us in our purpose.

   a. NO CHANGE
   b. We always believed that we were a democracy, searching for freedom, and that belief has strengthened our purpose.
   c. We always believed that we were democratic, involved in the search for freedom, but that belief has not strengthened our purpose.
   d. We have always believed that we are part of democracy, until recently, we have searched for freedom to give us purpose.

76. my longing
   a. NO CHANGE
   b. their longing
   c. the longing
   d. our longing

77. Which of the examples fits best in the paragraph?

We've learned that piling up material goods cannot fill the emptiness of lives which have no confidence or purpose.

   a. NO CHANGE
   b. no wealth or investments
   c. no progress or innovation
   d. no children or neighbors

78. country a majority
   a. NO CHANGE
   b. country, a majority
   c. country... a majority
   d. country; a majority

79. relevance
   a. NO CHANGE
   b. reassurance
   c. ramification
   d. reluctance

80. generation; years
   a. NO CHANGE
   b. generation: years
   c. generation, years
   d. generation. Years

Quantitative Reasoning

81. A college student views a number of isosceles triangles and makes the following statement:

   All isosceles triangles have a right angle.

Which of the following is a counterexample that disproves the above statement?
   a. A triangle with side lengths of 1 and a hypotenuse of $\sqrt{2}$
   b. A triangle with two equal angles of 45°
   c. An equilateral triangle
   d. A triangle with side lengths of 4 and a hypotenuse of $4\sqrt{2}$

82. An animal shelter had 5 cats for every dog. The total number of cats and dogs was 186. How many cats did it have?
   a. 62
   b. 130
   c. 155
   d. 31

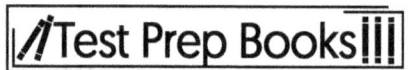

83. What is the solution to $4\frac{1}{3} + 3\frac{3}{4}$?
   a. $6\frac{5}{12}$
   b. $8\frac{1}{12}$
   c. $8\frac{2}{3}$
   d. $7\frac{7}{12}$

84. What would the equation be for the following problem?

   3 times the sum of a number and 7 is greater than or equal to 32

   a. $3(7n) > 32$
   b. $3 \times n + 7 \geq 32$
   c. $3n + 21 > 32$
   d. $3(n + 7) \geq 32$

85. What is the equation of a circle whose center is (1,5) and whole radius is 4?
   a. $(x-1)^2 + (y-25)^2 = 4$
   b. $(x-1)^2 + (y-25)^2 = 16$
   c. $(x+1)^2 + (y+5)^2 = 16$
   d. $(x-1)^2 + (y-5)^2 = 16$

86. What is the volume of a rectangular prism with a height of 3 cm, a width of 5 cm, and a depth of 11 cm?
   a. 19 cm^3
   b. 165 cm^3
   c. 225 cm^3
   d. 150 cm^3

87. If the sine of $30° = x$, the cosine of what angle, in degrees, also equals x?
   a. 30°
   b. 45°
   c. 60°
   d. 90°

88. Jake can mow 6 yards in 5 hours. Jackson can mow 8 yards in 5 hours. Working together, how many hours does it take to mow 4 yards? Round up to the nearest whole number.
   a. 1 hour
   b. 2 hours
   c. 3 hours
   d. 4 hours

Practice Test #1

89. All the children in an art class have at least one pet. Given this information, which of the following must be true?
   a. At least one child has a dog.
   b. All of the girls have a cat.
   c. All of the boys have a pet.
   d. None of the children have two pets.

90. What is the solution to $3\frac{2}{3} - 1\frac{4}{5}$?
   a. $1\frac{13}{15}$
   b. $\frac{14}{15}$
   c. $2\frac{2}{3}$
   d. $\frac{4}{5}$

91. What is the solution to the following system of equations?

$$x^2 - 2x + y = 8$$

$$x - y = -2$$

   a. $(-2, 3)$
   b. There is no solution.
   c. $(-2, 0)(1, 3)$
   d. $(-2, 0)(3, 5)$

92. What is the equation for the line passing through the origin and the point (2,1)?
   a. $y = 2x$
   b. $y = \frac{1}{2}x$
   c. $y = x - 2$
   d. $2y = x + 1$

93. Today, the price of a magazine is $5.29. In 2000, the price of the same magazine was $3.79. What is the percent change from 2000 to today? Round to the nearest tenth of a percent.
   a. 39.6%
   b. 29.7%
   c. 19.6%
   d. 15.0%

94. The second angle of a triangle is double the first. The third angle is 20 degrees less than the first. What is the measure of the first angle?
   a. 80°
   b. 20°
   c. 100°
   d. 50°

95. The length of arc $AB = 3\pi$ cm. The length of $\overline{OA} = 12$ cm. What is the degree measure of $\angle AOB$?

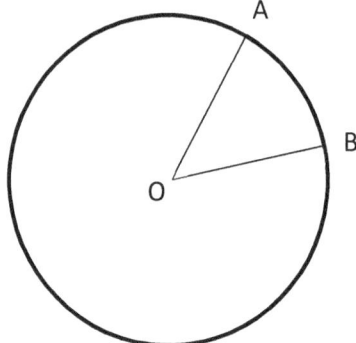

a. 30°
b. 40°
c. 45°
d. 55°

96. What is the next number in the following series: $1, 3, 6, 10, 15, 21, \ldots$?
a. 26
b. 27
c. 28
d. 29

97. Let x be an integer that is negative and odd. Then $2x$ must be:
a. Odd and positive
b. Even and negative
c. Odd and negative
d. Even and positive

98. A line goes through the points (2, 4) and (4, 10) in the (x, y)-coordinate plane. Which of the following is FALSE?
a. The slope of the line is positive.
b. The y-intercept is below the x-axis.
c. The y-intercept is above the x-axis.
d. The line goes through the point (3, 7).

99. A cord is cut into three pieces. The second piece is 6 times longer than the first, and the third piece is 8 times longer than the first. The length of the original cord is 210 feet. How long is the first piece of the cord?
a. 14 feet
b. 15 feet
c. 10 feet
d. 12 feet

Practice Test #1

100. If the volume of a sphere is 288π cubic meters, what are the radius and surface area of the same sphere?
    a. Radius: 6 meters, surface area: 144π square meters
    b. Radius: 36 meters, surface area a: 144π square meters
    c. Radius: 6 meters, surface area: 12π square meters
    d. Radius: 36 meters, surface area a: 12π square meters

101. Using trigonometric ratios for a right angle, what is the value of the angle whose opposite side is equal to 25 centimeters and whose hypotenuse is equal to 50 centimeters?
    a. 15°
    b. 30°
    c. 45°
    d. 90°

102. A line passes through the point (1,2) and crosses the y-axis at $y = 1$. Which of the following is an equation for this line?
    a. $y = 2x$
    b. $y = x + 1$
    c. $x + y = 1$
    d. $y = \frac{x}{2} - 2$

103. Which of the following inequalities is equivalent to $3 - \frac{1}{2}x \geq 2$?
    a. $x \geq 2$
    b. $x \leq 2$
    c. $x \geq 1$
    d. $x \leq 1$

104. A line is graphed in the (x,y)-coordinate plane. The equation of the line is $y = -2x + 5$. Which of the following is true?
    a. The slope of a perpendicular line is $-\frac{1}{2}$.
    b. The y-intercept is (5,0).
    c. The line decreases from left to right.
    d. The line goes through the point (1,7).

105. x is an integer and is a factor of 28. Which of the following must also be true?
    a. x is a factor of 4.
    b. x is a factor of 56.
    c. x is a multiple of 4.
    d. x is a factor of 16.

106. Pond 1 has half as many frogs as Pond 2. Pond 2 has one-fourth as many frogs as Pond 3. What is the ratio of frogs in Pond 1 to Pond 3?
    a. 1:4
    b. 1:8
    c. 2:3
    d. 8:1

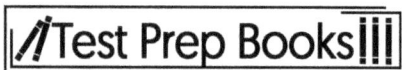

107. How will the following algebraic expression be simplified: $(5x^2 - 3x + 4) - (2x^2 - 7)$?
   a. x^5
   b. $3x^2 - 3x + 11$
   c. $3x^2 - 3x - 3$
   d. $x - 3$

108. An isosceles right triangle has two sides that each measure 7 cm. What is the perimeter of this triangle? Round to the nearest tenth of a centimeter.
   a. 14 cm
   b. 21.3 cm
   c. 24.3 cm
   d. 23.9 cm

109. If the point $(-3, -4)$ is reflected over the x-axis, what new point does it make?
   a. $(-3, -4)$
   b. $(3, -4)$
   c. $(3, 4)$
   d. $(-3, 4)$

110. The current exchange rate in Mexico is 1 US dollar = 16.99 pesos. Also, 1 US dollar is equivalent to 0.912 euros. If someone has 90 pesos, how many euros could they exchange it for? Round to the nearest hundredth of a euro.
   a. 4.83 euros
   b. 1,667 euros
   c. 5.80 euros
   d. 120.23 euros

111. How many integers between -10 and 10 (inclusive) meet both conditions below?
   I. $|x| > 0$
   II. $x^2 = 1$
   a. 3
   b. 2
   c. 1
   d. 0

112. What is 3 out of 8 when expressed as a percent?
   a. 37.5%
   b. 37%
   c. 26.7%
   d. 2.67%

Practice Test #1

113. Katie has four purses. Two of the purses are red. One of the purses has a chain strap. If the previous three sentences are true, which of the following is also true?

        I: Katie has a red purse with a chain strap.
        II: Katie has three shoulder bags.
        III: Katie only likes red purses.

a. I only
b. II only
c. II and III only
d. Not enough information is given.

114. Kylie's score was 18 percentage points higher than London's score. London received an 18 out of 30. What was Kylie's score?

a. 18.18 out of 30
b. 24.4 out of 30
c. 23.4 out of 30
d. 28.4 out of 30

115. The perimeter of a 6-sided polygon is 56 cm. The lengths of three sides are 9 cm each. The lengths of two other sides are 8 cm each. What is the length of the final side?

a. 11 cm
b. 12 cm
c. 13 cm
d. 10 cm

116. What is the midpoint of a line segment with endpoints $(-1, 2)$ and $(3, -6)$?

a. $(1, 2)$
b. $(1, 0)$
c. $(-1, 2)$
d. $(1, -2)$

117. What is the value of x if $4x - 3 = 5$?

a. 4
b. 8
c. 1
d. 2

118. An isosceles triangle has one angle that measures 90°. What are the measures of the two other angles?

a. 45° and 45°
b. 50° and 50°
c. 30° and 60°
d. There isn't enough information to answer this question.

119. What is the function that forms an equivalent graph to $y = \cos(x)$?
   a. $y = \tan(x)$
   b. $y = \csc(x)$
   c. $y = \sin\left(x + \frac{\pi}{2}\right)$
   d. $y = \sin\left(x - \frac{\pi}{2}\right)$

120. A rectangle has a length that is 5 feet longer than three times its width. If the perimeter is 90 feet, what is the length in feet?
   a. 10
   b. 20
   c. 25
   d. 35

Answer Explanations #1

Verbal Reasoning

1. B: Choice B reflects Helios calling Hades "no unfitting husband" for Demeter's daughter for a short list of reasons. Helios would not speak so highly of Hades if he saw him as Choice A does. Choice C is incorrect because Helios notes Demeter's anger and would not see her distress as a sign of Hades being a good brother. Choice D directly contradicts what Helios says about Hades in his response to Demeter.

2. C: Choice C is correct because the passage tells the story of Demeter's search for her daughter after her kidnapping. Choice A describes how Demeter might tell the story but not how Homer is telling it. Choice B would require the passage to tell the reader to avoid or do something to avoid Persephone's fate. Choice D is incorrect because, while descriptive, the main purpose of the description is to tell a story.

3. A: Choice A employs the correct meaning of the word *awful*, in the archaic sense of awesome power. Choices B, C, and D each would work only if one assumes the modern, purely negative connotation of *awful*, with C and D also demanding a negative view of Demeter that the passage does not show.

4. D: It is written in Choice D that Hades took Persephone "by leave of Zeus," meaning with Zeus' permission. Choices A and B only support the fact that Persephone was kidnapped by Hades. Choice C shows Helios telling Demeter not to fret but to consider Hades a good match for her daughter, but it does not imply that he was personally involved in the event he just finished recounting.

5. A: Choice A acknowledges the obstacles stacked against Demeter in the passage: Zeus, Persephone's father, gave his brother permission to kidnap her; and Helios, the first god who can tell Demeter what happened, immediately declares her daughter's kidnapper a good match. Choice B is unlikely to occur due to Zeus having given Hades permission to take Persephone. We see no indication in the passage that Demeter will give up easily, as stated in Choice C, nor are we given any reason to assume that Helios can be swayed in his opinion, as stated in Choice D.

6. B: Choice B correctly notes that knowing how unhappy Persephone was during the kidnapping helps to drive home the injustice of the situation and to give proper weight to Demeter's struggle. Choice A would require Helios to have claimed that Persephone went willingly, which he does not. Choice C is incorrect because the passage is indeed about Demeter's search for her daughter. Choice D implies a connection that does not exist between Persephone's unwillingness and the idea that Hades will make a good husband for her.

7. D: Choice D is most accurate to Demeter calling Persephone the child she *bare*, or bore. Choice A acts as though the word *bare* is being used as a noun when it functions as a verb in this sentence. Choice B does not fit because there is no suggestion of Demeter showing Persephone to anyone, and Choice C implies that Demeter had eyes on Persephone when she was abducted.

8. C: In Choice C, Helios, the first other god Demeter and Hectate approach for help explains what happened but proceeds to declare that Hades is "no unfitting husband" for Persephone and to explain his reasoning. Choices A and B both focus on Persephone's anguish or hope, respectively, and Choice D contains only Hecate's speech to Demeter.

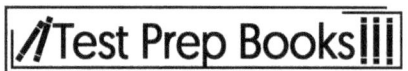

Answer Explanations #1

9. B: Choice *B* correctly places the parent in the first position: Hyperion is Helios's father, and Demeter is Persephone's mother. Choice *A* places Demeter's mother, Rhea, second in the analogy. Choices *C* and *D* involve relationships other than parent-child.

10. A: Choice *A* compares the idea of the explicitly unwilling Persephone being willingly taken with the idea of Hecate, who has exclusively been helpful to Demeter in the story, being unhelpful to her. Choices *B* and *C* are not the direct opposite of how Demeter or the passage views either character, and the passage does nothing to establish whether she or we should view Cronos in Choice *D* as fatherly.

11. A: Choice *A* is the correct answer because it accurately identifies the main focus of the passage. In this passage, Darwin is discussing natural selection and then uses a metaphor to describe how natural selection affects species and overall evolution. Choice *B* is incorrect because the passage touches on how diversity in descendants can affect survival, but it does not discuss specific struggles. Choice *C* is incorrect because trees are not mentioned except as a metaphor for natural selection. Choice *D* is incorrect because although species are discussed, their communication methods are not.

12. B: Choice *B* is the correct answer because the passage argues that natural selection is a way for nature to create diversity of character. This is directly mentioned in Paragraph 1, Sentence 3. The more diversity, the better the chance for survival. Choice *A* is incorrect because although the area that the species live in is mentioned, the destruction of the habitat is not. Choice *C* is incorrect because geological disasters are not a form of natural selection. Choice *D* is incorrect because although fatal genetic modifications may be a part of natural selection and diversity, they are not the main purpose of natural selection.

13. C: Choice *C* is the correct answer because it accurately identifies the way the passage connects the classification of species with the Tree of Life. The Tree of Life is serving as a metaphor for how species evolve and diversify over time. The point of natural selection is to create divergence of character and increase the possibility of survival for a species. The Tree of Life shows this process. Choice *A* is incorrect because although the struggle for survival is a part of the evolutionary process, it is not the main tether between species and the Tree of Life. Choice *B* is incorrect because the threat of extinction is something that species face, but it is not what the Tree of Life is displaying overall. Choice *D* is incorrect because although the Tree of Life is technically showing mutations and diversifications, Choice *C* is overall a more accurate way to state this.

14. A: Choice *A* is the correct answer because the author brings up these species as an example of how the different branches connect. Darwin states that these animals connect two larger branches due to their affinities. Choice *B* is incorrect because the passage does not state that these animals are extinct. Choice *C* is incorrect because the decaying branches are mentioned earlier in the passage. Choice *D* is incorrect because readers cannot be sure that the two animals have adapted due to their geographical location.

15. C: Choice *C* is the correct answer because it is a fair inference based on the information provided in the passage. In the first paragraph, Darwin says that increased divergence leads to more living beings in an area. He then goes on to say that the changes in structure, habits, and constitution increase their chances in the battle for life. Choices *A* and *B* are incorrect because, as Darwin states, there is a connection between diversity (which comes from divergence in character) and improved survival. Choice *D* is incorrect because diversity does not generally lead to ultimate extinction.

Answer Explanations #1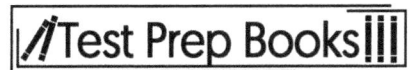

16. D: Choice *D* is the correct answer because it is the meaning that best fits the word *incessant*. In this passage, the word *incessant* is being used to describe a never-ending struggle for species. Therefore, to say that the word aligns with *ceaseless* is accurate. Choices *A*, *B*, and *C* do not fit the context of the passage or the common meaning of the word *incessant*.

17. B: Choice *B* is the correct answer because it accurately identifies the purpose of the two paragraphs. The first paragraph focuses on how natural selection affects nature and creates diversification. The second paragraph is about the Tree of Life, which is a metaphor for the diversification and survival of various species. Choice *B* is the option that identifies these two purposes. Choice *A* is incorrect because while the first paragraph does discuss survival chances, the second paragraph does not focus on specific dominant traits. Choice *C* is incorrect because the first paragraph mentions survival and extinction but never evolution as a concept. Choice *D* is incorrect because the second paragraph does not focus on specific species that have been affected by natural selection.

18. A: Choice *A* is the correct answer because it accurately identifies what the author meant in the sentence about ramifying branches. The word *ramifying* means to form offshoots. In this case, within the context of the rest of the passage, the author is referring to the branches of the tree increasing in number and how it represents the different species. Choice *B* is incorrect because the dying branches are discussed in a different sentence. Choice *C* is incorrect because the budding twigs are a part of the ramifying branches metaphor for species classification. Choice *D* is incorrect because the ramifying branches concept is a metaphor, not an actual reference to branches.

19. D: Choice *D* is the correct answer because it is the analogy that best fits with the original pairing. As seen in the passage, natural selection leads to divergence in character. So for the matching analogy, the first term must be something that leads to the second. In this case, Choice *D* is correct because studying leads to good grades. Choices *A*, *B*, and *C* are incorrect because the first term does not lead to the second term.

20. B: Choice *B* is the correct answer because it is the analogy that best fits with the original pairing. In the passage, the Tree of Life paragraph describes that the budding twigs grow into branches, much like a foal grows into a steed. Choices *A*, *C*, and *D* are incorrect because they do not have a similar analogous relationship.

21. A: Choice *A* is the correct answer. Descartes is discussing the qualities of good sense in all humans and his intellectual journey pursuing truth and knowledge. Choice *B* is incorrect because the author believes that all people have equal good sense. Choice *C* is incorrect because the author is sharing his experience of pursuing knowledge but does not use persuasive tactics. Choice *D* is incorrect because the author cites listening to philosophers neutrally. He does not share any negative thoughts regarding philosophers.

22. D: Choice *D* is the correct answer because it shows that the author considers the possibility of being incorrect in his beliefs. Choice *A* is incorrect because it is about the possibilities of different minds. It does not mention the author's own beliefs. Choice *B* is incorrect because the author is talking about his views on his mind's capabilities when compared to others. This is not about the possibility of being incorrect. Choice *C* is incorrect because the author is discussing how he feels proud of his progress in advancing his mind. It does not mention the possibility of being incorrect.

23. B: Choice *B* is the correct answer because it is a reasonable inference that can be made from the text. The author of this text shares his experiences with good sense and the pursuit of truth and

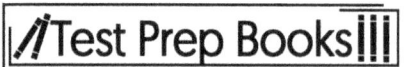

Answer Explanations #1

knowledge. He believes that all men have good sense, as mentioned in the first line of the text. He then goes on to say that the requisite for having good sense is to apply it. Therefore, we can reasonably infer that those who do not use the good sense they were born with are simply lacking the conviction to use it. In Paragraph 4, the author discusses that his opinions on the subject may be incorrect since we often think of things delusionally when they relate to ourselves. However, this does not tell us that the author makes mistakes often, which eliminates Choice *A*. Choice *C* is incorrect because the author does not speak on what attributes make somebody a good leader or if that leads to obligation. Choice *D* is incorrect because the author expresses himself humbly, namely in Paragraph 2, where he states that he has never thought of himself as being better than anyone.

24. B: Choice *B* is the correct answer because it best explains why the author feels strongly about this subject. In this line, the author states that good sense is what makes humans unique; good sense separates humans from brutes. Choice *A* is incorrect because it discusses the importance of using good sense, but it does not explain why good sense is important in humans. Choice *C* is incorrect because the author is discussing how he has increased his knowledge, which is not generally why good sense in humans is unique. Choice *D* is incorrect because the author is talking about how he will continue his journey, which is not related to why good sense is important.

25. D: Choice *D* is the correct answer because it accurately identifies the shared theme between the two paragraphs. While the first paragraph focuses on general thoughts regarding good sense and mankind, Paragraph 2 and Paragraph 3 are focused on the author's experiences. Paragraph 2 discusses the author's thoughts regarding his abilities and progress when compared to other people. Paragraph 3 discusses the author's efforts to pursue truth and knowledge and how he feels positively about them. In this case, both paragraphs are focused on the author's thoughts and experiences. Choice *A* is incorrect because these two paragraphs do not speak about the pros and cons of good sense. They are centered around the author's experiences. Choice *B* is incorrect because these two paragraphs do not question philosophers; philosophers are only briefly mentioned. Choice *C* is incorrect because the text is not directed at the reader for encouragement.

26. A: Choice *A* is the correct answer because it accurately identifies the opinion of the author based on evidence within the passage. In Paragraph 1, the author discusses opinions. He states that although all humans have good sense, they have differing opinions and thoughts. He claims that this comes from the fact that we conduct our thoughts in different ways. This is present in Sentence 2. Choice *B* is incorrect because the author does not state that facts invalidate opinions. Choice *C* is incorrect because the author does not say that opinions should be celebrated. Choice *D* is incorrect because the author does not mention childhood in any capacity.

27. C: Choice *C* is the correct answer because it accurately identifies an inference that can be made from Paragraph 3. In this paragraph, the author is discussing his experience with gaining as much knowledge as his mind will allow. He also states that he had derived much satisfaction from this path and that he believes it to be the most important path a man can take. From this, the reader can infer that the author values the willpower required to gain more knowledge and skills more than he values abilities obtained at birth. Choice *A* is incorrect because the author states that his mind is not endlessly capable and that he only attempts to live up to his full potential. Choice *B* is incorrect because the author does not state any of his beliefs in a way that is derogatory to those who do not pursue the same path as him. Choice *D* is incorrect because the author states that he continues to have goals for the future.

28. C: Choice *C* is the correct answer because it illustrates a visual representation of a concept to help the reader understand what is being said. Choice *A* is incorrect because empirical evidence requires observation and documentation of what the author is talking about. Choice *B* is incorrect because anecdotal evidence requires the author to tell his own or another person's story to demonstrate the concepts that he is discussing. Choice *D* is incorrect because circumstantial evidence requires a fact that the reader can infer another fact from. In this case, the author is talking about broad concepts that align more with opinion than fact.

29. C: Choice *C* is the correct answer because it is the analogy that is most like the one featured in the question. In this passage, the author states that all men have good sense. In this analogy, all birds have feathers. Choice *A* is incorrect because communism is a type of political ideology. While communism would affect the state of an economy, the relationship is not analogous to the original terms. Choice *B* is incorrect because chemistry is a type of science; this does not fit the original analogy. Choice *D* is incorrect because a president is someone who helps to govern citizens, creating a political and social relationship that does not fit the original analogy.

30. A: Choice *A* is the correct answer because it is the analogy that is most like the one featured in the question. The original analogy shows a relationship of something inexpensive versus something expensive. Glass is relatively cheap compared to expensive diamonds. Choice *A* is correct because plastic is a cheap material whereas platinum is expensive. Choice *B* is incorrect because cotton and fleece are two types of fabric of similar value. Choice *C* is incorrect because a pebble is a small rock, while a boulder is a large rock; this is a size comparison rather than one of price. Choice *D* is incorrect because tigers and bears are different animals that are not assigned a monetary value.

31. A: Choice *A* is the correct answer because both passages discuss the role of those who govern compared to the role of those who are governed. They touch on the nature of man and how it functions within politics. Choice *B* is incorrect because foreign countries are not the focus of either paragraph. Choice *C* is incorrect because although the passages discuss the nature of governance, Passage B specifically does not mention corruption. Choice *D* is incorrect because political factions are the focus of Passage B, but not Passage A.

32. C: Choice *C* is the correct answer because it correctly identifies what both passages are saying about liberty. Passage A focuses on the role of the individual and how some people are fit to govern while others are meant to be governed. Passage B focuses on factions within society and how liberty is essential for political function. Choice *A* is incorrect because the first passage does not focus on communicating that slavery is an inevitability; it is more focused on the role of all individuals within society. Choice *B* is incorrect because the first passage does not mention testing for leadership attributes. Choice *D* is incorrect because the second passage does not state that liberty is part of the ego.

33. D: Choice *D* is the correct answer because it identifies what Aristotle believes regarding corruption. Aristotle acknowledges that corruption is a part of mankind. He also states that those who govern should be perfect in mind and body to prevent such corruption. Choice *A* is incorrect because Aristotle claims that there is a way to prevent corruption. Choice *B* is incorrect because Aristotle does not mention that democracy must run its course to get rid of corruption. Choice *C* is incorrect because Aristotle does not recommend protest at any point.

34. A: Choice *A* is correct because it is how Madison supports his argument about factionalism. Madison explains how diverse opinions and interests lead to factions. This is seen in Paragraph 3, Sentence 2. Choice *B* is incorrect because Madison does not provide any specific examples. Choice *C* is incorrect

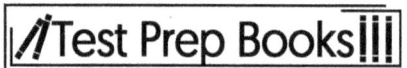

because although Madison discusses human beliefs and passion, he does not emphasize passion. Choice D is incorrect because Madison does not discuss various types of government.

35. A: Choice A is the correct answer because Aristotle asserts that those with a perfect soul and body are the type of people who should govern others; he believes these people are less prone to corruption. This is seen in the last sentence of the paragraph. Choice B is incorrect because according to Aristotle, the soul and body are relevant to those who govern. Choice C is incorrect because Aristotle claims that those who govern can be corrupt. Choice D is incorrect because Aristotle does not speak about body and soul separately.

36. C: Choice C is correct because it is the best quote to illustrate Aristotle's thoughts on natural order. Aristotle believes that some people are more naturally suited to govern, while others are born to be governed. Choice C illustrates this point. Choices A, B, and D focus on other points made by Aristotle.

37. B: Choice B is correct because while both passages focus on similar topics, they do so in different manners. Passage A is concerned with individual roles in society. For example, Aristotle touches on the idea of slavery. Passage B is about factions in society and how those factions come to be. Choice A is incorrect because Passage A mentions slavery, but it is not the focus. Choice C is incorrect because corruption is not the focus of Passage A; corruption is only mentioned to state the kind of person best suited for governance. Choice D is incorrect because Passage B does not mention civil unrest.

38. D: Choice D is the correct answer because *unconquerable* is the word that best fits the meaning of *insuperable*. In this context, *insuperable* means that the obstacle is insurmountable as it talks about the uniformity of interests in men. The word *unconquerable* aligns with this meaning. Choice A is incorrect because *achievable* has the opposite meaning to the author's intention. Choice B is incorrect because there is no element of surprise in this context. Choice C is incorrect because although the obstacle may be considered difficult, that is not the purpose of the word *insuperable*.

39. C: Choice C is the correct answer because it is the analogy that best fits with the original pairing. As seen in Passage B, diverse opinions lead to factions. Therefore, the paired analogy should be one thing that leads to another. In this case, a spark leads to fire, and this is an appropriate analogy. Choice A is incorrect because labor does not necessarily lead to taxation. Choice B is incorrect because legislation and laws are nearly synonyms. Choice D is incorrect because a diplomat can be considered a peacekeeper, so there is no cause-and-effect relationship.

40. A: Choice A is the correct answer because it is the analogy that best fits with the original pairing. In this analogy and as read in Passage A, corruption is destructive to government. Therefore, the paired analogy should fit that negative relationship. Crops are affected negatively by disease, so it is an appropriate pairing. Choice B is incorrect because a school is run by a principal; there is no negative relationship. Choice C is incorrect because the afterlife is not something that is destructive to life. Choice D is incorrect because exercise positively affects health.

Grammar and Writing

41. B: Choice B is the correct answer because the colon is used to introduce the concepts of moral basis and social application for eugenics. Choice A is incorrect because a semicolon is used to separate two independent clauses; the two clauses the semicolon would separate are not independent of each other. Choice C is incorrect because dashes separate different ideas within a sentence or signify a break in thought. For introducing ideas, a colon works better. Choice D is incorrect because there is no need for a purposeful pause, which is the main function of ellipses.

42. D: Choice D is the correct answer because it uses the correct tense and phrasing for the sentence. It follows the standard form for infinitive verbs (to + the base form of the verb) and functions with the main verb *obliged*. Choice A is incorrect because *sacrificed* is a past tense verb and does not work with the grammatical structure of the sentence. Choice B is incorrect because *sacrificial* is an adjective and not a verb, and a verb is what is needed in this sentence. Choice C is incorrect because sacrificing is not an infinitive verb; an infinitive verb is necessary because the original sentence is expressing a potential action, not an ongoing one.

43. C: Choice C is the correct answer because it is the most concise while maintaining all of the information provided in the original sentence. This includes the main idea that we tend to focus on one partner within a union when considering potential outcomes in relationships. Choice A is incorrect because the sentence is not as concise as Choice C. Choice B is incorrect because, although it is concise, it does not accurately convey the same idea of the original sentence, as it states that the focus is on both partners. Choice D is incorrect because it does not express the connection to biology that the original sentence includes.

44. D: Choice D is the correct answer because it is the sentence that is the most concise while conveying all of the information in the original sentence. This includes the idea of procreation being the aim of marriage and that of some people attributing procreation to God and others to nature. Choice A is incorrect because the sentence is lengthier than the other options presented. Choice B is incorrect because it states that the opinions on procreation were well-defined when the original sentence states the opposite. Choice C is incorrect because it adds the idea that those who believed that procreation was an act of nature were misled. This is not stated in the original sentence. It also leaves out the author's labeling of the people who believed these things as sane.

45. A: Choice A is the correct answer because the word *whom* functions as the object of the preposition *towards* in this sentence. Choice B is incorrect because whose indicates possession, which is not applicable in this sentence. Choice C is incorrect because whom is preferrable to which when referring to people. Choice D is incorrect because *them* is a pronoun used for plural nouns and does not work grammatically in the sentence.

46. C: Choice C is the correct answer because the two clauses are comparing the reasons behind the actions of the women and the knight. The first clause explains why the women of the harem would praise the hero. The second clause explains why the Christian knight would help his wife off her horse. Choice A is incorrect because there is no indication of the women and men having different levels of concern about posterity. Choice B is incorrect because, although the two clauses are given in the form of one sentence, the two actions described are not directly related. Choice D is incorrect because nothing about the women's actions suggests that they are not concerned with morals. The text is simply making a comparison between the dues of men and women.

47. C: Choice C is the correct answer because it is the option that best fits the context of the sentence and overall passage. As the topic is posterity and sex relations, the hopes of those mentioned would be to produce healthy children. The need for strong children is also mentioned later in the text. Choice A is incorrect because strong investments are not mentioned anywhere else in the text. Choice B is incorrect because, even though beautiful sons are mentioned in the next sentence, there is nothing to suggest

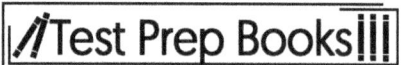

that people hoped for only male children. Choice *D* is incorrect because there is nothing in the text that suggests the children would be used as laborers.

48. B: Choice *B* is the correct answer because it uses the correct punctuation for the sentence. There must be a comma before the beginning of the quote. A direct quote should also use double quotation marks. Choice *A* is incorrect because there is no comma before the quote. Choice *C* is incorrect because ellipses are not appropriate before the quote. Choice *D* is incorrect because, although there is a comma before the quote, it only uses single quotation marks.

49. D: Choice *D* is the correct answer because *impious* is the best word for the sentence. The word *impious* means not showing reverence for God. This works in the context of the Christian and Muslim beliefs regarding procreation and marriage. Choice *A* is incorrect because *imminent* means about to happen, which does not make sense in this context. Choice *B* is incorrect because *idealistic* means striving for perfection or believing good things can happen, which doesn't fit this sentence. Choice *C*, *illustrious*, means famous, outstanding, or highly respected, which also doesn't work in this sentence.

50. C: Choice *C* is the correct answer because it uses a comma before the word *but*. Commas are generally used before conjunctions. Choice *A* is incorrect because a semicolon is not normally used before a conjunction but rather between two independent clauses. Choice *B* is incorrect because there should be a comma before the conjunction to separate the two clauses. Choice *D* is incorrect because it is better to join a clause beginning with a conjunction with the preceding sentence than to have it stand as a sentence on its own.

51. C: Choice *C* is the correct answer because the subject of the sentence is Poe, and the pronoun who is appropriate in reference to a person. Choice *A* is incorrect because the word *that* typically refers to inanimate objects, not people. Choice *B* is incorrect because the pronoun *whom* functions as the object of a verb, but the antecedent in this case is the subject, *Poe*. Choice *D* is incorrect because the word *he* would be appropriate at the beginning of a new clause, which is not the case at this point in the sentence.

52. D: Choice *D* is the correct answer because there should be commas between the day and the year, between the city and the state, and after each element set off by commas. A comma is also needed at the end of introductory phrases, which is another reason why this sentence needs a comma after "Massachusetts." Choice *A* is incorrect because there is no comma between the day and the year. Choice *B* is incorrect because there is no comma between the city and the state. Choice *C* is incorrect because there is no comma after the state.

53. A: Choice *A* is the correct answer because the sentence is referring to the fact that Poe became successful despite the challenges that could have held him back. These challenges are the unfortunate events of his childhood. Choice *B* is incorrect because the text never indicates that macabre writing was unpopular. Choice *C* is incorrect because the text never mentions interruptions by either fans or contemporaries. Choice *D* is incorrect because there is nothing to suggest that Poe's peers were critical of him or his writing.

54. C: Choice *C* is the correct answer because the word *turbulent*, meaning disorderly or chaotic, best fits the description of Poe's childhood. Choice *A* is incorrect because *taciturn* describes a person who is quiet or uncommunicative and thus cannot describe Poe's childhood. Choice *B* is incorrect because *tedious* means dull or monotonous. Poe's childhood was not monotonous. Choice *D* is incorrect because *tenuous* means weak. Although Poe's upbringing was difficult, it's not accurate to refer to it as weak.

Answer Explanations #1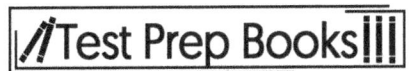

55. C: Choice C is the correct answer because the subject of the sentence (a few of Poe's works), which the verb must agree with, is plural. Additionally, the paragraph is about Poe's lasting legacy, meaning the works are still being read and celebrated, so the present tense is appropriate. Therefore, the verb *are* makes sense in the sentence. Choice A is incorrect because the verb, *is*, is singular. Choice B is incorrect because the verb *be* is not grammatically correct in the sentence. *Be* is the base form of the verb, which needs to be conjugated into *are* to fit the sentence. Choice D is incorrect because *were* is a past tense verb, and the works mentioned are still celebrated in the present.

56. D: Choice D is the correct answer because there should be a comma after Dupin's name as a new clause begins. Choice A is incorrect because the comma before Dupin's name is unnecessary. A name is only set off by commas if it is a non-essential clause or basically synonymous with the descriptor it follows ("the main character of 'The Murders in the Rue Morgue,' C. Auguste Dupin," is an example, whereas in the given sentence, Dupin is just one character out of many). Choice B is incorrect because there needs to be a comma before the clause starting with "who." Choice C is incorrect because there should be a comma after Dupin's name, not a period. The clause beginning with "who" is not independent and cannot stand alone.

57. C: Choice C is the correct answer because the tone of the sentence is somber, meaning gloomy or depressing. It is discussing Poe's depression after the death of his wife. Choice A is incorrect because no one is being accused of anything. Choice B is incorrect because a *cynical* tone suggests that Poe's feelings or motivations were self-serving or insincere; nothing indicates this. Choice D is incorrect because the text does not have a caustic—harsh or sarcastic—tone; it is a serious and uncritical account of Poe's struggles.

58. B: Choice B is the correct answer because there is no need for any punctuation after the word *included*. In this sentence, it is appropriate to flow straight into the examples of Poe's struggles. Choice A is incorrect because the semicolon is not separating two independent clauses. Choice C is incorrect because there is no grammatical need for a comma after *included*. Choice D is incorrect because there is no need for a purposeful pause in this sentence, thus making ellipses unnecessary.

59. D: Choice D is the correct answer because *laudatory* means expressing praise, and the sentence is celebrating Poe's achievement of becoming a cultural icon. Choice A is incorrect because the sentence does not state anything regarding hopefulness for future events. Choice B is incorrect because the sentence is praising Poe, not criticizing him. Choice C is incorrect because the sentence does not express a negative or hateful opinion about Poe; it is simply stating a positive fact about Poe.

60. A: Choice A is the correct answer because the rest of the text indicates that Poe's writing was very macabre. Earlier in the text, Poe's fixation on the human psyche is mentioned. These are key clues that the current sentence is correct. Choice B is incorrect because Poe focused on the negative aspects of human experience rather than humanity's strengths. Choice C is incorrect because, based on this text, scientific discovery was not a significant part of Poe's writing. Choice D is incorrect because, although Poe seemed to appreciate psychology, there is no mention of chronic illness in the text.

61. C: Choice C is the correct answer because the word *pedantic* describes someone who is overly focused on small errors. This works in the sentence because the author is saying the reader should understand his meaning as long as they aren't too nitpicky. Choice A is incorrect because *patriotic* means having pride in one's nation, and there is no discussion about any nation. Choice B is incorrect because *penitent* means showing regret, and the reader being regretful does not make sense in this

context. Choice *D* is incorrect because *perfidious* means untrustworthy. A person being untrustworthy has nothing to do with the clarity of the author's text.

62. C: Choice *C* is the correct answer because *their* is a plural pronoun and accurately refers to the plural antecedent *rods*. The word *lengths* should be used because it is plural, and the author is discussing the lengths of multiple rods, not just one. Choice *A* is incorrect because the word *its* is a singular possessive pronoun, not plural. Choice *B* is incorrect because the word *the* is a definite article and does not create a relationship of possession. Choice *D* is incorrect because *length* should be pluralized to *lengths*.

63. D: Choice *D* is the correct answer because *square* must be singular due to it being preceded by the indefinite article *a*. The corresponding verb, *belongs*, must be singular as well. This eliminates Choices *A*, *B*, and *C*.

64. D: Choice *D* is the correct answer because the author is expressing awe at the fact that the experiment can take place without issue. Therefore, it makes sense to say he is *appreciative*. Choice *A* is incorrect because the author is genuinely pleased, rather than ironic or mocking. Choice *B* is incorrect because the author is not warning the reader of anything. Choice *C* is incorrect because the author is pleased, which is the opposite of *disappointed*.

65. B: Choice *B* is the correct answer because it is the logical option when considering the content of the sentence. The sentence states that two sides of the square have been laid. Since a square has four sides, the remaining number of sides is two. Choices *A*, *C*, and *D* are incorrect because they are not mathematically logical.

66. D: Choice *D* is the correct answer because a comma separates the main information provided in the first part of the sentence from the author's additional thoughts. Choice *A* is incorrect because a semicolon is only appropriate when combining two independent clauses. Choice *B* is incorrect because there should be a comma to separate the clauses. Choice *C* is incorrect because a colon should be used when presenting a list, which this sentence does not have.

67. D: Choice *D* is the correct answer because the word *construction* in this sentence is referencing what the author describes building in their previous instructions. These instructions include both the slab and rods put together. Choice *A* is incorrect because the quadrilateral figure is not a part of the model that the author constructs. Choices *B* and *C* are incorrect because while they are both partially accurate, Choice *D* includes them both, thus creating the full answer.

68. C: Choice *C* is the correct answer because the pronoun *our* agrees with *we* at the beginning of the sentence. Choices *A*, *B*, and *D* are incorrect because the proposed pronouns do not agree with *we* in person or in number.

69. B: Choice *B* is the correct answer because it is the most clear and concise way to convey all of the information in the original sentence. Choice *B* accurately states that the squares are disordered when heated and that the central region expands, while the outer region does not. Choice *A* is incorrect because the sentence can be made more concise. Choice *C* is incorrect because it inaccurately states that the outer part expands. Choice *D* is incorrect because it states that the squares come into order, when they come into disorder.

70. D: Choice *D* is the correct answer because there is no need for punctuation after the word *manner* in this sentence. There are no separate clauses, ideas, or information to set off with punctuation; the entire sentence flows seamlessly. Choice *A* is incorrect because there is no need for a comma between *manner* and *by*. Choice *B* is incorrect because a colon is used before a list, which is not featured in this sentence. Choice *C* is incorrect because a semicolon is used to separate two related independent clauses, and this sentence does not have more than one independent clause.

71. A: Choice *A* is the correct answer because the commas are used to create emphasis. Carter wishes to emphasize that, *of course*, he recognizes the importance of government action. In this case, the commas are used correctly to single out that emphasized portion of text. Choice *B* is incorrect because neither the first nor the second part of the original sentence functions on its own, and the sentence should not be split into two sentences. Choice *C* is incorrect because a semicolon should only be used between two independent clauses. Choice *D* is incorrect because there need to be commas within that section of text to emphasize the phrase *of course*.

72. B: Choice *B* is the correct answer because the plural pronoun *they* corresponds to the political and civil liberties mentioned in the previous sentence. Choice *A* is incorrect because the word *it* is a singular pronoun. Choices *C* and *D* are incorrect because the author is referring to political and civil liberties, not to himself or other people, so a first-person pronoun does not make sense.

73. D: Choice *D* is the correct answer because it conveys the purpose of the original sentence while eliminating excess wording. Choice *A* is incorrect because the sentence can be made more concise. Choice *B* is incorrect because it states that America is not at peace when it is. Choice *C* is incorrect because it says that Carter is speaking of America's strength, when he was stating that he was not.

74. C: Choice *C* is the correct answer because it best complements the surrounding paragraph. In the same paragraph, Carter discusses families and their faith that their children would live better lives than their own. In this case, it is accurate to say that confidence connects generations of people. Choice *A* is incorrect because nowhere in this portion of text does Carter mention other nations. Choice *B* is incorrect because, although cultures are connected throughout America, in the context of this specific paragraph, *generations* is a better word choice. Choice *D* is incorrect because different species are never mentioned in this speech.

75. B: Choice *B* is the correct answer because it concisely states all of the information provided in the original sentence. The original sentence is claiming that the belief in democracy has strengthened the purpose of Americans. Choice *A* is incorrect because the sentence could be more concise. Choice *C* is incorrect because it states that the belief has not strengthened our purpose. Choice *D* is incorrect because it presents freedom and democracy as separate ideas, whereas the original sentence connects the two.

76. D: Choice *D* is the correct answer because the pronoun *our* maintains agreement in the sentence. The beginning of the sentence uses the word *we've*, which refers to Carter and Americans as a whole. The pronoun *our* matches *we've* in person and number. Choices *A* and *B* do not use the correct pronoun. Choice *C* is too vague, making the relationship between *we've* and *longing* unclear.

77. A: Choice *A* is the correct answer because it fits the sentence and the overall message of the text the best. In this speech, Carter is addressing why America is suffering. He claims it is due to a lack of confidence or purpose, which damages not only the nation but also an individual's quality of life. Choice *B* is incorrect because Carter does not stress the importance of anything monetary. Choice *C* is incorrect because, although America is facing issues with halted progress, it is ultimately because of a lack of confidence and purpose. Choice *D* is incorrect because neither this paragraph nor the passage focuses on having children or neighbors.

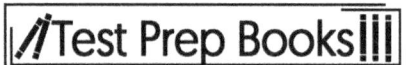

78. B: Choice B is the correct answer because a comma is necessary to separate the introductory phrase from the rest of the sentence. Choice A is incorrect because it does not have the necessary punctuation. Choice C is incorrect because this is not a spot where a purposeful pause would be needed. Choice D is incorrect because a semicolon should only be used to separate independent clauses, and the first clause is not independent.

79. B: Choice B is the correct answer because the paragraph and passage focus on negative changes in America, and it makes sense to say the change described in the previous sentence does not provide *reassurance*. The fact that it is "not a message of happiness" is another clue. Choice A is incorrect because the change described is relevant to the overall topic. Choice C is incorrect because Carter does present the changes he describes as consequential, which is synonymous with having ramifications. Choice D is incorrect because *reluctance* is a negative word, which does not make sense here.

80. C: Choice C is the correct answer because a comma is appropriate for separating the first idea from additional context about the generation. Choice A is incorrect because a semicolon is used to separate two related independent clauses. That is not the case in this sentence, as the second part is not an independent clause. Choice B is incorrect because a colon is used before a list, which this sentence does not have. Choice D is incorrect because the information starting with *years* is not an independent clause and cannot stand as its own sentence.

Quantitative Reasoning

81. C: An equilateral triangle has three 60° angles, so it cannot have a 90° right angle. Choices A, B, and D are all isosceles right triangles. If an isosceles right triangle has side length s, then it has a hypotenuse length of $\sqrt{2}s$. In Choice A, $s = 1$, and in Choice D, $s = 4$. In Choice B, the unknown angle measures $180 - 45 - 45 = 90°$ since the three angles have a sum of 180°.

82. C: Let x be the number of dogs and $5x$ be the number of cats. We are given that the total number of cats and dogs is 186; therefore, $x + 5x = 6x = 186$. Dividing both sides by 6 results in $x = 31$. Therefore, there were 31 dogs and $5(31) = 155$ cats.

83. B: First, separate out and add the whole numbers from the mixed fractions:

$$4\frac{1}{3} + 3\frac{3}{4}$$

$$4 + 3 + \frac{1}{3} + \frac{3}{4}$$

$$7 + \frac{1}{3} + \frac{3}{4}$$

Adding the fractions gives:

$$\frac{1}{3} + \frac{3}{4} = \frac{4}{12} + \frac{9}{12}$$

$$\frac{13}{12} = 1 + \frac{1}{12}$$

Thus,

$$7 + \frac{1}{3} + \frac{3}{4} = 7 + 1 + \frac{1}{12} = 8\frac{1}{12}$$

84. D: 3 times the sum of a number and 7 is greater than or equal to 32 can be translated into equation form utilizing mathematical operators and numbers.

85. D: Subtract the center from the x- and y-values of the equation and square the radius on the right side of the equation. Choice A is not the correct answer because the radius of the equation must be squared. Choice B is not the correct answer because you do not square the centers of the equation. Choice C is not the correct answer because you need to subtract (not add) the centers of the equation.

86. B: The volume of a rectangular prism is the $length \times width \times height$, and $3\ cm \times 5\ cm \times 11\ cm$ is $165\ cm^3$. Choice A is not the correct answer because that is 3 cm + 5 cm + 11 cm. Choice C is not the correct answer because that is 15^2. Choice D is not the correct answer because that is $3\ cm \times 5\ cm \times 10\ cm$.

87. C: When x and y are complementary angles, the sine of x is equal to the cosine of y. The complementary angle of 30 is $90 - 30 = 60°$. Therefore, the answer is 60°.

88. B: Jake can mow 6 yards in 5 hours, so his rate of work is $\frac{6}{5}$. Jackson can mow 8 yards in 5 hours, so his rate of work is $\frac{8}{5}$. Let x be the number of hours needed to mow 4 yards. Therefore, $\frac{6}{5}x + \frac{8}{5}x = 4$. This becomes $\frac{14}{5}x = 4$. Multiply each side by $\frac{5}{14}$ to obtain $x = \frac{20}{14} \approx 1.4$ hours, which rounds up—as per the question—to 2 hours.

89. C: The statement says that all of the children have at least one pet. We don't know what type of pet they have or whether they have two pets. We do know that, because all children have a pet, all of the boys have a pet.

90. A: Convert the mixed fractions to improper fractions: $\frac{11}{3} - \frac{9}{5}$. Subtract using 15 as a common denominator and rewrite to get rid of the improper fraction:

$$\frac{11}{3} - \frac{9}{5} = \frac{55}{15} - \frac{27}{15} = \frac{28}{15} = 1\frac{13}{15}$$

91. D: This system of equations involves one quadratic function and one linear function, as seen from the degree of each equation. One way to solve this is through substitution.

Solving for y in the second equation yields:

$$y = x + 2$$

Plugging this equation in for the y of the quadratic equation yields:

$$x^2 - 2x + x + 2 = 8$$

Simplifying the equation, it becomes:

$$x^2 - x + 2 = 8$$

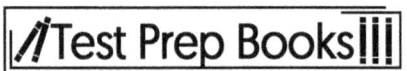

Answer Explanations #1

Setting this equal to zero and factoring, it becomes:

$$x^2 - x - 6 = 0 = (x-3)(x+2)$$

Solving these two factors for x gives the zeros:

$$x = 3, -2$$

To find the y-value for the point, each number can be plugged in to either original equation. Solving each one for y yields the points $(3, 5)$ and $(-2, 0)$.

92. B: The slope will be given by $\frac{1-0}{2-0} = \frac{1}{2}$.

The y-intercept will be 0, since it passes through the origin. Using slope-intercept form, the equation for this line is $y = \frac{1}{2}x$.

93. A: The old price was $3.79, and the new price is $5.29. The percent change is calculated as:

$$\frac{5.29 - 3.79}{3.79} \approx 39.6\%.$$

94. D: The three angles have a sum of 180°. Let x be the first angle. Therefore, $2x$ is the second angle, and $x - 20$ is the third angle. Together, we have $x + 2x + x - 20 = 180$, which simplifies to $4x - 20 = 180$, or $4x = 200$. Dividing each side of the equation by 4 results in $x = 50$, so the measure of the first angle is 50°.

95. C: The formula to find arc length is $s = \theta r$, where s is the arc length, θ is the radian measure of the central angle, and r is the radius of the circle. Substituting the given information produces:

$$3\pi \text{ cm} = \theta \times 12 \text{ cm}$$

Solving for θ yields $\theta = \frac{\pi}{4}$. To convert from radian to degrees, multiply the radian measure by $\frac{180°}{\pi}$:

$$\frac{\pi}{4} \times \frac{180°}{\pi} = 45°$$

96. C: Each number in the sequence is adding one more than the difference between the previous two.

For example, $10 - 6 = 4, 4 + 1 = 5$.

Therefore, the next number after 10 is $10 + 5 = 15$.

Going forward, $21 - 15 = 6, 6 + 1 = 7$. The next number is:

$$21 + 7 = 28$$

Therefore, the difference between numbers is the set of whole numbers starting at 2: $2, 3, 4, 5, 6, 7, …$

97. B: Multiplying a negative integer by 2 results in a negative integer since a negative integer times a positive integer is always negative. Also, an odd integer is of the form $2k + 1$ for some $k = 1, 2, 3, …$ Multiplying this by 2 results in $2(2k + 1) = 4k + 2$, which is the form of an even integer. Therefore, $2x$ is both even and negative.

Answer Explanations #1

98. C: The slope of the line is $m = \frac{10-4}{4-2} = \frac{6}{2} = 3$. Therefore, the slope is positive. The equation of the line is $y - 4 = 3(x - 2)$, which simplifies to $y = 3x - 2$. The point $(3,7)$ lies on this line. The y-intercept is -2, which is below the x-axis. Therefore, Choice C is false.

99. A: Let x be the length of the first cord. Therefore, $6x$ is the length of the second cord, and $8x$ is the length of the third cord. The sum of the three cords is 210 feet. Therefore, $x + 6x + 8x = 210$, which simplifies to $15x = 210$. Dividing each side of the equation by 15 results in $x = 14$ feet.

100. A: The volume of the sphere is 288π cubic meters. Using the formula for sphere volume, we see:

$$\frac{4}{3}\pi r^3 = 288\pi$$

This equation is solved for r to obtain a radius of 6 meters. The formula for surface area is $4\pi r^2$, so $SA = 4\pi 6^2 = 144\pi$ square meters.

101. B: The sine of an angle is equal to the opposite side over the hypotenuse. $\frac{25}{50} = \frac{1}{2}$. The sine of 30° is equal to $\frac{1}{2}$. Choice A is not the correct answer because the sine of 15° is 0.2588. Choice C is not the answer because the sine of 45° is 0.7071. Choice D is not the answer because the sine of 90° is 1.

102. B: We can use slope-intercept form, $y = mx + b$. We are told that the y-intercept (b) is 1, which gives us $y = mx + 1$. Now we can plug in the x and y values from our point, $(1,2)$, to find the slope: $2 = m(1) + 1$, so m=1. This gives us $y = x + 1$.

103. B: To simplify this inequality, subtract 3 from both sides to get $-\frac{1}{2}x \geq -1$. Then, multiply both sides by -2 (remembering this flips the direction of the inequality) to get $x \leq 2$.

104. C: The slope of the given line is -2, and the slope of a perpendicular line is the negative reciprocal of -2, which is $\frac{1}{2}$. The y-intercept is $(0,5)$, and the line goes through the point $(1,3)$, not $(1,7)$. The slope of the line is negative, which means that the line decreases from left to right. Choice C is true.

105. B: 56 is a multiple of 28. Therefore, a factor of 28 is also a factor of 56. The other three options are not true. 7 is a factor of 28, but it is not a factor of 4 or 16, nor is it a multiple of 4.

106. B: Let P_1 be the number of frogs in Pond 1, P_2 the number of frogs in Pond 2, and P_3 the number of frogs in Pond 3. From the information, we are given that $2P_1 = P_2$ and $\frac{1}{4}P_3 = P_2$. Therefore, $\frac{1}{4}P_3 = 2P_1$. Multiplying each side by 4 results in $P_3 = 8P_1$. Therefore, for every 1 frog in Pond 1 there are 8 in Pond 3.

107. B: By distributing the implied 1 in front of the first set of parentheses and the -1 in front of the second set of parentheses, the parentheses can be eliminated:

$$1(5x^2 - 3x + 4) - 1(2x^2 - 7)$$

$$5x^2 - 3x + 4 - 2x^2 + 7$$

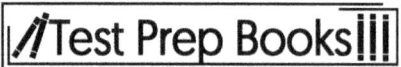

Next, like terms (same variables with same exponents) are combined by adding the coefficients and keeping the variables and their powers the same:

$$5x^2 - 3x + 4 - 2x^2 + 7 = 3x^2 - 3x + 11$$

108. D: The Pythagorean theorem can be used to find the missing side length, which is the hypotenuse c. $7^2 + 7^2 = c^2$. This simplifies into $c^2 = 98$, or $c \approx 9.9$ cm. The perimeter of the triangle is the sum of the three sides, so the perimeter is $7 + 7 + 9.9 = 23.9$ cm.

109. D: When a point is reflected over an axis, the sign of at least one of the coordinates must change. When it's reflected over the x-axis, the sign of the y-coordinate must change. The x-value remains the same. Therefore, the new point is $(-3, 4)$.

110. A: First, convert pesos to US dollars. Divide 90 by 16.99 to obtain 5.30 US dollars. Then, convert US dollars to euros by multiplying 5.30 by 0.912. The correct answer is 4.83 euros.

111. B: All of the integers between -10 and 10 besides 0 have an absolute value greater than 0. The only two integers that satisfy $x^2 = 1$ are -1 and 1. Therefore, there are 2 integers that satisfy both conditions.

112. A: Solve this by setting up the percent formula:

$$\frac{3}{8} = \frac{\%}{100}$$

Multiply 3 by 100 to get 300. Then divide 300 by 8:

$$\frac{300}{8} = 37.5\%$$

Note that with the percent formula, 37.5 is automatically a percentage and does not need to have any further conversions.

113. D: Not enough information is given to support these statements. The purse with the chain strap might be a color other than red, she might have three other types of purses, and, although she has red purses, we do not know what color purses she likes.

114. C: London received an 18 out of 30, which is equivalent to $\frac{18}{30} = 0.6 = 60\%$. Kylie received a score that was 18 percentage points higher, which equals 78%. Multiply 0.78 by 30 to obtain 23.4. Kylie received a 23.4 out of 30.

115. C: The perimeter is found by calculating the sum of all sides of the polygon:

$$9 + 9 + 9 + 8 + 8 + s = 56$$

where s is the missing side length. Therefore, $43 + s = 56$. The missing side length is 13 cm.

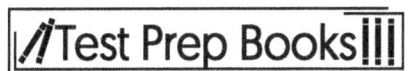

116. D: The midpoint formula should be used to get the average of both points.

$$M = \left(\frac{x_1 + x_2}{2}, \frac{y_1 + y_2}{2}\right)$$

$$\left(\frac{-1 + 3}{2}, \frac{2 + (-6)}{2}\right) = (1, -2)$$

117. D: Add 3 to both sides to get $4x = 8$. Then divide both sides by 4 to get $x = 2$.

118. A: An isosceles triangle has two angles of equal measure. The sum of the three angles in the triangle is 180°, so there cannot be another 90° angle. The additional two angles must be equal and have a sum of 90°. Divide 90° by 2 to find that each angle must be 45°.

119. C: Graphing the function $y = \cos(x)$ would show that the curve starts at $(0, 1)$, has an amplitude of 2, and a period of 2π. This same curve can be constructed using the sine graph, by shifting the graph to the left $\frac{\pi}{2}$ units. This equation is in the form $y = \sin\left(x + \frac{\pi}{2}\right)$.

120. D: Denote the width as w and the length as l. Then, $l = 3w + 5$. The perimeter is $2w + 2l = 90$. Substituting the first expression for l into the second equation yields:

$$2(3w + 5) + 2w = 90$$

$$6w + 10 + 2w = 90$$

$$8w = 80$$

$$w = 10$$

Putting this into the first equation, it yields:

$$l = 3(10) + 5 = 35$$

Practice Test #2

Verbal Reasoning

Passage: Literature

This passage is adapted from Niccolò Machiavelli's The Prince, *originally published in 1532.*

[1] Coming now to the other qualities mentioned above, I say that every prince ought to desire to be considered clement and not cruel. Nevertheless he ought to take care not to misuse this clemency. Cesare Borgia was considered cruel; notwithstanding, his cruelty reconciled the Romagna, unified it, and restored it to peace and loyalty. And if this be rightly considered, he will be seen to have been much more merciful than the Florentine people, who, to avoid a reputation for cruelty, permitted Pistoia to be destroyed. Therefore a prince, so long as he keeps his subjects united and loyal, ought not to mind the reproach of cruelty; because with a few examples he will be more merciful than those who, through too much mercy, allow disorders to arise, from which follow murders or robberies; for these are wont to injure the whole people, whilst those executions which originate with a prince offend the individual only.

[2] And of all princes, it is impossible for the new prince to avoid the imputation of cruelty, owing to new states being full of dangers. Hence Virgil, through the mouth of Dido, excuses the inhumanity of her reign owing to its being new, saying:

[3] *"Res dura, et regni novitas me talia cogunt / Moliri, et late fines custode tueri."*

[4] Nevertheless he ought to be slow to believe and to act, nor should he himself show fear, but proceed in a temperate manner with prudence and humanity, so that too much confidence may not make him incautious and too much distrust render him intolerable.

[5] Upon this a question arises: whether it be better to be loved than feared or feared than loved? It may be answered that one should wish to be both, but, because it is difficult to unite them in one person, it is much safer to be feared than loved, when, of the two, either must be dispensed with. Because this is to be asserted in general of men, that they are ungrateful, fickle, false, cowardly, covetous, and as long as you succeed they are yours entirely; they will offer you their blood, property, life, and children, as is said above, when the need is far distant; but when it approaches they turn against you. And that prince who, relying entirely on their promises, has neglected other precautions, is ruined; because friendships that are obtained by payments, and not by greatness or nobility of mind, may indeed be earned, but they are not secured, and in time of need cannot be relied upon; and men have less scruple in offending one who is beloved than one who is feared, for love is preserved by the link of obligation which, owing to the baseness of men, is broken at every opportunity for their advantage; but fear preserves you by a dread of punishment which never fails.

[6] Nevertheless a prince ought to inspire fear in such a way that, if he does not win love, he avoids hatred; because he can endure very well being feared whilst he is not

hated, which will always be as long as he abstains from the property of his citizens and subjects and from their women. But when it is necessary for him to proceed against the life of someone, he must do it on proper justification and for manifest cause, but above all things he must keep his hands off the property of others, because men more quickly forget the death of their father than the loss of their patrimony. Besides, pretexts for taking away the property are never wanting; for he who has once begun to live by robbery will always find pretexts for seizing what belongs to others; but reasons for taking life, on the contrary, are more difficult to find and sooner lapse. But when a prince is with his army, and has under control a multitude of soldiers, then it is quite necessary for him to disregard the reputation of cruelty, for without it he would never hold his army united or disposed to its duties.

[7] Among the wonderful deeds of Hannibal this one is enumerated: that having led an enormous army, composed of many various races of men, to fight in foreign lands, no dissensions arose either among them or against the prince, whether in his bad or in his good fortune. This arose from nothing else than his inhuman cruelty, which, with his boundless valor, made him revered and terrible in the sight of his soldiers, but without that cruelty, his other virtues were not sufficient to produce this effect. And short-sighted writers admire his deeds from one point of view and from another condemn the principal cause of them. That it is true his other virtues would not have been sufficient for him may be proved by the case of Scipio, that most excellent man, not only of his own times but within the memory of man, against whom, nevertheless, his army rebelled in Spain; this arose from nothing but his too great forbearance, which gave his soldiers more license than is consistent with military discipline. For this he was upbraided in the Senate by Fabius Maximus, and called the corrupter of the Roman soldiery. The Locrians were laid waste by a legate of Scipio, yet they were not avenged by him, nor was the insolence of the legate punished, owing entirely to his easy nature. Insomuch that someone in the Senate, wishing to excuse him, said there were many men who knew much better how not to err than to correct the errors of others. This disposition, if he had been continued in the command, would have destroyed in time the fame and glory of Scipio; but, he being under the control of the Senate, this injurious characteristic not only concealed itself, but contributed to his glory.

1. Which of the following best describes the movement of the passage?
    a. Academic assessment to impassioned plea
    b. Reasoned suggestion to specific example
    c. Calm statement to pressing demand
    d. Persuasive argument to dramatic narrative

2. Which of these sentences best sums up Machiavelli's argument in this passage?
    a. Paragraph 2, Sentence 1 ("And of all princes...dangers.")
    b. Paragraph 7, Sentence 3 ("And shortsighted...of them.")
    c. Paragraph 1, Sentence 1 ("Coming...not cruel.")
    d. Paragraph 5, Sentence 2 ("It may be...dispensed with.")

3. The word *clement* in Paragraph 1, Sentence 1 most closely means
   a. Personable
   b. Relaxed
   c. Merciful
   d. Accommodating

4. According to the passage, cruelty in a prince is
   a. Often a necessary evil owing to the dangers inherent to the start of one's reign
   b. A regrettable practice that ought to be avoided if at all possible
   c. An unacceptable way for one in such a position to behave
   d. The only way to maintain the respect of one's people

5. The relationship between forbearance and leniency is most similar to that between
   a. Dirt and soil
   b. Sand and glass
   c. Heat and cold
   d. Fear and delusion

6. Which paragraph in the passage provides the best evidence in support of the idea that leniency can be dangerous?
   a. Paragraph 1
   b. Paragraph 7
   c. Paragraph 4
   d. Paragraph 6

7. Which choice best describes the tone of the passage?
   a. Delicately implying the true nature of princes
   b. Passionately demanding that princes rearrange their priorities
   c. Coldly contemplating the depths of princes' cruelty
   d. Respectfully explaining the potential courses of action for a prince

8. What purpose does Paragraph 4 serve for the argument presented in Paragraph 1?
   a. It presents evidence to support the argument introduced earlier.
   b. It builds upon previous statements by repeating them using stronger language.
   c. It presents a nuance without which taking the advice in Paragraph 1 may go awry.
   d. It offers a counterargument to an earlier statement.

9. Cesare Borgia : Hannibal ::
   a. Strong leader : depraved madman
   b. Effective ruler : strong leader
   c. Foot soldier : general
   d. Destroyer of Pistoia : commander of a massive army

10. Hannibal : Scipio ::
    a. Fighter : lover
    b. Torturer : rescuer
    c. Disciplinarian : friend
    d. Monster : man

Passage: Science

This passage is adapted from Gregor Mendel's "Experiments on Plant Hybrids."

[1] If two plants that are constantly different in one or more characters are united through fertilization, the characters in common are transmitted unchanged to the hybrids and their progeny, as numerous experiments have shown; each pair of differing characters, however, unites in the hybrid to form a new character that generally is subject to variation in the progeny. To observe these variations for each pair of differing characters and to ascertain a law according to which they occur in succeeding generations was the objective of the experiment. This experiment, therefore, breaks up into just as many individual experiments as there are constantly differing characters in the experimental plants.

[2] The different pea forms selected for fertilization show differences in the length and color of the stem; in the size and form of the leaves; in the placement, color, and size of the flowers; in the length of the flower peduncles; in the color, form, and size of the pods; in the form and size of the seeds; and in the color of the seed coat and of the albumen. Some of these characters, however, do not permit certain and sharp separation because the difference rests on a "more or less" that is difficult to determine. Such characters could not be used for the individual experiments, which had to be limited to characters that appear clearly and decidedly in the plants. A successful result would finally show whether they all are observed as portraying identical behavior in hybrid union and whether, as a result, a judgment is possible about those characters that typically are inferior in their importance.

[3] Of a larger number of plants of the same kind, only the most vigorous were selected for fertilization. Feeble specimens always yield uncertain results, because even in the first generation of the hybrids, and even more so in the following generations, some of the offspring either do not succeed in flowering or produce only few and inferior seeds.

[4] Further, in all experiments reciprocal crosses were undertaken in this manner: One of the two kinds that served as seed plants for a number of fertilizations was used as the pollen plant for the other.

[5] The plants were raised in garden beds, a small number of them in pots, and were kept in the natural upright position by means of poles, tree branches, and taut cords. For each experiment a number of potted plants were placed in a glasshouse during the flowering period. They served as a control for the main garden experiment in case of possible disturbance by insects.

[6] The experiments conducted with ornamental plants in past years already produced evidence that hybrids, as a rule, do not represent the precise intermediate form between the original parents. With individual characters that are particularly noticeable, like those related to the form and size of the leaves and to the pubescence of the individual parts, the intermediate form is in fact almost always apparent; in other cases, however, one of the two original parental characters possesses such an overwhelming

dominance that it is difficult or quite impossible to find the other in the hybrid. Such is exactly the behavior of the Pisum hybrids.

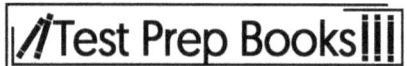

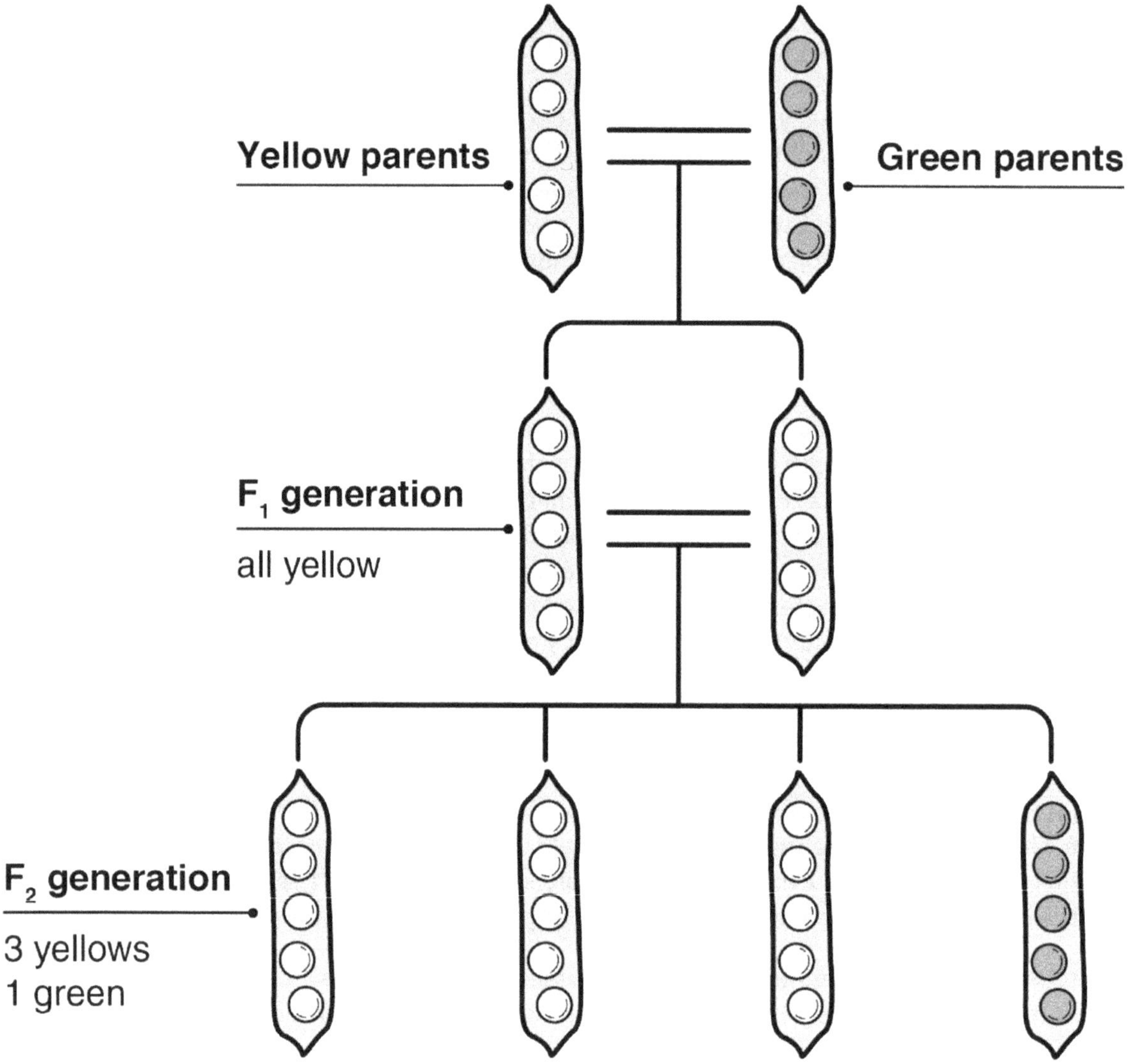

11. What was the primary goal of the experiment described in this passage?
    a. To determine the best variations for pea plants set to go to market
    b. To create pea plant hybrids that only have dominant traits
    c. To observe the variations in succeeding generations of hybrid pea plants
    d. To prove that feeble pea plant specimens can function just as effectively for experimentation

12. Which of the following is NOT a characteristic used in the pea plant experiment?
    a. Petal color variation
    b. Size and form of leaves
    c. Form of seeds
    d. Length of flower peduncles

Practice Test #2

13. How does the passage support its claim about how hybrids compare to their original parents?
    a. By describing the process of reciprocal crosses
    b. By explaining the dominance of parental traits
    c. By discussing the elimination of feeble specimens
    d. By giving examples of hybrid plants in the wild

14. What is the author's attitude toward the process of hybridization?
    a. Enthusiastic
    b. Skeptical
    c. Bewildered
    d. Apathetic

15. What was the purpose of the potted plants in the glasshouse?
    a. To measure the importance of temperature variation
    b. To create a control group in case of insect disturbance
    c. To prevent the interference of wildlife such as rabbits or deer
    d. To observe the process of photosynthesis in the plants

16. How does the information provided in Paragraph 6 relate to the findings of the rest of the passage?
    a. It provides more specific evidence regarding the behavior of hybrids.
    b. It offers information regarding a new experimental method.
    c. It contradicts observations made in previous paragraphs.
    d. It provides examples of the best characteristics for pest resistance.

17. What was the purpose of selecting the most robust plants for fertilization?
    a. To control for the possibility of insect disturbance
    b. To reserve the feeble plants for secondary experiments
    c. To provide more variations for observation
    d. To ensure a higher likelihood of successful fertilization

18. How are Paragraph 3 and Paragraph 4 connected?
    a. Paragraph 4 introduces various characteristics that can change in the hybridization process described in Paragraph 3.
    b. Paragraph 3 provides introductory information about pea plants, while Paragraph 4 goes into depth.
    c. Paragraph 4 is a continuation of Paragraph 3's discussion on how the plants were selected.
    d. Paragraph 3 describes the hybridization hypothesis, while Paragraph 4 provides evidence.

19. Flower : stem ::
    a. Church : worship
    b. Train : caboose
    c. Ocean : waves
    d. Oranges : citrus

20. Feeble specimens : uncertain results ::
    a. Scalpel : surgery
    b. Painter : impressionism
    c. Photosynthesis : sunlight
    d. Solar panel : energy

209

Passage: Philosophy/Religion

This passage is adapted from Augustine of Hippo's The Confessions of Saint Augustine, *created around 397-400 AD.*

[1] Great art Thou, O Lord, and greatly to be praised; great is Thy power, and Thy wisdom infinite. And Thee would man praise; man, but a particle of Thy creation; man, that bears about him his mortality, the witness of his sin, the witness that Thou resistest the proud: yet would man praise Thee; he, but a particle of Thy creation. Thou awakest us to delight in Thy praise; for Thou madest us for Thyself, and our heart is restless, until it repose in Thee. Grant me, Lord, to know and understand which is first, to call on Thee or to praise Thee? and, again, to know Thee or to call on Thee? for who can call on Thee, not knowing Thee? for he that knoweth Thee not, may call on Thee as other than Thou art. Or, is it rather, that we call on Thee that we may know Thee? but how shall they call on Him in whom they have not believed? or how shall they believe without a preacher? and they that seek the Lord shall praise Him: for they that seek shall find Him, and they that find shall praise Him. I will seek Thee, Lord, by calling on Thee; and will call on Thee, believing in Thee; for to us hast Thou been preached. My faith, Lord, shall call on Thee, which Thou hast given me, wherewith Thou hast inspired me, through the Incarnation of Thy Son, through the ministry of the Preacher.

[2] And how shall I call upon my God, my God and Lord, since, when I call for Him, I shall be calling Him to myself? and what room is there within me, whither my God can come into me? whither can God come into me, God who made heaven and earth? is there, indeed, O Lord my God, aught in me that can contain Thee? do then heaven and earth, which Thou hast made, and wherein Thou hast made me, contain Thee? or, because nothing which exists could exist without Thee, doth therefore whatever exists contain Thee? Since, then, I too exist, why do I seek that Thou shouldest enter into me, who were not, wert Thou not in me? Why? because I am not gone down in hell, and yet Thou art there also. For if I go down into hell, Thou art there. I could not be then, O my God, could not be at all, wert Thou not in me; or, rather, unless I were in Thee, of whom are all things, by whom are all things, in whom are all things? Even so, Lord, even so. Whither do I call Thee, since I am in Thee? or whence canst Thou enter into me? for whither can I go beyond heaven and earth, that thence my God should come into me, who hath said, I fill the heaven and the earth.

[3] Do the heaven and earth then contain Thee, since Thou fillest them? or dost Thou fill them and yet overflow, since they do not contain Thee? And whither, when the heaven and the earth are filled, pourest Thou forth the remainder of Thyself? or hast Thou no need that aught contain Thee, who containest all things, since what Thou fillest Thou fillest by containing it? for the vessels which Thou fillest uphold Thee not, since, though they were broken, Thou wert not poured out. And when Thou art poured out on us, Thou art not cast down, but Thou upliftest us; Thou art not dissipated, but Thou gatherest us. But Thou who fillest all things, fillest Thou them with Thy whole self? or, since all things cannot contain Thee wholly, do they contain part of Thee? and all at once the same part? or each its own part, the greater more, the smaller less? And is, then one part of Thee greater, another less? or, art Thou wholly every where, while nothing contains Thee wholly?

Practice Test #2

21. What does the passage claim about the role of vessels for God?
    a. It claims that only humans who are worthy of God's grace are filled with his presence.
    b. It states that vessels are used when God needs to be closer to Earth.
    c. It argues that God fills his human vessels with his essence but his presence dissipates when the vessel is broken.
    d. It suggests that humans are used to contain God's essence on Earth but are not necessary to support him.

22. What is the author's main purpose for this passage?
    a. To question why humans face multiple limitations despite God's grace
    b. To reflect on the nature of God and his relationship with mankind
    c. To condemn preachers for attempting to speak for God
    d. To celebrate theology for enriching mankind's knowledge regarding God

23. Which line from the text provides evidence for the author's devotion?
    a. Paragraph 1, Sentence 3 ("Thou awakest us… repose in Thee.")
    b. Paragraph 1, Sentence 12 ("My faith… ministry of the Preacher.")
    c. Paragraph 2, Sentence 1 ("And how… calling Him to myself?")
    d. Paragraph 3, Sentence 5 ("for the vessels… not poured out.")

24. What purpose does the framework of the passage serve?
    a. The lack of conceptual progression shows the author's scattered thoughts on theology.
    b. The shortened sentences and questions show the author's concern about being cast down to Hell.
    c. The interrogative structure shows that the author is questioning his faith due to lack of concrete evidence.
    d. The use of question marks creates a contemplative tone meant to stimulate the reader's thoughts.

25. What does the author believe about the human heart and restlessness?
    a. That humans feel restless due to their sins that they need to atone for
    b. That God made the human heart restless so that we must find peace with him
    c. That restlessness is a result of the devil's work and requires God's healing
    d. That restlessness fades from our body once we pass on to Heaven

26. What does the word *repose* in Paragraph 1, Sentence 3 most nearly mean?
    a. Finds peace
    b. Expresses anger
    c. Yearns for forgiveness
    d. Goes to sleep

211

27. How does Paragraph 1 logically connect with Paragraph 2?
    a. Paragraph 1 encourages readers to accept God's place in their life, while Paragraph 2 explains how to do that.
    b. Paragraph 1 allows the author to express his views on God, while Paragraph 2 offers an opposing view.
    c. Paragraph 1 seeks to understand why God makes us suffer, while Paragraph 2 gives a pathway to ease suffering.
    d. Paragraph 1 explains why humans seek God, and Paragraph 2 ponders the capacity that humans have to take in God.

28. What shared theme do Paragraph 2 and Paragraph 3 have?
    a. The role of the preacher
    b. Vessels
    c. God's containment
    d. The requirements for Heaven

29. Vessels : God ::
    a. River : boat
    b. Sunset : horizon
    c. Pitcher : water
    d. Volcano : eruption

30. Preacher : belief ::
    a. Teacher : exam
    b. Military : general
    c. Jet : pilot
    d. Environmentalist : conservation

Passage: Historical/Founding Documents

Passage A
This passage is adapted from The Analects of Confucius, *likely compiled between 476-221 BC.*

> [1] Tsze-chang asked Confucius, saying, 'In what way should a person in authority act in order that he may conduct government properly?' The Master replied, 'Let him honor the five excellent, and banish away the four bad, things;— then may he conduct government properly.' Tsze-chang said, 'What are meant by the five excellent things?' The Master said, 'When the person in authority is beneficent without great expenditure; when he lays tasks on the people without their repining; when he pursues what he desires without being covetous; when he maintains a dignified ease without being proud; when he is majestic without being fierce.'
>
> [2] Tsze-chang said, 'What is meant by being beneficent without great expenditure?' The Master replied, 'When the person in authority makes more beneficial to the people the things from which they naturally derive benefit;— is not this being beneficent without great expenditure? When he chooses the labors which are proper, and makes them labor on them, who will repine? When his desires are set on benevolent government, and he secures it, who will accuse him of covetousness? Whether he has to do with many people or few, or with things great or small, he does not dare to indicate any

disrespect;— is not this to maintain a dignified ease without any pride? He adjusts his clothes and cap, and throws a dignity into his looks, so that, thus dignified, he is looked at with awe;— is not this to be majestic without being fierce?'

[3] Tsze-chang then asked, 'What are meant by the four bad things?' The Master said, 'To put the people to death without having instructed them;— this is called cruelty. To require from them, suddenly, the full tale of work, without having given them warning;— this is called oppression. To issue orders as if without urgency, at first, and, when the time comes, to insist on them with severity;— this is called injury. And, generally, in the giving pay or rewards to men, to do it in a stingy way;— this is called acting the part of a mere official.'

Passage B
This passage is adapted from John Locke's Second Treatise of Government, *published in 1689.*

[1] Man being born, as has been proved, with a title to perfect freedom, and an uncontrolled enjoyment of all the rights and privileges of the law of nature, equally with any other man, or number of men in the world, hath by nature a power, not only to preserve his property, that is, his life, liberty and estate, against the injuries and attempts of other men; but to judge of, and punish the breaches of that law in others, as he is persuaded the offence deserves, even with death itself, in crimes where the heinousness of the fact, in his opinion, requires it.

[2] But because no political society can be, nor subsist, without having in itself the power to preserve the property, and in order thereunto, punish the offences of all those of that society; there, and there only is political society, where every one of the members hath quitted this natural power, resigned it up into the hands of the community in all cases that exclude him not from appealing for protection to the law established by it. And thus all private judgment of every particular member being excluded, the community comes to be umpire, by settled standing rules, indifferent, and the same to all parties; and by men having authority from the community, for the execution of those rules, decides all the differences that may happen between any members of that society concerning any matter of right; and punishes those offences which any member hath committed against the society, with such penalties as the law has established: whereby it is easy to discern, who are, and who are not, in political society together.

[3] Those who are united into one body, and have a common established law and judicature to appeal to, with authority to decide controversies between them, and punish offenders, are in civil society one with another: but those who have no such common appeal, I mean on earth, are still in the state of nature, each being, where there is no other, judge for himself, and executioner; which is, as I have before shewed it, the perfect state of nature.

31. How do these two passages differ in their approach towards governance?
    a. Passage A focuses on the importance of morals and virtues in a ruler, while Passage B focuses on the formation of political societies to maintain order.
    b. Passage A believes in democracy and collective power, while Passage B encourages an authoritarian approach towards government.
    c. Passage A emphasizes the rights of individuals and freedom from governance, while Passage B believes in a rigid system that dictates society.
    d. Passage A believes in harsh punishment and a militant approach to maintaining order, while Passage B encourages benevolence and dignity in dealings between government and citizen.

32. According to Passage A, what qualities are essential for those in authoritative positions?
    a. Severity and cruelty
    b. Greed and ambition
    c. Benevolence and dignity
    d. Tranquility and caution

33. In Passage B, what purpose does the author assign to political society?
    a. To establish common rules and authority
    b. To maintain the natural state of humanity
    c. To share resources and responsibility
    d. To deny criminals their individual freedom

34. How do both passages approach their discussion of punishment?
    a. Passage A believes in lenient punishments, while Passage B argues for punishments such as the death penalty.
    b. Passage A states that punishment is a way to maintain order, while Passage B discusses it as a function of a political society.
    c. Passage A says that punishment should be decided by a singular leader, while Passage B encourages a community-based decision.
    d. Passage A encourages punishment to be focused on rehabilitation, while Passage B encourages a prison system.

35. What does Passage A mean by "being beneficent without great expenditure"?
    a. It means to be selective about who receives money and who doesn't.
    b. It means to care about the welfare of the people while being mindful of resources.
    c. It means to only be generous with those who do not plan to excessively spend money.
    d. It means to focus most government spending on issues other than citizen welfare.

36. Which quote from Passage A illustrates Confucius' thoughts on the killing of citizens?
    a. "To issue orders as if without urgency, at first, and, when the time comes, to insist on them with severity;— this is called injury."
    b. "...when he pursues what he desires without being covetous; when he maintains a dignified ease without being proud; when he is majestic without being fierce.'"
    c. "The Master said, 'To put the people to death without having instructed them;— this is called cruelty."
    d. "Whether he has to do with many people or few, or with things great or small, he does not dare to indicate any disrespect..."

37. What quote from Passage B provides the best evidence for Locke's position on those who do not participate in political society?
   a. "And thus all private judgment of every particular member being excluded, the community comes to be umpire, by settled standing rules, indifferent, and the same to all parties…"
   b. "Those who have no such common appeal, I mean on earth, are still in the state of nature, each being, where there is no other judge for himself, and executioner; which is, as I have before shewed it, the perfect state of nature."
   c. "Those who are united into one body, and have a common established law and judicature to appeal to, with authority to decide controversies between them, and punish offenders, are in civil society one with another…"
   d. "Man being born, as has been proved, with a title to perfect freedom, and an uncontrolled enjoyment of all the rights and privileges of the law of nature, equally with any other man, or number of men in the world…"

38. In Passage A, Paragraph 1, Sentence 2, the word *covetous* most nearly means
   a. Greedy
   b. Shameful
   c. Arrogant
   d. Charitable

39. Breaking the law : penalties ::
   a. Medicine : doctor
   b. Tornado : destruction
   c. Breakfast : lunch
   d. Hibernation : winter

40. Benevolent : oppressive ::
   a. Motivated : determined
   b. Robust : complex
   c. Generous : greedy
   d. Communism : socialism

Grammar and Writing

Passage One: Philosophy/Religion

This passage is adapted from Jonathan Edwards' Selected Sermons of Jonathan Edwards.

Man hath now a greater dependence on the grace of God than [41] she had before the fall. He depends on the free goodness of God for much more than he did then: then he depended on God's goodness for conferring the reward of [42] perfect obedience: for God was not obliged to promise and bestow that reward: but now we are dependent on the grace of God for much more. We stand in need of grace, not only [43] bestowed glory upon us, but to deliver us from hell and eternal wrath. Under the first covenant we depended on God's goodness to give us the reward of [44] righteousness; and so we do now. [45] And not only so, but we stand in need of God's free and sovereign grace to give us that righteousness; and yet not only so, but we stand in need of his grace to pardon our sin and release us from the guilt and infinite demerit of it.

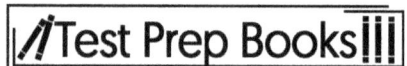

And as we are dependent on the goodness of God for more now than under the first covenant, so we are dependent on a much greater, more free and wonderful goodness. We are now more dependent on God's arbitrary and sovereign good pleasure. We were in our first estate dependent on God for holiness: we had our original righteousness from him; but then holiness was not bestowed in such a way of sovereign good pleasure as it is now. [46] Man was created holy, and it became God to create holy all the reasonable creatures he created: it would have been a disparagement to the holiness of God's nature, if he had made an intelligent creature unholy. But now when a man is made holy, it is from mere and arbitrary grace; God may forever deny holiness to the fallen creature if he pleases, without any disparagement to any of his perfections.

And we are not only indeed more dependent on the grace of God, but our dependence is much more conspicuous, because our own [47] insufficiency and helplessness in ourselves is much more apparent in our fallen and undone state than it was before we were either sinful or miserable. We are more apparently dependent on God for holiness, because we are first sinful, and utterly polluted, and afterward holy: so the production of the effect is sensible, and its derivation from God more obvious. If man was ever holy and always was so, it would not be so apparent, that he had not holiness necessarily, as an inseparable qualification of human nature. [48] So - we are more apparently dependent on free grace for the favor of God, for we are first justly the objects of his displeasure and afterwards are received into favor. We are more apparently dependent on God for [49] happiness; being first miserable and afterwards happy. It is more apparently free and without merit in us, because we are actually without any kind of excellency to merit, if there could be any such thing as merit in creature excellency. And we are not only without any true excellency, but are full of, and wholly defiled with, that which is infinitely odious. All our good is more apparently from God, because we are first naked and wholly without any good, and afterwards [50] fight against our nature.

41. she
   a. NO CHANGE
   b. he
   c. we
   d. they

42. Which of the examples fits best in the sentence?

   He depends on the free goodness of God for much more than he did then: then he depended on God's goodness for conferring the reward of perfect obedience...

   a. NO CHANGE
   b. unwavering abstinence
   c. consistent prayer
   d. unforgivable sin

43. bestowed
   a. NO CHANGE
   b. to bestow
   c. bestowing
   d. to bestowed

Practice Test #2

44. righteousness; and
    a. NO CHANGE
    b. righteousness, and
    c. righteousness - and
    d. righteousness. And

45. Which of the following choices represents the clearest and most concise way to convey all the information in the sentence?

    And not only so, but we stand in need of God's free and sovereign grace to give us that righteousness; and yet not only so, but we stand in need of his grace to pardon our sin and release us from the guilt and infinite demerit of it.

    a. NO CHANGE
    b. We stand in need of God's free and sovereign grace to give us righteousness, but we cannot stand in need of his grace to pardon our sins and release us from gift.
    c. We stand in need of God's free and sovereign grace to give us righteousness, pardon our sins, and release us from the guilt and infinite demerit of it.
    d. We stand in need of God's free and sovereign grace to give us righteousness.

46. Which of the following choices represents the clearest and most concise way to convey all the information in the sentence?

    Man was created holy, and it became God to create holy all the reasonable creatures he created: it would have been a disparagement to the holiness of God's nature, if he had made an intelligent creature unholy.

    a. NO CHANGE
    b. Man is the only reasonable creature created by God that is holy, all other intelligent creatures are unholy and are a disparagement to God's holy nature.
    c. Man and all reasonable creatures created by God are holy, as it would be a disparagement of God's holy nature to make an intelligent creature unholy.
    d. Man was created holy yet act in ways that are a disparagement to the holy nature of God, as he makes all reasonable creatures holy from the beginning.

47. insufficiency
    a. NO CHANGE
    b. independence
    c. idealism
    d. impudence

48. So - we
    a. NO CHANGE
    b. So: we
    c. So, "we
    d. So, we

217

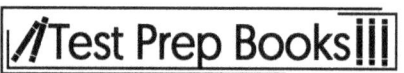

49. happiness; being
    a. NO CHANGE
    b. happiness... being
    c. happiness, being
    d. happiness being

50. Which of the examples fits best in the sentence?

    All our good is more apparently from God, because we are first naked and wholly without any good, and afterwards <u>fight against our nature</u>.

    a. NO CHANGE
    b. suffer for our sins
    c. beg for mercy from God
    d. enriched with his good

Passage Two: Historical Profile

Galileo Galilei, born on February 15, 1564, in Pisa, Italy, was a polymath whose contributions to astronomy, physics, and mathematics forever altered the course of scientific history. His work [51] <u>taken</u> place during the Renaissance era. This was a period marked by a celebration of gaining new knowledge and a shift toward empirical observation. Galileo's work was unique in that it challenged prevailing beliefs and laid the foundation for modern science.

As a child, Galileo was sent to a monastery, where he gained an education and decided to become a monk. However, this [52] <u>displeases</u> his father, who encouraged his son to become a medical doctor. Giving up his chosen path for a career in medicine, Galileo enrolled at the University of Pisa. However, his academic pursuits took a different turn when he discovered his passion for mathematics and natural philosophy. Galileo remained reluctant to study medicine and eventually gave up his studies to teach mathematics instead.

The turning point in Galileo's career came in 1609, when he heard about the invention of a spyglass in the Netherlands. [53] <u>Recognizing its</u> [54] <u>potential Galileo quickly constructed his own telescope that would surpass the performance of the original spyglass, and thus, he created an instrument that would revolutionize his observations of the night sky</u>. In addition, he sold the rights to the telescope to the Venetian Senate, which would use the telescope on its ships.

Galileo's telescopic observations began with the Moon. He discovered craters, mountains, and valleys on the lunar surface, challenging centuries-old beliefs that the Moon was smooth. He observed Jupiter's moons and the phases of Venus. He also provided compelling evidence for the heliocentric model proposed by Copernicus, which stated that the Earth and other planets revolved around the Sun.

Galileo's support for the heliocentric model was not well-received. It put him in a [55] <u>pragmatic</u> situation, where his life's work was threatened. His belief in the model was in direct conflict with the prevailing geocentric worldview upheld by the Catholic Church. [56] <u>The Church saw Galileo's support for heliocentrism as a challenge to its authority</u>

Practice Test #2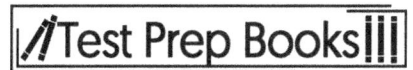

and the beliefs put forth in scripture, so in 1616, they declared heliocentrism to be heretical, and Galileo could no longer spread the word about his discoveries.

Despite the Church's threats, Galileo continued his work and observations. In 1632, he published his findings in a book titled *Dialogue Concerning the Two Chief World Systems*. This work cleverly presented a dialogue between characters discussing the merits of heliocentrism and geocentrism. This publication led to Galileo facing the Roman Inquisition in 1633. The Inquisition found him guilty of heresy. He was sentenced to lifelong imprisonment through house arrest. Despite the restrictions, Galileo continued his [57] scientific pursuits to learn more about our world.

During his imprisonment, Galileo wrote *Two New Sciences* in 1638. It was one of his most notable works, as it explored the strength of materials and the science of motion. He discussed the concept of inertia and the law of falling bodies. This would become the foundation for Isaac Newton's development of classical mechanics, as well as the scientific method.

Galileo completed his work and had it smuggled [58] out of Florence, Italy. It was then taken to Holland to be published, ensuring his legacy. Unfortunately, Galileo was often ill, as he was nearing 70 years old at this time. In 1640, he designed the first pendulum clock but was unable to bring the design to life, as he died a mere two years later. His son would go on to attempt to create the design himself but ultimately failed.

Galileo's legacy holds strong today. Scientists continue to find inspiration in Galileo's curiosity and dedication to pursuing the truth, despite the [59] deadly illness he faced. Heliocentrism eventually triumphed, and it was largely thanks to the observations and experimentation that Galileo had dedicated his life to. Astronomy and physics [60] is forever changed by Galileo's contributions.

51. taken
    a. NO CHANGE
    b. takes
    c. took
    d. take

52. displeases
    a. NO CHANGES
    b. displeased
    c. displeasing
    d. displease

53. Which of the following choices represents the clearest and most concise way to convey all the information in the sentence?

> Recognizing its potential Galileo quickly constructed his own telescope that would surpass the performance of the original spyglass and thus he had created an instrument that would revolutionize his observations of the night sky.

a. NO CHANGE
b. Galileo believed he could create something better and thus made the telescope, which was an invaluable instrument for his night sky observations.
c. Galileo created the spyglass before evolving it into the telescope, which revolutionized his observations of the night sky.
d. Galileo recognized the potential of the spyglass and constructed a superior telescope that revolutionized his observations of the night sky.

54. potential Galileo
   a. NO CHANGE
   b. potential; Galileo
   c. potential… Galileo
   d. potential, Galileo

55. pragmatic
   a. NO CHANGE
   b. pecuniary
   c. precarious
   d. precocious

56. Which of the following choices represents the clearest and most concise way to convey all the information in the sentence?

> The Church saw Galileo's support for heliocentrism as a challenge to its authority and the beliefs put forth in the scripture, so in 1616 they declared heliocentrism to be heretical, and Galileo could no longer spread the word about his discoveries.

a. NO CHANGE
b. The Church banned Galileo from speaking about heliocentrism as it went against the scripture and Church beliefs, therefore it was declared to be heretical, and Galileo was forced to give up on the theory.
c. The Church found heliocentrism to be unprovable and thus heretical, thus banning Galileo from spreading the word about his discoveries.
d. In 1616, the Church deemed heliocentrism to be heretical as it challenged their authority and scripture, so they banned Galileo from spreading the word about his discoveries.

Practice Test #2

57. Which of the examples fits best in the paragraph?

Despite the restrictions, Galileo continued his scientific pursuits to learn more about our world.

   a. NO CHANGE
   b. work that was dedicated to sharing unproven theories in order to inspire others
   c. plan of getting back at the Roman Catholic Inquisition for his imprisonment
   d. dreams of proving his father wrong about not becoming a doctor

58. out of Florence, Italy
   a. NO CHANGE
   b. out of, Florence, Italy
   c. out of Florence Italy
   d. out, of Florence, Italy

59. Which of the examples fits best in the paragraph?

Scientists continue to find inspiration in Galileo's curiosity and dedication to pursue the truth, despite deadly illness.

   a. NO CHANGE
   b. family tragedies
   c. strong opposition
   d. struggles with motivation

60. is
   a. NO CHANGE
   b. can be
   c. was
   d. were

Passage Three: Science

This passage is adapted from Alfred North Whitehead's An Introduction to Mathematics, *published in 1911.*

The study of mathematics is apt to commence in disappointment. The important applications of the science, the theoretical interest of its ideas, and the logical rigor of its methods, all generate the expectation of a speedy introduction to processes of interest. We are told that by its aid the stars are weighed and the billions of molecules in a drop of water [61] are counting. Yet, like the ghost of Hamlet's father, this great science eludes the efforts of our mental weapons to grasp it—" 'Tis here, 'tis there, 'tis gone"—and what we do see does not suggest the same excuse for [62] infirmity as sufficed for the ghost, that it is too noble for our gross methods. "A show of violence," if ever excusable, may surely be "offered" to the trivial results which occupy the pages of some elementary mathematical treatises.

The reason for this failure of the science to live up to its reputation is that its fundamental ideas are not explained to the student disentangled from the technical procedure which has been invented to facilitate their exact presentation in particular

221

instances. [63] Accordingly, the unfortunate learner finds himself struggling to acquire a knowledge of a mass of details which are not illuminated by any general conception. [64] Without a doubt, technical facility is a first requisite for valuable mental activity: we shall fail to appreciate the rhythm of Milton, or the passion of Shelley, so long as we find it necessary to spell the words and are not quite certain of the forms of the individual letters. In this sense there is no royal road to learning. But it is equally an error to confine attention to technical processes, excluding consideration of general ideas. Here lies the road to pedantry.

The first acquaintance which most people have with mathematics is through arithmetic. That two and two make four is usually taken as the type of a simple mathematical proposition which everyone will have heard of. Arithmetic, therefore, will be a good subject to consider [65] in order to discover, if possible, the most obvious characteristic of the science. Now, the first noticeable fact about arithmetic is that it applies to everything, to tastes and to sounds, to apples and to angels, to the ideas of the mind and to the bones of the body. The nature of the things is perfectly indifferent, all things it is true that two and two make four. [66] Thus we write down as the leading characteristic of mathematics that it deals with properties and ideas which are applicable to things just because they are things, and apart from any particular feelings, or emotions, or sensations, in any way connected with them. This is what is meant by calling mathematics an abstract science.

The result which we have reached deserves attention. [67] It is natural to think that an abstract science cannot be of much importance in the affairs of human life, because it has omitted from its consideration everything of real interest. It will be remembered that [68] Swift, in his description of Gulliver's voyage to Laputa is of two minds on this point. He describes the mathematicians of that country as silly and useless dreamers, whose attention has to be awakened by flappers. Also, the mathematical tailor measures his height by a quadrant, and deduces his other dimensions by a rule and compasses, [69] producing a suit of very ill-fitting clothes. On the other hand, the mathematicians of Laputa, by their marvelous invention of the magnetic island floating in the air, ruled the country and maintained their ascendency over their subjects. [70] Swift, indeed, lived at a time peculiarly unsuited for gibes at contemporary mathematicians. Newton's Principia had just been written, one of the great forces which have transformed the modern world. Swift might just as well have laughed at an earthquake.

61. are counting
    a. NO CHANGE
    b. are counted
    c. is counted
    d. is counting

62. infirmity
    a. NO CHANGE
    b. idiosyncrasy
    c. indemnity
    d. illusiveness

Practice Test #2

63. Accordingly:
   a. NO CHANGE
   b. Accordingly;
   c. Accordingly,
   d. Accordingly…

64. Which of the following choices represents the clearest and most concise way to convey all the information in the sentence?

   Without a doubt, technical facility is a first requisite for valuable mental activity: we shall fail to appreciate the rhythm of Milton, or the passion of Shelley, so long as we find it necessary to spell the words and are not quite certain of the forms of the individual letters.

   a. NO CHANGE
   b. Technical facility is essential for meaningful mental activity; understanding the rhythm of Milton, or the passion of Shelley, is impossible without the fundamental skills.
   c. We fail to understand Milton and Shelly because we focus too much on technical writing skills, such as the formation of letters and spelling.
   d. Poets such as Milton and Shelly are underappreciated due to their expert technical facility, which is not shared by most individuals.

65. Which of the examples fits best in the paragraph?

   Arithmetic, therefore, will be a good subject to consider <u>in order to discover</u>, if possible, the most obvious characteristic of the science.

   a. NO CHANGE
   b. in order to critique
   c. in order to teach
   d. in order to disprove

66. Which of the following choices represents the clearest and most concise way to convey all the information in the sentence?

   Thus we write down as the leading characteristic of mathematics that it deals with properties and ideas which are applicable to things just because they are things, and apart from any particular feelings, or emotions, or sensations, in any way connected with them.

   a. NO CHANGE
   b. Mathematics focuses on the feelings, emotions, and sensations that are attached to things.
   c. Mathematics often applies to properties and ideas of things regardless of their feelings, emotions, or sensations.
   d. The characteristics of mathematics are similar to the feelings, emotions, and sensations that are connected to things and thus must be approached in the same manner.

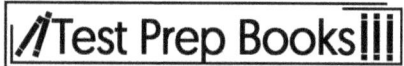

67. Which previous line(s) from the text refutes the belief mentioned here?

   It is natural to think that an abstract science cannot be of much importance in the affairs of human life, because it has omitted from its consideration everything of real interest.

   a. The reason for this failure of the science to live up to its reputation is that its fundamental ideas are not explained to the student disentangled from the technical procedure which has been invented to facilitate their exact presentation in particular instances.
   b. The first acquaintance which most people have with mathematics is through arithmetic.
   c. In this sense there is no royal road to learning. But it is equally an error to confine attention to technical processes, excluding consideration of general ideas.
   d. Now, the first noticeable fact about arithmetic is that it applies to everything, to tastes and to sounds, to apples and to angels, to the ideas of the mind and to the bones of the body.

68. Swift, in his description of Gulliver's voyage to Laputa is
   a. NO CHANGE
   b. Swift in his description of Gulliver's voyage to Laputa is,
   c. Swift, in his description of Gulliver's voyage to Laputa, is
   d. Swift, in his description of Gullivers voyage to Laputa, is

69. producing
   a. NO CHANGE
   b. produces
   c. produced
   d. production

70. Swift, indeed, lived
   a. NO CHANGE
   b. Swift indeed lived
   c. Swift indeed lived,
   d. Swift, indeed lived

Passage Four: Modern/Influential Thinker

This passage is adapted from Mahatma Gandhi's A Guide to Health, *published in 1921.*

Ordinarily that man is considered healthy who eats well and moves about, and does not resort to a doctor. But a little thought will convince us that this idea is wrong. There are many cases of men being [71] diseased, in spite of their eating well and freely moving about. They are under the delusion that they are healthy, simply because they are too indifferent to [72] thinks about the matter.

In fact, perfectly healthy men hardly exist anywhere over this wide world.

As has been well said, only that man can be said to be really healthy, [73] she who has a sound mind in a sound body. The relation between the body and the mind is so intimate that, if either of them got out of order, the whole system would suffer. Let us take the analogy of the rose-flower. Its color stands to its fragrance in the same way as the body to the mind or the soul. No one [74] regard an artificial paper-flower as a sufficient substitute for the natural flower, for the obvious reason that the fragrance, which forms the essence of the flower, cannot be reproduced. So too, we instinctively honor the man of a pure mind and a [75] nebulous character in preference to the man who shows only [76] physical prowess. Of course, the body and the soul are both essential, but the latter is far more important than the former. No man whose character is not pure can be said to be really healthy. The body which contains a diseased mind can never be anything but diseased. Hence it follows that a pure character is the foundation of health in the real sense of the term; and we may say that all evil thoughts and evil passions are but different forms of disease.

[77] Thus considered, we may conclude that that man alone is perfectly healthy whose body is well formed, whose teeth as well as eyes and ears are in good condition, whose nose is free from dirty matter, whose skin exudes perspiration freely and without any bad smell, whose mouth is also free from bad smells, whose hands and legs perform their duty properly, who is neither too fat nor too thin, and whose mind and senses are constantly under his control. As has already been said, it is very hard to gain such health, but it is harder still to retain it, when once it has been acquired. The chief reason why we are not truly healthy is that our parents were not. An eminent writer has said that, if the parents are in perfectly good condition their children would certainly be superior to them in all respects. A perfectly healthy man has no reason to fear [78] death: our terrible fear of death shows that we are far from being so healthy. It is, however, the clear duty of all of us to [79] make a goal to avoid the doctor. We will, therefore, proceed to consider in the following pages how such health can be attained, and how, when once attained, it can also be retained forever.

The world is compounded of the five elements,—earth, water, air, fire, and ether. So too is our body. It is a sort of miniature world. [80] Hence the body stands in need of all the elements in due proportion,—pure earth, pure water, pure fire or sunlight, pure air, and open space, thus when any one of these falls short of its due proportion, illness is caused in the body.

71. diseased, in
    a. NO CHANGE
    b. diseased… in
    c. diseased: in
    d. diseased; in

72. thinks
    a. NO CHANGE
    b. thought
    c. thoughts
    d. think

73. she
    a. NO CHANGE
    b. he
    c. they
    d. them

74. regard
    a. NO CHANGE
    b. regarded
    c. regards
    d. regarding

75. nebulous
    a. NO CHANGE
    b. naive
    c. noble
    d. nefarious

76. Which of the examples fits best in the paragraph?

    So too, we instinctively honor the man of a pure mind and a nebulous character in preference to the man who shows only physical prowess.

    a. NO CHANGE
    b. great intelligence
    c. restraint from sinning
    d. parenting success

77. Which of the following choices represents the clearest and most concise way to convey all the information in the sentence?

    Thus considered, we may conclude that that man alone is perfectly healthy whose body is well formed, whose teeth as well as eyes and ears are in good condition, whose nose is free from dirty matter, whose skin exudes perspiration freely and without any bad smell, whose mouth is also free from bad smells, whose hands and legs perform their duty properly, who is neither too fat nor too thin, and whose mind and senses are constantly under his control.

    a. NO CHANGE
    b. A man cannot be considered healthy so long as he has poor eyesight, hearing, or body odor.
    c. The perfectly healthy man cannot exist as there is a long list of criteria, such as: healthy eyes and ears, a clean nose, perspiration without smell, a mouth with no smell, functioning limbs, a moderate weight, and a strong mind.
    d. A perfectly healthy man has a well formed body that functions well while remaining clean and free of bad smells, as well a healthy weight and strong mind.

78. death: our
    a. NO CHANGE
    b. death... our
    c. death; our
    d. death – our

Practice Test #2

79. Which of the examples fits best in the paragraph?

A perfectly healthy man has no reason to fear death; our terrible fear of death shows that we are far from being so healthy. It is, however, the clear duty of all of us to make a goal to avoid the doctor.

   a. NO CHANGE
   b. avoid accidents leading to death
   c. aim to do better than our parents
   d. strive for perfect health

80. Which of the following choices represents the clearest and most concise way to convey all the information in the sentence?

Hence the body stands in need of all the elements in due proportion,—pure earth, pure water, pure fire or sunlight, pure air, and open space, thus when any one of these falls short of its due proportion, illness is caused in the body.

   a. NO CHANGE
   b. The body needs adequate pure earth, water, fire or sunlight, air, and open space, otherwise it will become ill.
   c. The body requires certain elements depending on its needs, such as, pure earth, water, fire or sunlight, air, and open space.
   d. When the body has an illness, we need elements such as pure earth, pure water, pure fire or sunlight, pure air, and open space in order to heal it.

Quantitative Reasoning

81. If $\sqrt{5+x} = 5$, what is x?
   a. 10
   b. 15
   c. 20
   d. 25

82. What is the solution to $9 \times 9 \div 9 + 9 - 9 \div 9$?
   a. 0
   b. 17
   c. 81
   d. 9

83. The area of a given rectangle is 24 cm². If the measure of each side is multiplied by 3, what is the area of the new figure?
   a. 48 cm²
   b. 72 cm²
   c. 216 cm²
   d. 13,824 cm²

84. A mathematics student states that all right triangles have three sides with different lengths. Which of the following is a counterexample that disproves this statement?
   a. An isosceles right triangle
   b. An obtuse triangle with an angle measuring 120°
   c. An equilateral triangle
   d. An acute triangle

85. The triangle shown below is a right triangle. What's the value of x?

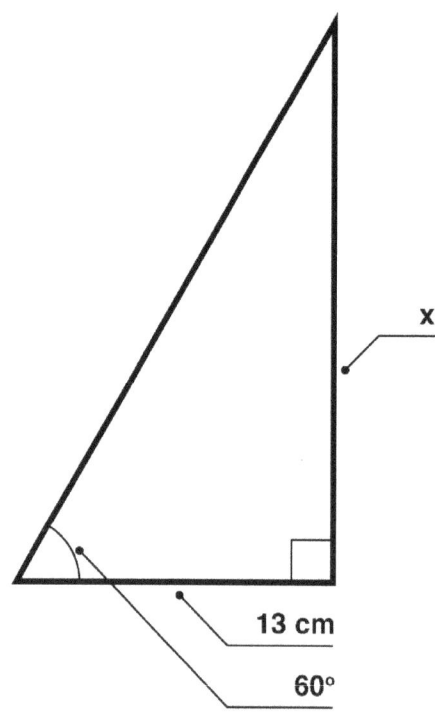

   a. $x = 1.73$
   b. $x = 0.57$
   c. $x = 13$
   d. $x = 22.52$

86. How many integers between 11 and 81 (inclusive) meet both of the following conditions?
   I. The last digit of the integer is a non-negative solution to $x^3 + x^2 - 6x = 0$.
   II. The sum of the integer's digits is greater than 5.
   a. 13
   b. 10
   c. 16
   d. 7

87. "The sum of two composite numbers has to be another composite number." Which of the following is a counterexample that disproves this statement?
   a. $12 + 21$
   b. $3 + 7$
   c. $16 + 5$
   d. $8 + 9$

88. If the point $(6, 2)$ is reflected over the y-axis, what new point does it make?
   a. $(6, 2)$
   b. $(-6, 2)$
   c. $(-6, -2)$
   d. $(6, -2)$

89. If $\frac{5}{2} \div \frac{1}{3} = n$, then n is between:
   a. 5 and 7
   b. 1 and 3
   c. 3 and 5
   d. 7 and 9

90. How could the following equation be factored to find the zeros?

$$y = x^3 - 3x^2 - 4x$$

   a. $0 = x^2(x - 4), x = 0, 4$
   b. $0 = 3x(x + 1)(x + 4), x = 0, -1, -4$
   c. $0 = x(x + 1)(x + 6), x = 0, -1, -6$
   d. $0 = x(x + 1)(x - 4), x = 0, -1, 4$

91. For the following similar triangles, what are the values of x and y (rounded to one decimal place)?

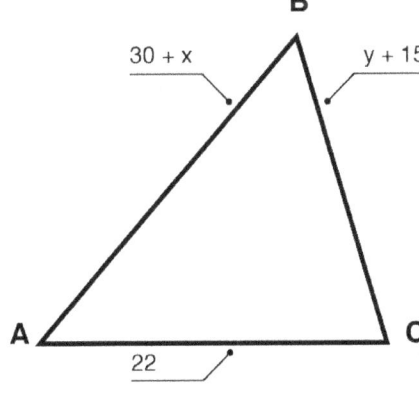
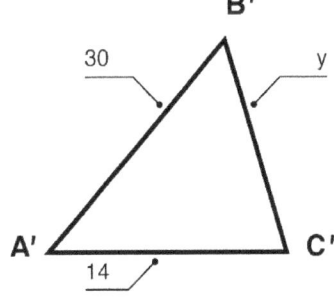

   a. $x = 16.5, y = 25.1$
   b. $x = 19.5, y = 24.1$
   c. $x = 17.1, y = 26.3$
   d. $x = 26.3, y = 17.1$

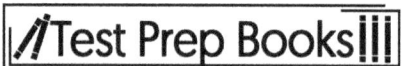

92. A box of mini chocolate chip cookies contains 64 items. Special edition packages contain 12% more. How many cookies are in the special edition boxes? Round to the nearest whole number.
    a. 8 cookies
    b. 72 cookies
    c. 76 cookies
    d. 12 cookies

93. A mathematics teacher taught an algebra class every year from 2018 through 2021. The average class size was 25.5. What is the lowest possible class size if no class has exceeded 28 students?
    a. 18 students
    b. 19 students
    c. 20 students
    d. 21 students

94. Kristina purchased a laptop at 14% off and received an additional discount of $200. If the laptop cost her $1,250, what was the original price of the laptop? Round to the nearest dollar.
    a. $1,450
    b. $1,247
    c. $1,686
    d. $1,453

95. Using trigonometric ratios for a right angle, what is the value of the closest angle whose adjacent side is equal to 7.071 centimeters and whose hypotenuse is equal to 10 centimeters?
    a. 15°
    b. 30°
    c. 45°
    d. 90°

96. A positive integer k^2, whose digits have a sum of 10, is the square of a positive integer k. What is one possible value of $k^3 + 3$?
    a. 1334
    b. 1003
    c. 346
    d. 515

97. Last year, the New York City area received approximately $27\frac{3}{4}$ inches of snow. The Denver area received approximately 3 times as much snow as New York City. How much snow fell in Denver?
    a. 60 inches
    b. $27\frac{1}{4}$ inches
    c. $9\frac{1}{4}$ inches
    d. $83\frac{1}{4}$ inches

Practice Test #2

98. What is the solution for the following equation?

$$\frac{x^2 + x - 30}{x - 5} = 11$$

  a. $x = -6$
  b. $x = 5$
  c. $x = 16$
  d. There is no solution.

99. What are the center and radius of a circle with equation $4x^2 + 4y^2 - 16x - 24y + 51 = 0$?
  a. Center $(3, 2)$ and radius $1/2$
  b. Center $(2, 3)$ and radius $1/2$
  c. Center $(3, 2)$ and radius $1/4$
  d. Center $(2, 3)$ and radius $1/4$

100. The sum of four consecutive odd numbers is 5,064. What is the third number?
  a. 1,263
  b. 79
  c. 1,267
  d. 1,011

101. A garden is shaped in the form of a right triangle. The hypotenuse of the garden measures 15 feet, and one of the other sides is 6 feet long. What is the area of the garden? Round your answer to the nearest tenth of a square foot.
  a. 41.1 ft²
  b. 45.0 ft²
  c. 82.2 ft²
  d. 120.0 ft²

102. Using trigonometric ratios, what is the value of an angle whose opposite side is equal to 1 inch and whose adjacent side is equal to the square root of 3 inches?
  a. 15°
  b. 30°
  c. 45°
  d. 90°

103. Kenya was selling magazines for a school fundraiser. She ended up selling 89 magazines, which was 56% of the allotted magazines for her class. How many magazines were allotted for her class? Round to the nearest whole number of magazines.
  a. 50 magazines
  b. 159 magazines
  c. 39 magazines
  d. 202 magazines

104. What is the equation of a circle whose center is (0, 0) and whole radius is 5?
   a. $(x-5)^2 + (y-5)^2 = 25$
   b. $(x)^2 + (y)^2 = 5$
   c. $(x)^2 + (y)^2 = 25$
   d. $(x+5)^2 + (y+5)^2 = 25$

105. A student gets an 85% on a test with 20 questions. How many questions did the student solve correctly?
   a. 15 questions
   b. 16 questions
   c. 17 questions
   d. 18 questions

106. If x is not zero, then $\frac{3}{x} + \frac{5u}{2x} - \frac{u}{4} =$
   a. $\frac{12+10u-ux}{4x}$
   b. $\frac{3+5u-ux}{x}$
   c. $\frac{12x+10u+ux}{4x}$
   d. $\frac{12+10u-u}{4x}$

107. The area of circle O is 49π m. What is the area of the sector formed by $\angle AOB$?

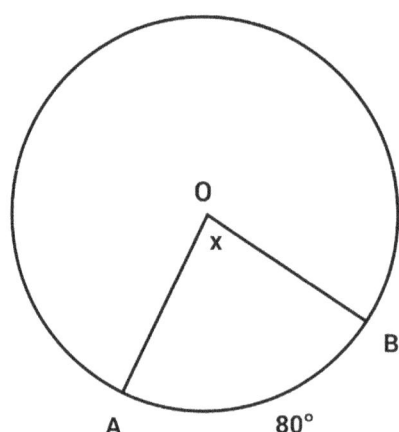

   a. 80π m
   b. 10.9π m
   c. 4.9π m
   d. 10π m

Practice Test #2

108. Line A is on the (xy)-coordinate plane and is represented by the equation $2x + 4y = 9$. Which of the following is false?
   a. The line $y = -2x + 6$ is perpendicular to Line A.
   b. The line $y = -\frac{1}{2}x + 5$ is parallel to Line A.
   c. The line $y = 2x + 10$ is perpendicular to Line A.
   d. The point $\left(1, \frac{7}{4}\right)$ is on Line A.

109. How many positive integers between 120 and 190 (inclusive) are divisible by 9 and are odd?
   a. 4
   b. 6
   c. 8
   d. 10

110. The ratio of pens to pencils in Christina's desk is 10:3. However, she then trades 4 pens for pencils and the ratio is now 10:5. How many pens did she start with?
   a. 10
   b. 70
   c. 100
   d. 30

111. What is the y-intercept for $y = x^2 + 3x - 4$?
   a. $y = 1$
   b. $y = -4$
   c. $y = -3$
   d. $y = 4$

112. "If a number is added to itself, the sum is greater than or equal to the original number." Which of the following is a counterexample?
   a. $-4 + (-4)$
   b. $12 + 12$
   c. $12 + (-12)$
   d. $0 + 0$

113. What is the simplified quotient of $\frac{5x^3}{3x^2y} \div \frac{25}{3y^9}$?
   a. $\frac{125x}{9y^{10}}$
   b. $\frac{x}{5y^8}$
   c. $\frac{5}{xy^8}$
   d. $\frac{xy^8}{5}$

114. What is the value of $x^2 - 2xy + 2y^2$ when $x = 2$ and $y = 3$?
   a. 6
   b. 10
   c. 12
   d. 18

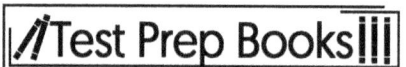

Practice Test #2

115. What is the length of the hypotenuse of a right triangle with one leg equal to 3 centimeters and the other leg equal to 4 centimeters?
   a. 7 cm
   b. 5 cm
   c. 25 cm
   d. 12 cm

116. In the *xy*-plane, the graph of $y = x^2 + 2$ and the circle with center $(0, 1)$ and radius 1 have how many points of intersection?
   a. 0
   b. 1
   c. 2
   d. 3

117. What is the simplified form of the expression $tan\theta \, cos\theta$?
   a. $sin\theta$
   b. 1
   c. $csc\theta$
   d. $\frac{1}{sec\theta}$

118. A right triangle has an interior angle that measures 30° and a hypotenuse that measures 20 cm. What is the length of the shortest side?
   a. 17 cm
   b. 15 cm
   c. 10 cm
   d. 5 cm

119. A line passes through the origin and through the point $(-3,4)$. What is the slope of the line?
   a. $-\frac{4}{3}$
   b. $-\frac{3}{4}$
   c. $\frac{4}{3}$
   d. $\frac{3}{4}$

120. Cassandra has four cats. Two of the cats are black and two are white. Half of the cats are male. If the first three sentences are true, which of the following must also be true?
           I: At least one male is black.
           II: Two of the cats are female.
           III: The males are white.
   a. I only
   b. II only
   c. II and III only
   d. None are true.

Answer Explanations #2

Verbal Reasoning

1. B: Choice B matches the movement of the passage from Machiavelli suggesting that a prince should aim to be seen as clement rather than cruel to him giving the specific example of how Hannibal and Scipio ruled. Choice A demands desperation that is not present in the final paragraph nor in any other part of the passage. Choice C also requires the passage's final paragraph to carry emotion that it does not. Choice D is incorrect because the last paragraph is not presented as a story being told about Hannibal.

2. D: In Choice D, Machiavelli declares it better to be feared than loved if one must be chosen, which is his thesis in this passage. Choice A is incorrect because it gives a generalization that Machiavelli believes applies to the world. Choice B is incorrect because it describes the conflicted manner in which writers discuss Hannibal. Choice C is incorrect because Machiavelli says it is best not to be seen as cruel, but he later goes on to say that it can still be the better choice for a prince to be cruel, especially at the start of his reign.

3. C: Choice C fits best with the idea of clemency as the opposite of cruelty. Choices A and B do not provide a strong enough contrast to the concept of cruelty to make either of them a suitable replacement for the word *clement*. Choice D presents the same problem in addition to being a quality Machiavelli would absolutely not support in a ruler based on the rest of the passage.

4. A: Choice A correctly notes Machiavelli's support of some cruelty if necessary, especially at the start of a prince's reign. Choice B and Choice C both present a too uniformly negative view of cruelty. Choice D is too uniformly uncritical of cruelty; this contradicts the opening statement of the passage that it is better to be seen as merciful rather than cruel.

5. A: Choice A makes it clear that these words are synonyms. Choice B implies that forbearance creates leniency, Choice C makes them out to be opposites, and Choice D compares an emotion to a state of mind that might sometimes accompany it.

6. B: Choice B supports this idea by comparing the example of the cruel Hannibal with the forbearing Scipio, noting that it is the latter whose troops rebelled against him. Choice A gives the example of Cesare Borgia being successful due to his cruelty, but no strong examples in which clemency caused the opposite outcome. In Choices C and D, Machiavelli does not provide evidence to support this assertion. While Paragraph 1 does give the example of "the Florentine people, who, to avoid a reputation for cruelty, permitted Pistoia to be destroyed," Paragraph 7 is more persuasive because it provides greater detail.

7. D: Choice D correctly marks Machiavelli's tone as respectful as he explains to the potential prince reading his book how he may act to ensure the loyalty of his people. Choice A would require a more timid and hesitant use of language, Choice B would require that the passage be much more emotionally charged, and Choice C would require it to pass harsh judgment on the cruel behavior of the princes it uses as points of reference.

8. C: Choice C is the correct answer because Paragraph 4 includes the nuance that a prince should be slow to act and should not appear to act out of fear. This prevents Paragraph 1's support of necessary

Answer Explanations #2

cruelty from being misinterpreted as encouragement for rulers to react to all problems with immediate, harsh punishments. Choice *A* is incorrect because Paragraph 4 makes an assertion but does not include evidence to support it. Choice *B* is incorrect because Paragraph 4 adds to the argument rather than simply repeating it. Choice *D* is incorrect because Paragraph 4 does not contradict anything stated in Paragraph 1.

9. B: Choice *B* acknowledges that Cesare Borgia and Hannibal are praised in very similar ways for what their cruelty did for their leadership qualities in their respective paragraphs. Choice *A* is incorrect because the passage does not regard Hannibal as a madman. Choice *C* is incorrect because the passage does not imply that Cesare Borgia was of low rank. Choice *D* is incorrect because it falsely states that Cesare Borgia was the one to destroy Pistoia.

10. C: Choice *C* best expresses Machiavelli's view that Hannibal's inhuman cruelty spared him the rebellion that he says Scipio caused by being too forbearing with his men. Choice *A*'s oversimplification neglects the fact that these men both commanded an army. Choice *B* implies that Scipio saved Hannibal's men from him. Choice *D* states an unflattering opinion of Hannibal that does not match Machiavelli's in the passage.

11. C: Choice *C* is the correct answer because it accurately identifies the primary goal of the experiment. Mendel used pea plants to study variations between parent plants and their hybrid offspring. Choice *A* is incorrect because the market is not mentioned as a destination for the plants. Choice *B* is incorrect because the study is about hybridization, not only about dominant traits. Choice *D* is incorrect because the feeble specimens were discarded in this experiment.

12. A: Choice *A* is the correct answer because the color variation of petals is never mentioned. The passage lists characteristics such as length and color of the stem, size and form of leaves, placement and color of flowers, and form and size of seeds. However, the passage does not mention color variation in the petals. Choices *B, C,* and *D* are incorrect because they are all characteristics that are specifically mentioned in the passage.

13. B: Choice *B* is the correct answer because it identifies how the author supports their claims about hybrid plants in comparison to their parent plants. This is discussed most in Paragraph 2 and Paragraph 6. Choice *A* is incorrect because the process of reciprocal crosses does not change how the hybrids compare to their parents. Choice *C* is incorrect because eliminating feeble specimens was for the quality of the experiment; it is not relevant to the comparison. Choice *D* is incorrect because pea plants and ornamental plants are the only types of plants described.

14. A: Choice *A* is the correct answer because the author seems enthusiastic about the work that he is doing. This is evidenced by the long descriptions and detail he uses to recount the experiment. There is nothing to suggest that the author is skeptical or bewildered, as the passage comes across confidently. This eliminates Choices *B* and *C*. Choice *D* is incorrect because the author's attention to detail shows that he is not apathetic towards the work.

15. B: Choice *B* is the correct answer because Paragraph 5 explains the glasshouse was used to create a control group in case of possible disturbance by insects. Choice *A* is incorrect because although temperature consistency may be a benefit of using the glasshouse, it is not discussed. Choice *C* is incorrect because insects are the only creature mentioned. Choice *D* is incorrect because photosynthesis as a process is not discussed explicitly.

Answer Explanations #2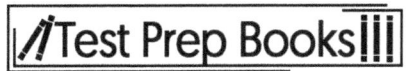

16. A: Choice *A* is the correct answer because it accurately describes the purpose of the information in Paragraph 6. Paragraph 6 provides additional evidence about how hybrids behave genetically. Specifically, it is about how certain visual characteristics from the parent plants transfer to the hybrids. Choice *B* is incorrect because Paragraph 6 does not introduce a new experimental method. Choice *C* is incorrect because there is no contradictory information in this passage. Choice *D* is incorrect because there are no examples of pest-resisting characteristics.

17. D: Choice *D* is the correct answer because it accurately identifies the purpose of using only robust plants in the experiment. The robust plants were used to ensure successful fertilization and to avoid uncertain results from feeble specimens. Choice *A* is incorrect because the glasshouse was used to prevent insect disturbance. Choice *B* is incorrect because the feeble plants were not said to be used for other purposes. Choice *C* is incorrect because the passage does not state that robust plants have more variations than others, just that they fertilize more successfully.

18. C: Choice *C* is correct because it best states how Paragraphs 3 and 4 relate to one another. Paragraph 3 discusses how and why plants were selected for fertilization and the reciprocal cross process. Paragraph 4 is a continuation of that discussion. Choice *A* is incorrect because the focus of Paragraph 3 is the strength of specimens. Paragraph 4 discusses reciprocal crosses. The paragraphs do not focus on specific characteristics. Choice *B* is incorrect because, although there is some information about feeble specimen defects, it is not introductory information. Choice *D* is incorrect because the hybridization hypothesis is discussed at the beginning of the passage.

19. B: Choice *B* is correct because it is the analogy that best fits the original pairing. A stem is part of the larger object, which is a flower. The relationship must match this. In this case, a caboose is part of the larger object, which is the train. Choices *A*, *C*, and *D* are incorrect because they do not have a Whole : Part relationship.

20. D: Choice *D* is correct because it is the analogy that best matches the relationship of the original pairing, which is a cause-and-effect relationship. Feeble specimens lead to uncertain results in the experiment. Choice *D* is correct because solar panels lead to energy creation. Choices *A*, *B*, and *C* are incorrect because the first term does not lead to the second term.

21. D: Choice *D* is the correct answer because it accurately identifies what the last paragraph in the passage is saying about God's vessels. The author writes about the role of the vessel while saying, "for the vessels which Thou fillest uphold Thee not, since, though they were broken, Thou wert not poured out," which confirms that God is not lost when a vessel is broken. This aligns with Choice *D*. Choice *A* is incorrect because the author claims that God fills humans in order to gather and uplift them, whether they uphold God or not. Choice *B* is incorrect because God fills His vessels in order to uplift them, not so that He can be closer to Earth. Based on the passage, God has infinite power so it would not make sense that He requires vessels to be closer to Earth. Choice *C* is incorrect because the passage states that God does not dissipate when the vessel is broken.

22. B: Choice *B* is the correct answer because the passage is the author's musings about the nature of God and how He connects with humans. Much of the passage is written in question form. This is the author wondering about God's omnipresence and how He lives within mankind. Choice *A* is incorrect because although the author brings up human's limitations, he is not questioning God's grace. He only suggests celebrating God. Choice *C* is incorrect because the author only briefly mentions preachers and it is not to condemn them. Choice *D* is incorrect because although the author is asking theological questions, he is not discussing theology as a subject.

237

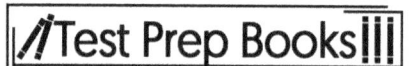

23. B: Choice *B* is the correct answer because it is the line from the text that explains where the author's devout nature came from. He cites the reasons that he feels inspired to worship God, including the resurrection of Jesus and the ministry of his preacher. Choice *A* is incorrect because that sentence is about calming a restless heart through God. However, it is not an explanation for why the author believes in God. Choice *C* is incorrect because that sentence is about the author calling God to himself to become full. That is an expression of his devotion but not an explanation. Choice *D* is incorrect because that sentence is about God using humans as vessels for His essence.

24. D: Choice *D* is the correct answer because it is the statement about the passage's format that is most logical and accurate. The passage is interrogative in nature and features numerous questions regarding theology. This shows the author's questioning of God's abilities, and it creates a contemplative tone. This contemplative tone is meant to encourage readers to consider their own thoughts on the subject. Choice *A* is incorrect because there is conceptual progression shown throughout the text. There are themes and ideas that connect the separate paragraphs. Choice *B* is incorrect because the author does not express that he is concerned about Hell. The short sentences and questions are not indicators of fear but rather the author's style. Choice *C* is incorrect because the author is strong in his faith, and this does not seem to waver in the text.

25. B: Choice *B* is the correct answer because the author's thoughts on this are made clear in Paragraph 1. The sentence reads, "Thou awakest us to delight in Thy praise; for Thou madest us for Thyself, and our heart is restless, until it repose in Thee," and connects restlessness in the human heart with God. It claims that a person will cease to be restless once they have found God. Choice *A* is incorrect because sins are not mentioned anywhere in the text. Choice *C* is incorrect because no reason is provided for the restlessness, except for the theory that God made it that way so people would come to Him. Choice *D* is incorrect because the text cites God as the reason for restlessness fading, not Heaven. The two are connected but not the same.

26. A: Choice *A* is the correct answer because it is what the word *repose* most nearly means. The author is discussing the restless heart and how God is meant to help with that. In this case, *repose* would mean to find peace in God's presence. It means to find calm rest. Choice *B* is incorrect because the author is not suggesting expressing anger towards God but praising him. Choice *C* is incorrect because no sins are mentioned that would require forgiveness. Choice *D* is incorrect because although *repose* can mean to go to sleep, that is not its meaning here.

27. D: Choice *D* is the correct answer because that is the logical connection between the themes discussed in Paragraph 1 and Paragraph 2. The first paragraph is about how humans have a restless heart until they devote themselves to God. It also explains how preachers spread the belief. Paragraph 2 then moves into a logical subject change about how people can take in God and God's ability to connect with humans. Choice *A* is incorrect because, although Paragraph 1 speaks highly of God, it does not directly encourage the reader. Choice *B* is incorrect because, although Paragraph 1 does show the author's views on God, the second paragraph is not focused on an opposing view. Choice *C* is incorrect because the first paragraph does not explain why humanity suffers despite God's presence.

28. C: Choice *C* is the correct answer because it is the shared theme between Paragraph 2 and Paragraph 3. Paragraph 2 discusses God's containment in Heaven and Earth, while Paragraph 3 discusses His containment in mankind as vessels. Choice *A* is incorrect because preachers are mentioned in Paragraph 1, not Paragraph 2 or Paragraph 3. Choice *B* is incorrect because vessels are only mentioned as a concept in Paragraph 3. Choice *D* is incorrect because, although Heaven is mentioned, the requirements to get there are not.

Answer Explanations #2

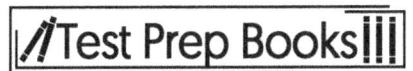

29. C: Choice *C* is the correct answer because it is the analogy that best fits the meaning of the original. The original analogy is that of something that contains another thing. Vessels contain God's essence. The best analogy would be a pitcher, which is an item that contains water or another liquid. Choice *A* is incorrect because a river is something that a boat sails upon, not something that contains it. Choice *B* is incorrect because the sunset is something that is situated along the horizon. There is no containment. Choice *D* is incorrect because an eruption is an action of a volcano. This is not analogous with the original terms.

30. D: Choice *D* is the correct answer because it is the analogy that best fits the meaning of the original. Preacher is the role of the person, while belief is what the preacher attempts to teach people about and convince them to have. Choice *D* is appropriate because a climate activist's goal would be to teach people about environmentalism and encourage belief in it. This is analogous with the original terms. Choice *A* is incorrect because an exam is something that a teacher gives to students, not a concept they hope to impress on their students. Choice *B* is incorrect because a general is a role within the military. Choice *C* is incorrect because a jet is the vehicle that a pilot is responsible for.

31. A: Choice *A* is correct because it correctly identifies the focus of both Passage A and Passage B. Passage A emphasizes the morality and virtues that should be present in those who rule over others. Passage B emphasizes that political societies form in order to maintain order and specifically points out that they preserve property. Choice *B* is incorrect because Passage B never encourages an authoritarian government. Choice *C* is incorrect because the first passage does not go into depth about those who choose to be free from governance. Choice *D* is incorrect because the severity of punishment is not mentioned in either passage. Punishment is only mentioned briefly.

32. C: Choice *C* is correct because it identifies the qualities that are important for those holding political positions. Confucius states that leaders should show benevolence and dignity. In Paragraph 1, he states that they should be "beneficent without great expenditure" and maintain "a dignified ease" when ruling. Choices *A* and *B* are not positive enough. Confucius focuses on the positive traits that a leader needs. Choice *D* is incorrect because, although Confucius seemingly would agree that leaders need tranquility and caution, they are not mentioned in the text.

33. A: Choice *A* is correct because it accurately describes the purpose of political society, according to Passage B. The author asserts that political society is created to establish common rules and authority. Specifically, the author mentions that protecting property is an important part of political society. Choice *B* is incorrect because the author states that those who do not participate in society are in a perfect state of nature, but that does not mean that is the purpose of political society. Choice *C* is incorrect because the author focuses on how political society maintains order, not how it enables people to share resources. Choice *D* is incorrect because criminals are not the focus of the passage.

34. B: Choice *B* is correct because it identifies how both passages address the idea of punishment. Passage A mentions that punishment is a way to maintain order, while Passage B suggests that it is a necessary function of society. Choice *A* is incorrect because the severity of punishment is not described in great detail in either passage. Choice *C* is incorrect because Passage A does not state that punishment should only be decided by one person. Choice *D* is incorrect because rehabilitation and the prison system are not mentioned.

35. B: Choice *B* is correct because it describes what Passage A means by that quote. Confucius is stating that rulers should freely share wealth with the citizens of their nation while still paying attention to the resources of the nation overall. Choice *A* is incorrect because, although that may be an implied point,

239

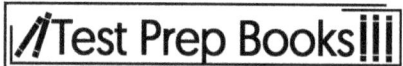

there is nothing to suggest that Confucius does not refer to giving welfare to every person. Choice C is incorrect because it is the ruler's responsibility to keep track of spending. Choice D is incorrect because Confucius is still claiming that the ruler should help the people, just that they should be mindful of the total amount spent.

36. C: Choice C is correct because it is the best quote for illustrating Confucius' thoughts on capital punishment. He says that it is a cruelty to put people to death without instructing them or giving them guidance and understanding. Choices A, B, and D are incorrect because they do not address the topic of a government or ruler putting its people to death.

37. B: Choice B is correct because it is the best quote for showing Locke's views on those who do not participate in political society. He believes that there are some men who wish to function under an established law. The chosen quote states that men who do not have that desire are left completely to their own lives and are in the perfect state of nature. Choices A, C, and D are incorrect because they do not address the man who does not wish to participate in political society.

38. A: Choice A is correct because it is the closest meaning to the word *covetous*. In context, the word *covetous* is used to describe somebody who pursues desires but does not want everything for themselves. The best synonym for this would be *greedy*. Choices B and C are appropriately negative, but they do not fit the context. Choice D is a positive trait and does not fit the overall sentence.

39. B: Choice B is the correct answer because the first term leads to the second term in this analogy. Breaking the law leads to penalties. In the same manner, a tornado leads to destruction. This is an appropriate pairing because the analogy relationship is nearly the same. Choices A, C, and D are incorrect because the first term does not lead to the second term.

40. C: Choice C is the correct answer because the original analogy pairing shows antonymous words. Benevolent and oppressive mean nearly opposite things. Therefore, generous and greedy are an appropriate pairing since they have opposite meanings. Choices A, B, and D are incorrect because the terms are not antonymous with one another.

Grammar and Writing

41. B: Choice B is the correct answer because the pronoun *he* agrees with the noun *man* at the beginning of the sentence. Choice A is incorrect because it uses *she*, which would be used in the case of a female subject. Choice C is incorrect because the text refers to man in the third person and requires a third-person pronoun. Choice D is incorrect because, although *they* is sometimes used as a gender-neutral singular pronoun, *he* better matches the male-gendered subject.

42. A: Choice A is the correct answer because the sentence is saying that people are more dependent on the grace of God now than they were before the fall, when they were free from sin or, in other words, perfectly obedient. Choice B is incorrect because abstinence is not mentioned as one of the requirements for God's grace. Choice C is incorrect because the text does not mention prayer. Choice D is incorrect because sin would not be rewarded.

43. B: Choice B is the correct answer because the infinitive form of the verb fits the sentence grammatically and is consistent with the form of "to deliver." Choice A is incorrect because it is in the past tense, which is not used in this sentence. Choice C is incorrect because *bestowing* is the present

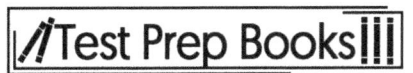

Answer Explanations #2

participle, which does not fit the sentence's verb form. Choice D is incorrect because "to bestowed" is never grammatically correct.

44. B: Choice B is the correct answer because a comma is the best punctuation to use before a conjunction followed by an independent clause. Choice A is incorrect because a semicolon separates two independent clauses that are not joined by a conjunction, which is not the case here. Choice C is incorrect because there is no need for an em dash here. An em dash is typically used before an interjection or for a stronger, more emphatic pause. Choice D is incorrect because it is better to connect the clause starting with *and* to the rest of the sentence than to have it stand alone as a sentence.

45. C: Choice C is the correct answer because it is the most concise and clear sentence that features all relevant information from the original sentence. The original sentence states that we need God's grace to give us righteousness, pardon sins, and release us from guilt. Choice A is incorrect because the original sentence can be made more concise. Choice B is incorrect because it changes information from the original sentence by stating that we cannot stand in need of God's grace to pardon our sins or release us from guilt. Choice D is incorrect because it fails to mention the sins and guilt that the original sentence does.

46. C: Choice C is the correct answer because it is the most concise and clear sentence while maintaining all relevant information from the original sentence. The original sentence is stating that man and all reasonable creatures are created holy because it would be a disparagement to God's holiness to make an intelligent creature unholy. Choice A is incorrect because the sentence can be made shorter. Choice B is incorrect because it states that man is the only reasonable creature, when this is not what the original sentence states. Choice D is incorrect because the original sentence does not comment on man's behavior.

47. A: Choice A is the correct answer because the sentence states that humans are dependent on the grace of God due to their helplessness, and *insufficiency*, or inadequacy, is a related quality that fits the sentence. Choice B is incorrect because the sentence is stating that humans are dependent on God, not independent. Choice C is incorrect because *idealism* does not function with the characterization of people as hopeless and sinful. Choice D is incorrect because *impudence* means not having respect for others, and while that may be true for sinful people, the word *insufficiency* better aligns with what the author is saying.

48. D: Choice D is the correct answer because a comma is most appropriate here. The word *so* is functioning similarly to *therefore* and warrants a comma, which is standard after a transition word or phrase. Choice A is incorrect because an em dash is used before an interjection or for strong emphasis and is not necessary here. Choice B is incorrect because a colon should be used before a list. Choice C is incorrect because the author is sharing original thoughts and not paraphrasing a quote.

49. C: Choice C is the correct answer because a comma is the most appropriate punctuation to set off the additional information starting with *being*. Choice A is incorrect because the second half of the sentence is not an independent clause and cannot stand on its own after a semicolon. Choice B is incorrect because ellipses are used to indicate a purposeful pause, which there is no need for in this location. Choice D is incorrect because there should be a break between the two thoughts.

50. D: Choice D is the correct answer because the text has repeatedly stated that it is God's goodness that enriches human life and saves people from their sinful nature. Therefore, Choice D is the best fit. Choice A is incorrect because the text never states that humans fight their nature. Choice B is incorrect

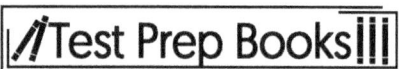

because, according to the text, God forgives people's sins. Choice C is incorrect because the text does not state that humans must beg for mercy from God.

51. C: Choice C is the correct answer because it is the form of the word *take* that fits best with the sentence. Since Galileo's work occurred in the past, the verb should be in the past tense. Choice A is incorrect because *taken* is the past participle and should only be used when an auxiliary verb is present, such as the word *has*. Choices B and D are not in past tense and are therefore incorrect.

52. B: Choice B is the correct answer because it is the right form of the word *displease* for the sentence, which is in past tense. Choice A is incorrect because it is in present tense. Choice C is incorrect because it is a participle and does not work with the sentence construction. Choice D is incorrect because *displease* is the base form of the word or one of its present-tense forms and does not work grammatically in the sentence.

53. D: Choice D is the correct answer because it is the most concise option that maintains all relevant information. The original sentence states that Galileo took inspiration from the spyglass to create a superior telescope that revolutionized his sky observations. Choice D conveys all of this information in a more concise manner. Choice A is incorrect because the sentence can be made shorter. Choice B is incorrect because it does not mention the spyglass that Galileo drew inspiration from. Choice C is incorrect because the spyglass was not Galileo's invention.

54. D: Choice D is the correct answer because a comma is the right punctuation to separate the introductory phrase from the rest of the sentence. Choice A is incorrect because a comma is needed after the introductory phrase. Choice B is incorrect because a semicolon should only be used between two independent clauses. Choice C is incorrect because there is no need for a purposeful pause here.

55. C: Choice C is the correct answer because the sentence states that the criticism of Galileo's heliocentric model put Galileo in a bad position—ultimately, he was sentenced to life in prison. Therefore, it is appropriate to say that his situation was *precarious* or dangerously uncertain. Choice A is incorrect because *pragmatic* would mean that his situation was well thought out and practical. Considering the response by the church, this is false. Choice B is incorrect because *pecuniary* means related to money. His situation was not related to money. Choice D is incorrect because *precocious* means indicative of early development in children, which is unrelated to the topic of this sentence.

56. D: Choice D is the correct answer because it is the most concise answer while maintaining all of the relevant information of the original sentence. The original sentence states that Galileo's support for heliocentrism was heretical, and the Church put a stop to his teachings. Choice A is incorrect because it is needlessly wordy and can be shortened. Choice B is incorrect because it is not as concise as Choice D and states that Galileo was forced to give up on the theory instead of saying that he could no longer spread the word about it. Choice C is incorrect because the Church did not deem heliocentrism heretical because it was unprovable but rather because it challenged scripture.

57. A: Choice A is the correct answer because the example featured in the sentence is the best choice for the context of the overall work. Galileo went on to contribute more works, per the text, so it is safe to say that he continued his scientific pursuits. Choice B is incorrect because the text does not state that Galileo's goal was ever to inspire others, although he did happen to do so. Choice C is incorrect because there is no indication that Galileo ever attempted revenge on the Church. Choice D is incorrect because the text never states that Galileo cared about his father's beliefs regarding his career.

58. A: Choice A is the correct answer because a comma should always come between a city name and country name. There is no need for commas at any other point in the highlighted text. Choice B is incorrect because there does not need to be a comma after the word *of*. Choice C is incorrect because there should be a comma after *Florence*. Choice D is incorrect because there is no need for a comma before the word *of*.

59. C: Choice C is the correct answer because Galileo faced opposition to his pursuits throughout his life. First, his family wished for him to take a different path than he did. Second, the Roman Catholic Church opposed his scientific beliefs. Despite the opposition, he continued on due to his curiosity and dedication to science. Choice A is incorrect because it is not stated that Galileo faced illness throughout his life, only at the end. Choice B is incorrect because there are no family tragedies mentioned in the text. Choice D is incorrect because, due to Galileo's persistence, it is apparent that he did not struggle with motivation in a significant way.

60. D: Choice D is the correct answer because it uses the correct form of the verb *be* for the sentence. Since it corresponds to two subjects, astronomy and physics, the word should be *were*. Choice A is incorrect because the verb *is* is not plural and does not work in this sentence. Choice B is incorrect because the sentence is not saying there is potential for astronomy and physics to be changed by Galileo's contributions; they already have been changed. Choice C is incorrect because *was* is not a plural verb.

61. B: Choice B is the correct answer because the verb *count* is being used in passive voice, in which it is conjugated as *counted* and preceded by a form of the verb *be*—in this case *are*, as the subject, stars and molecules, is plural. Choices A and D use the participle form of *count*, which does not work here, and Choice D also uses *is* instead of *are*. Choice C is incorrect because *is* would only work with a singular subject.

62. D: Choice D is the correct answer because *illusiveness* means deceptive or hard to make sense of, which makes sense in the context of comparing mathematics to a ghost. Choice A is incorrect because *infirmity* means the state of being unhealthy. This has nothing to do with mathematics. Choice B is incorrect because *idiosyncrasy* means a strange habit or personal feature. This is not something that typically applies to an abstract concept. Choice C is incorrect because *indemnity* means security against a loss, which does not apply to the context of this sentence or text.

63. C: Choice C is the correct answer because introductory adverbial words should generally be followed by a comma. Choices A, B, and D are incorrect because they are not standard forms of punctuation that come after an introductory word. A colon is unnecessary, as there is no list that follows. A semicolon cannot be used, as it does not follow an independent clause. Ellipses are not appropriate, as there is no reason for a purposeful pause here.

64. B: Choice B is the correct answer because it is the most concise way to provide all of the information in the original sentence. The original sentence states that technical facility is needed in order to engage in more meaningful mental activity, such as appreciating a poet's passion and rhythm. Choice A is incorrect because the original sentence can be made more concise. Choice C is incorrect because the original sentence is not stating that we do not understand Milton and Shelly or that technical skills detract from this but rather that these skills are necessary to appreciate their work. Choice D is incorrect because it shifts the focus of the sentence to Milton and Shelley and changes its main ideas; the original sentence does not say that Milton and Shelley are underappreciated or that most people do not share their technical facility.

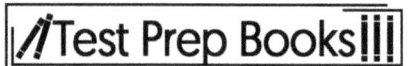

65. A: Choice A is the correct answer because the author is saying that arithmetic is an entry point for understanding mathematics on a broader scale. Thus, saying that the subject leads to discovery is accurate. Choice B is incorrect because the author does not encourage criticism of the science at any point. Choice C is incorrect because the focus of the author is on people who are learning, not teaching. Choice D is incorrect because the author does not discuss the possibility of disproving anything about mathematics.

66. C: Choice C is the correct answer because it is the option that conveys all of the information in the sentence in the most concise way. The original sentence states that mathematics applies to things just because they exist, without consideration for any feelings tied to the things. Choice C conveys this idea concisely. Choice A is incorrect because the sentence can be made more concise. Choice B is incorrect because the original sentence states that mathematics does not consider feelings, emotions, or sensations at all. Choice D is incorrect because the original sentence is saying that mathematics and feelings are separate, not that they are similar.

67. D: Choice D is the correct answer because it states that arithmetic relates to nearly everything that a person can think of, which refutes the idea that mathematics does not consider anything of real interest in human life. Choice A is incorrect because that sentence describes why most students fail to become interested in mathematics, but it does nothing to challenge the original sentence. Choice B is incorrect because it describes how most people are introduced to mathematics and not why it is important. Choice C is incorrect because it shares the author's opinion on the right way to learn mathematics, but it does not explain its significance.

68. C: Choice C is the correct answer because the phrase "in his description of Gulliver's voyage to Laputa," which interrupts the main clause to provide additional information, should be set off by commas at the beginning and end. Choice A is incorrect because a comma should come at the end of the phrase that features additional information. Choice B is incorrect because the word *is* is not a part of the phrase containing additional information, so placing a comma after that word and not before it is incorrect. Choice D is incorrect because the name *Gulliver's* requires its apostrophe in order to show ownership of the voyage that the person took.

69. A: Choice A is the correct answer because the phrase starting with *producing* modifies the preceding part of the sentence, indicating the result of the mathematical tailor's actions, and the *-ing* form of the verb is right in this case. Choice B is incorrect because it would have to be preceded by a conjunction like *and* to work grammatically in this sentence. Choice C is incorrect for the same reason, in addition to being in past tense, unlike the rest of the sentence. Choice D is incorrect because *production* is a noun rather than the verb needed.

70. A: Choice A is the correct answer because the commas surrounding the word *indeed* are purposefully placed there for emphasis. This is done to underscore the kinds of times Swift lived in. Choice B is an acceptable way to punctuate the sentence but not the best-suited for its purposes. Choice C is incorrect because there is no need for a comma after *lived*. Choice D is incorrect because there need to be commas on both sides of *indeed* or none at all.

71. A: Choice A is the correct answer because the use of the comma is appropriate before the adverbial phrase starting with *in spite of*, which provides information that contrasts with the first half of the sentence. Choice B is incorrect because there is no need to take an extended pause between the two parts of the sentence. Choice C is incorrect because a colon is primarily used before a list. This is not the

Answer Explanations #2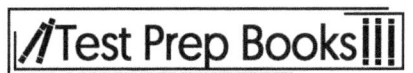

case in this sentence. Choice *D* is incorrect because the second half of the sentence is not an independent clause and cannot stand by itself; therefore, it is inappropriate to use a semicolon.

72. D: Choice *D* is the correct answer because *think* should be used in its base form, as it follows the preposition *to*. Choice *A* is incorrect since *thinks* is not the base form. Choice *B* is also not the base form; additionally, it is in the past tense, which does not work with the sentence. Choice *C* is incorrect because *thoughts* is a noun rather than a verb.

73. B: Choice *B* is the correct answer because the subject is *man*; therefore, the correct pronoun is *he*. Choice *A* is incorrect because it corresponds to the wrong gender. Choices *C* and *D* are incorrect because they are plural pronouns, which do not work with the subject-verb agreement of the sentence.

74. C: Choice *C* is the correct answer because the indefinite pronoun *no one* is singular and needs a singular verb. The word *regards* is the third-person singular form of the verb *to regard*. Choice *A* is incorrect because it corresponds to a plural noun. Choice *B* is incorrect because the sentence and overall text are not in the past tense. Choice *D* is incorrect because it is a participle or gerund, which does not work in this sentence.

75. C: Choice *C* is the correct answer because the word *noble*, meaning having high morals, is often used to describe a person's character. This fits the context of the sentence, which is discussing the mental characteristics that are valued in people. Choice *A* is incorrect because *nebulous* means vague or unclear. This is not a positive quality of the mind, so it does not fit the sentence. Choice *B* is incorrect because the word *naïve* means easily fooled and is not a positive quality for a person to have. Choice *D* is incorrect because *nefarious* means ill-intentioned, which is also not a positive quality.

76. A: Choice *A* is the correct answer because the sentence is making a comparison between people with positive mental and physical characteristics. Choice *B* is incorrect because the author does not mention intelligence as a factor of health, only that a sound mind is required. Choice *C* is incorrect because the author does not mention the concept of sin in this text. Choice *D* is incorrect because, although parenting is mentioned as being important in the text, it is not one of the main concepts.

77. D: Choice *D* is the correct answer because it is the option that provides the most clear and concise sentence while maintaining the integrity of the original sentence. This includes the examples of healthy features that a man should have. Choice *A* is incorrect because the original sentence is wordy and can be successfully shortened. Choice *B* is incorrect because it eliminates too much of the information provided in the original sentence, such as the mentions of a man's weight and mental state. Choice *C* is incorrect because the original sentence does not state that the perfectly healthy man cannot exist.

78. C: Choice *C* is the correct answer because the sentence features two clauses that can stand independently of one another and can thus be separated by a semicolon. Choice *A* is incorrect because a colon is generally used to introduce a list, not combine two independent clauses. Choice *B* is incorrect because there is no need for a purposeful pause in this sentence. Choice *D* is incorrect because a semicolon is the most standard punctuation (aside from a period) for separating two independent clauses.

79. D: Choice *D* is the correct answer because it is the example that best fits the sentence and overall text. The text tells readers that that all humans should strive to be healthy in both mind and body. Choice *A* is incorrect because it never states that the doctor should be avoided. Choice *B* is incorrect because accidents leading to death are not mentioned anywhere in the text. Choice *C* is incorrect

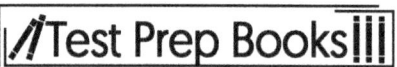

Answer Explanations #2

because, while the text mentions how good parents create good people, it does not mention the reader's responsibility in overcoming poor parenting.

80. B: Choice B is the correct answer because it is the most concise option while maintaining the purpose of the original sentence, which lists elements that the body needs in order to avoid illness. Choice B maintains both the information about the elements and the mention of illness. Choice A is incorrect because the original sentence is wordy and can be made more concise. Choice C is incorrect because, although it mentions that the body requires the elements, it does not state the other important point about how they stave off illness. Choice D is incorrect because the original sentence does not state that the elements are a cure for illness but rather that they can prevent it.

Quantitative Reasoning

81. C: To solve this equation, square both sides to eliminate the radical, resulting in $x + 5 = 25$. Subtracting 5 from both sides to solve for x gives $x = 20$.

82. B: According to the order of operations, multiplication and division must be completed first from left to right. Then, addition and subtraction are completed from left to right. Therefore:

$$9 \times 9 \div 9 + 9 - 9 \div 9$$

$$81 \div 9 + 9 - 9 \div 9$$

$$9 + 9 - 9 \div 9$$

$$9 + 9 - 1$$

$$18 - 1$$

$$17$$

83. C: Because area is a two-dimensional measurement, the dimensions are multiplied by a scale factor that is squared to determine the scale factor of the corresponding areas. The dimensions of the rectangle are multiplied by a scale factor of 3. Therefore, the area is multiplied by a scale factor of 3^2 (which is equal to 9):

$$24 \text{ cm}^2 \times 9 = 216 \text{ cm}^2$$

84. A: An isosceles right triangle has two angles measuring 45°. The sides opposite these angles are equal in length. This disproves the statement. An obtuse triangle with an angle measuring 120° is not a right triangle. Acute triangles and equilateral triangles cannot be right triangles.

85. D: We are given an angle (60°), the length of the opposite side (x), and the length of the adjacent side (13 cm). We can use the mnemonic "SOHCAHTOA," where the "TOA" reminds us that tangent equals the opposite side over the adjacent side. In other words, tan, $\tan 60° = \frac{x}{13}$.

Since $\tan 60° = \sqrt{3}$, we can calculate:

$$x = 13 \tan 60° = 13 \times \sqrt{3} = 22.52$$

246

Answer Explanations #2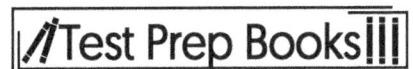

86. D: First, we need to solve $x^3 + x^2 - 6x = 0$. Factoring this equation, we obtain $x(x^2 + x - 6) = x(x + 3)(x - 2) = 0$. This equation has three solutions: 0, -3, and 2. Therefore, the only integers that can count end in either 0 or 2. The integers between 11 and 81 that have a sum greater than 5 that end in 0 or 2 are 42, 52, 60, 62, 70, 72, and 80. Therefore, there are 7 of them.

87. D: $12 + 21 = 33$, which is a composite number. $3 + 7$ is the sum of two prime numbers; therefore, they are not composite. $16 + 3$ is the sum of a composite and a prime number. In $8 + 9 = 17$, 8 and 9 are both composite, and 17 is prime. This is the counterexample.

88. B: When a point is reflected over an axis, the sign of at least one of the coordinates must change. When it's reflected over the y-axis, the sign of the x coordinate must change. The y value remains the same. Therefore, the new point is $(-6, 2)$.

89. D: $\frac{5}{2} \div \frac{1}{3} = \frac{5}{2} \times \frac{3}{1} = \frac{15}{2} = 7.5$.

90. D: Finding the zeros for a function by factoring is done by setting the equation equal to zero, then completely factoring. Since there is a common x for each term in the provided equation, that should be factored out first to get $x(x^2 - 3x - 4)$. Then, the quadratic that is left can be factored into two binomials, which are $(x + 1)(x - 4)$. This gives the factored equation $0 = x(x + 1)(x - 4)$.

91. C: Because the triangles are similar, the lengths of the corresponding sides are proportional. Therefore:

$$\frac{30 + x}{30} = \frac{22}{14} = \frac{y + 15}{y}$$

Using cross multiplication on the first two terms results in the equation:

$$14(30 + x) = 22 \times 30$$

When solved, this gives:

$$x \approx 17.1$$

Using cross multiplication on the last two terms results in the equation:

$$14(y + 15) = 22y$$

When solved, this gives:

$$y \approx 26.3$$

92. B: First, find 12% of 64. Multiply 0.12 by 64 to obtain 7.68, which rounds to 8. The special edition boxes contain 8 more cookies. Add this to 64 to obtain the total number of cookies: 72.

93. A: There were 4 classes from 2018 through 2021. The average class size was 25.5 students. Because the average is the total number of students over the four years divided by 4, the total number of students over the four years was $25.5(4) = 102$. The maximum class size was 28 students, which means three of the four classes could have had 28 students. Subtract $28(3) = 84$ from 102 to obtain 18. The smallest class size could have been 18 students.

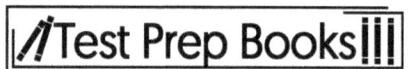

Answer Explanations #2

94. C: The cost of the laptop before the $200 discount was $1,250 + $200 = $1,450. There also was a 14% discount, meaning the laptop was sold at 100% − 14% = 86%. Divide $1,450 by 0.86 to obtain the original price of the laptop. $\frac{1450}{0.86} = \$1,686$.

95. C: The cosine of 45° is equal to 0.7071. Choice *A* is not the correct answer because the cosine of 15° is 0.9659. Choice *B* is not the correct answer because the cosine of 30° is 0.8660. Choice *D* is not correct because the cosine of 90° is 0.

96. D: We start by listing the squares and finding one that has digits that have a sum of 10. Here are the squares:

$$1, 4, 9, 16, 25, 36, 49, 64$$

64 is a square that has digits with a sum of 10. Take the square root of 64 to find that $k = 8$. For this value, $k^3 + 3 = 515$. The other options have values of k^2 that do not have a sum of 10.

97. D: To find Denver's total snowfall, 3 must be multiplied times $27\frac{3}{4}$. In order to easily do this, the mixed number should be converted into an improper fraction.

$$27\frac{3}{4} = \frac{27 \times 4 + 3}{4} = \frac{111}{4}$$

Therefore, Denver had approximately $\frac{3 \times 111}{4} = \frac{333}{4}$ inches of snow. The improper fraction can be converted back into a mixed number through division.

$$\frac{333}{4} = 83\frac{1}{4} \text{ inches}$$

98. D: We can try to solve the equation by factoring the numerator into $(x + 6)(x - 5)$. Since $(x - 5)$ is on the top and bottom, that factor cancels out. This leaves the equation $x + 6 = 11$. Solving the equation gives the answer $x = 5$. When this value is plugged into the equation, it yields a zero in the denominator of the fraction. Since this is undefined, there is no solution.

99. B: The technique of completing the square must be used to change the equation below into the standard equation of a circle:

$$4x^2 + 4y^2 - 16x - 24y + 51 = 0$$

First, the constant must be moved to the right-hand side of the equals sign and each term must be divided by the coefficient of the x^2-term (which is 4). The x- and y- terms must be grouped together to obtain:

$$x^2 - 4x + y^2 - 6y = -\frac{51}{4}$$

Then, the process of completing the square must be completed for each variable. This gives:

$$(x^2 - 4x + 4) + (y^2 - 6y + 9) = -\frac{51}{4} + 4 + 9$$

Answer Explanations #2

The equation can be written as:

$$(x-2)^2 + (y-3)^2 = \frac{1}{4}$$

Therefore, the center of the circle is $(2, 3)$ and the radius is:

$$\sqrt{\frac{1}{4}} = \frac{1}{2}$$

100. C: Let x be the first number. Therefore, $x + 2, x + 4$, and $x + 6$ are the three other consecutive odd numbers. The sum of these four numbers is equal to 5,064. Therefore, $x + x + 2 + x + 4 + x + 6 = 4x + 12 = 5,064$. Subtract 12 from both sides and divide by 4 to obtain that the first number is $x = 1,263$. Add 4 to obtain the third number of 1,267.

101. A: This is a right triangle, so the sides follow the Pythagorean theorem. Let x be the missing side length. Therefore, $x^2 + 6^2 = 15^2$. This simplifies to $x^2 + 36 = 225$, or $x^2 = 189$. Take the square root of both sides to obtain $x \approx 13.7$. Therefore, the missing side length is 13.7 ft. We can call this the height of the triangle and can call the side equaling 6 ft the base. The area of a triangle is $\frac{1}{2}bh$, so the area of this triangle is $\frac{1}{2}(6)(13.7) = 41.1$ ft².

102. B: The tangent of 30° is 1 over the square root of 3. Choice A is not the correct answer because the tangent of 15° is 0.2679. Choice C is not the correct answer because the tangent of 45° is 1. Choice D is not the correct answer because the tangent of 90° is undefined.

103. B: Kenya sold 89 magazines, which ended up being 56% of the total magazines allotted for the class. A common mistake would be to find 56% of 89, which would be 50 magazines. However, the fact is that 56% of the total number of magazines is equal to 89. Therefore, $.56x = 89$, where x is the total number of allotted magazines. Divide 89 by 0.56 to obtain $x \approx 159$ magazines.

104. C: Nothing is added to x and y since the center is 0 and 5^2 is 25. Choice A is not the correct answer because you do not subtract the radius from x and y. Choice B is not the correct answer because you must square the radius on the right side of the equation. Choice D is not the correct answer because you do not add the radius to x and y in the equation.

105. C: To get 85% of a number, multiply it by 0.85.

$$\frac{17}{20} \times \frac{20}{1} = 17$$

106. A: The common denominator here will be $4x$. Rewrite these fractions as:

$$\frac{3}{x} + \frac{5u}{2x} - \frac{u}{4}$$

$$\frac{12}{4x} + \frac{10u}{4x} - \frac{ux}{4x}$$

$$\frac{12 + 10u - ux}{4x}$$

107. B: Given the area of the circle, the radius can be found using the formula $A = \pi r^2$. In this case, $49\pi = \pi r^2$, which yields $r = 7$ m. A central angle is equal to the degree measure of the arc it inscribes; therefore, $\angle x = 80$. The area of a sector can be found using the formula:

$$A = \frac{\theta}{360°} \times \pi r^2$$

In this case:

$$A = \frac{80°}{360°} \times \pi(7)^2 = 10.9\pi \text{ m}$$

108. A: Line A, $2x + 4y = 9$, can be written in slope-intercept form as $y = -\frac{1}{2}x + \frac{9}{4}$. The point $\left(1, \frac{7}{4}\right)$ is on Line A. The slope of Line A is $-\frac{1}{2}$, and any other line with the same slope (including $y = -\frac{1}{2}x + 5$) is parallel to Line A. To be perpendicular to Line A, the slope of a line must be a negative reciprocal of $-\frac{1}{2}$, so 2. Therefore, the line $y = 2x + 10$ is perpendicular to Line A, and $y = -2x + 6$ is not perpendicular to Line A.

109. A: To be divisible by 9, the sum of the digits has to be a multiple of 9. The numbers between 120 and 190 that have sums of their digits that are multiples of 9 are 126, 135, 144, 153, 162, 171, 180, and 189. However, of these, the odd ones are 135, 153, 171, and 189. Therefore, there are four of them.

110. D: At the beginning, Christina had $10x$ pens and $3x$ pencils. She traded 4 pens for pencils, so now she has $10x - 4$ pens and $3x + 4$ pencils. The ratio is now 10:5. Therefore, we have the proportion

$$\frac{10x - 4}{3x + 4} = \frac{10}{5}.$$

Cross multiply to obtain $5(10x - 4) = 10(3x + 4)$. Distribute to obtain $50x - 20 = 30x + 40$. Adding 20 to both sides and subtracting $30x$ from both sides results in $20x = 60$. Then, divide both sides by 20 to obtain $x = 3$. Therefore, she started with $10(3) = 30$ pens.

111. B: The y-intercept of an equation is found where the x-value is zero. Plugging in zero for x in the equation, we get $0^2 + 3(0) - 4 = -4$.

112. A: $-4 + (-4) = -8$, which is less than the original number of -4. This is a counterexample that disproves the original statement. $12 + 12 = 24$ and $0 + 0 = 0$ are the only other two examples with the same number being added to itself, but their sums are greater than or equal to the original numbers.

113. D: Dividing rational expressions follows the same rule as dividing fractions. The division is changed to multiplication by the reciprocal of the second fraction. This turns the expression into:

$$\frac{5x^3}{3x^2y} \times \frac{3y^9}{25}$$

Answer Explanations #2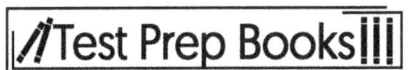

This can be simplified by finding common factors in the numerators and denominators of the two fractions.

$$\frac{x^3}{x^2y} \times \frac{y^9}{5}$$

Multiplying across creates:

$$\frac{x^3 y^9}{5x^2 y}$$

Simplifying leads to the final expression of:

$$\frac{xy^8}{5}$$

114. B: Start with the original equation: $x - 2xy + 2y$, then replace each instance of x with a 2, and each instance of y with a 3 to get:

$$2^2 - 2 \times 2 \times 3 + 2 \times 3^2$$

$$4 - 12 + 18 = 10$$

115. B: This answer is correct because $3^2 + 4^2$ is $9 + 16$, which is 25. Taking the square root of 25 is 5. Choice *A* is not the correct answer because that is $3 + 4$. Choice *C* is not the correct answer because that is stopping at $3^2 + 4^2$ is $9 + 16$, which is 25. Choice *D* is not the correct answer because that is 3×4.

116. B: The graph of $y = x^2 + 2$ has a vertex at (0, 2) on the *y*-axis. The circle with a center at (0, 1) also lies on the *y*-axis. With a radius of 1, the circle touches the parabola at one point: the vertex of the parabola (0, 2).

117. A: Using the trigonometric identity $\tan(\theta) = \frac{\sin(\theta)}{\cos(\theta)}$, the expression becomes $\frac{\sin\theta}{\cos\theta} \cos\theta$. The factors that are the same on the top and bottom cancel out, leaving the simplified expression $\sin\theta$.

118. C: The shortest side is the one opposite the 30° angle since that is the smallest angle. The other angle is 60° since all three angles have a sum of 180° and the third angle is 90°. We use a trigonometry ratio, $\sin 30° = \frac{opp}{hyp}$, to find the missing side length. We are given that the hypotenuse measures 20 centimeters, so $opp = 20\sin 30° = 10$. Therefore, the smallest side length is 10 cm.

119. A: The slope is given by:

$$m = \frac{y_2 - y_1}{x_2 - x_1}$$

$$\frac{0 - 4}{0 - (-3)}$$

$$-\frac{4}{3}$$

120. B: Both of the females could be black, so one male doesn't have to be black. Both of the males could be black as well, so in that case the males would not be white. Because half of the cats are male, two are female. The only true statement is option II.

Dear CLT Test Taker,

Thank you for purchasing this study guide for your CLT exam. We hope that we exceeded your expectations.

Our goal in creating this study guide was to cover all of the topics that you will see on the test. We also strove to make our practice questions as similar as possible to what you will encounter on test day. With that being said, if you found something that you feel was not up to your standards, please send us an email and let us know.

We have study guides in a wide variety of fields. Please search for it on Amazon or send us an email if you can't find what you are looking for.

Thanks Again and Happy Testing!
Product Development Team
info@studyguideteam.com

FREE Test Taking Tips Video/DVD Offer

To better serve you, we created videos covering test taking tips that we want to give you for FREE. **These videos cover world-class tips that will help you succeed on your test.**

We just ask that you send us feedback about this product. Please let us know what you thought about it—whether good, bad, or indifferent.

To get your **FREE videos**, you can use the QR code below or email freevideos@studyguideteam.com with "Free Videos" in the subject line and the following information in the body of the email:

    a. The title of your product

    b. Your product rating on a scale of 1-5, with 5 being the highest

    c. Your feedback about the product

If you have any questions or concerns, please don't hesitate to contact us at info@studyguideteam.com.

Thank you!